Lewis Spence (1874–1955) was a Scottish folklorist and mythologist. His many works included *A Dictionary of Mythology*, *The Myths of Mexico and Peru*, and *Myths and Legends of the North American Indians*.

Jon E. Lewis is the author of bestselling *The Mammoth Book of Native Americans* and *The Mammoth Book of the West*.

Highlights from the series

A BRIEF GUIDE TO

NATIVE AMERICAN MYTHS AND LEGENDS

LEWIS SPENCE

Updated material by Jon E. Lewis

Myths and Legends of the North American Indians,
by Lewis Spence, with an introduction and commentary
by Jon E. Lewis

RUNNING PRESS
PHILADELPHIA · LONDON

ROBINSON

Constable & Robinson Ltd
55–56 Russell Square
London WC1B 4HP
www.constablerobinson.com

Originally published as *Myths and Legends of the North American Indians*
in 1914 by George G. Harrap & Company.

This edition, with new material by Jon E. Lewis, published by Robinson,
an imprint of Constable & Robinson Ltd, 2013.

A copy of the British Library Cataloguing in Publication Data
is available from the British Library

UK ISBN 978-1-78033-787-6

1 3 5 7 9 10 8 6 4 2

This edition published in the United States in 2013 by Running Press Book Publishers,
A Member of the Perseus Books Group

Books published by Running Press are available at special discounts for bulk purchases in the United
States by corporations, institutions, and other organizations. For more information, please contact the
Special Markets Department at the Perseus Books Group, 2300 Chestnut Street, Suite 200,
Philadelphia, PA 19103, or call (800) 810-4145, ext. 5000, or e-mail
special.markets@perseusbooks.com.

US ISBN 978-0-7624-4802-9
US Library of Congress Control Number: 2012944546

9 8 7 6 5 4 3 2 1

Digit on the right indicates the number of this printing

Running Press Book Publishers
2300 Chestnut Street
Philadelphia, PA 19103-4371

Visit us on the web!
www.runningpress.com

Typeset by TW Typesetting, Plymouth, Devon

Printed and bound in the UK

CONTENTS

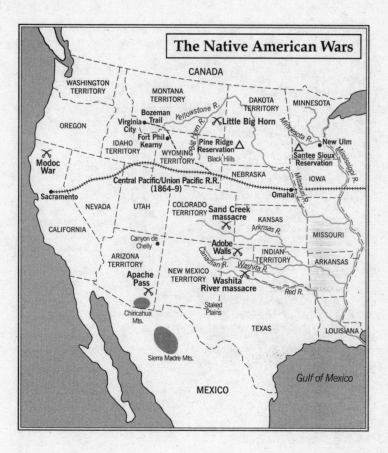

The Native American Wars

CANADA

WASHINGTON TERRITORY

OREGON

MONTANA TERRITORY

Bozeman Trail

Virginia City

Yellowstone R.

✕ **Little Big Horn**

DAKOTA TERRITORY

MINNESOTA

Fort Phil Kearny

IDAHO TERRITORY

Big Horn R.

Pine Ridge Reservation △

Minnesota R.

● New Ulm

✕ **Modoc War**

WYOMING TERRITORY

Black Hills

△ **Santee Sioux Reservation**

Mississippi R.

NEBRASKA

Missouri R.

IOWA

● Sacramento

Central Pacific/Union Pacific R.R.
(1864–9)

● Omaha

NEVADA

UTAH

COLORADO TERRITORY

Sand Creek massacre ✕

Arknsas R.

KANSAS

MISSOURI

CALIFORNIA

Canyon de Chelly ●

Adobe Walls ✕

Canadian R.

INDIAN TERRITORY

ARKANSAS

ARIZONA TERRITORY

NEW MEXICO TERRITORY

Washita R.

Apache Pass ✕

Washita River massacre ✕

Red R.

Chiricahua Mts.

Staked Plains

TEXAS

LOUISIANA

Sierra Madre Mts.

MEXICO

Gulf of Mexico

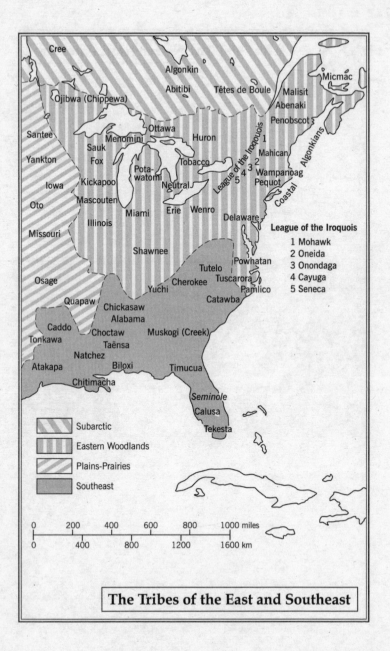

Cree

Ojibwa (Chippewa)

Algonkin

Abitibi   Têtes de Boule

Micmac

Malisit
Abenaki
Penobscot

Santee

Yankton

Iowa

Oto

Missouri

Menomini

Sauk

Fox

Kickapoo

Mascouten

Illinois

Pota-
watomi

Miami

Ottawa

Huron

Tobacco

Neutral

Erie   Wenro

Shawnee

Osage

Quapaw

Caddo

Tonkawa

Atakapa

Chitimacha

Chickasaw
Alabama

Choctaw

Taënsa

Natchez

Biloxi

Yuchi

Cherokee

Tutelo

Powhatan

Tuscarora

Catawba

Muskogi (Creek)

Timucua

Seminole

Calusa

Tekesta

Pamlico

Delaware

Mahican

Wampanoag
Pequot

1

2

3

4   2

5   5

League of the Iroquois

Coastal Algonkians

League of the Iroquois

1 Mohawk
2 Oneida
3 Onondaga
4 Cayuga
5 Seneca

Subarctic

Eastern Woodlands

Plains-Prairies

Southeast

| 0 | 200 | 400 | 600 | 800 | 1000 miles |

| 0 | 400 | 800 | 1200 | 1600 km |

The Tribes of the East and Southeast

The Tribes of the Northwest and North

Eskimo
Subarctic
Northwest Coast
Plateau
Plains-Prairies

0 200 400 600 800 1000 miles
0 400 800 1200 1600 km

Polar Eskimo
Greenland Eskimo
Angmagsalik

Baffinland Eskimo
Igulik
Netsilik
Copper Eskimo
Caribou Eskimo

Labrador Eskimo
Beothuk
Naskapi
Montagnais

Western Eskimo
Koyukon
Kutchin
Han
Hare
Mountain
Yellowknife
Dogrib
Slave
Chipewyan
Cree
Ojibwa
Plains Cree
Blackfoot

Aleut
Tatana
Ingalik
Ahtena
Eyak
Tlingit
Tutchone
Tagish
Kaska
Tahltan
Tsetsaut
Sekani
Carrier
Tsimshian
Bella Coola
Haida
Kwakiutl
Nootka
Salish
Shuswap
Okanagan
Kutenai
Sarsi

The Tribes of the West and Southwest

I

AN INTRODUCTION TO NATIVE AMERICANS AND MYTHOLOGY

Jon E. Lewis

The history of America does not begin in 1492. There were already millions of people living in the Americas when Christopher Columbus and his weary, salt-splattered white men stumbled ashore in the Bahamas. Columbus thought he had encountered the East Indies, so termed the welcoming natives 'Indios'. Indians.

Columbus was soon apprised of his mistake in geography, but his name for the aboriginals of the Americas stuck. To themselves, the inhabitants of the continent were usually 'The People'. Aside from the error in nomenclature, the European explorers also mistook the racial origins of the 'Red Men'. Commonly, the native people were regarded as being lost Phoenicians, migratory Hittites, or the lost Ten Tribes of Israel. Most fanciful of all were the early voyagers who found a blood link between the American Indian and the Welsh, with the former supposedly the multifarious offspring of the Welsh prince Madoc, son of Owen Gwyneth, who colonized the Gulf of Mexico in 1170.

It is easy to mock ethnographical explanations of earlier centuries, but modern Western science is surprisingly vague and divided about the first settlement of the land that would become known as America. Perhaps the first humans set foot there 30,000 years ago, but then it might have been as recent as 12,000 years ago. Or as far back in the mist of time as 60,000 years ago. What ethnologists do largely agree on, is that the first settlers walked there from Siberia via the land bridge known as Beringia, although 'bridge' is a misnomer for a tundra landmass five hundred miles wide. And that these pioneers – who were likely motivated by a hunger for big game, such as the mastodon and giant buffalo – were, anatomically, modern humans, *homo sapiens sapiens.* In other words, humans did not evolve in America, they migrated there. They were few in number, a scant handful of families, and from them, the DNA evidence suggests, descended 95 per cent of Native Americans – as America's aboriginals are now usually termed.

After landing in present day Alaska, the first Americans fanned out down the Continent via river valleys as the Ice Age reluctantly thawed; the inhabiting of the New World was a long process, with passage frequently blocked by the Laurentide ice sheet, which covered 5 million square miles of Canada and the USA, sometimes reaching 700 feet thick. According to some anthropologists, it may have taken man 25,000 years to spread from Alaska to Cape Horn. By that time, glacial meltwater had caused the seas to rise, submerging Berengia, and cutting off the New World from the Old. But just before waters lapped over Berengia, there were two late waves of migration, those of the Na-Dene and Eskimo-Aleuts, about 9,000 BC.

Something else modern Western scientific minds largely agree on: the first humans in America were Paleolithic, their culture characterized by the use of crude stone tools. A second stage of development (Upper Lithic or Paleo-American) beginning circa 20,000 BC, saw American aboriginals fashion stone knives and points for spears which were thin, flat and fluted; the spears themselves were launched from a wooden spear-thrower or atlatl. Then, around 10,000 years ago, either because of a shift in the Earth's axis or because of over-hunting, the giant Pleistocene herbivores that had enticed humans to the Americas vanished, forcing these so-called Clovis People (named after the archeological site near Clovis, New Mexico) to turn to the hunting of smaller game, and even farming. Milling stones and manos began to appear. In this 'Archaic Stage' the Native Peoples became spectacularly efficient in adapting to the environments in which they found themselves, whether it was the salmon-rich waters of the Pacific Northwest coast (the Tlingit), the wild rice bearing Great Lakes (the Menominee), or the harsh deserts of Arizona with their life-saving Mesquite trees (the Pima). As the tribes built relationships with their land, so they themselves changed, in shape, culture, religion, and tongue. From the single voice of the first settlers, there came a Babel of languages: Algonquian, Siouan, Iroquoian, Athapascan, Pi-man, Shoshonean, Shahaptian, Caddoan, Salishan among hundreds of others. The linguist Morris Swadesh estimated that when Columbus waded ashore in 1492, the inhabitants were speaking 2,200 languages.

Although the white latecomers like to talk of 'the Indian' when they gate-crashed the New World, 5 or so million original inhabitants living north of Mexico had long diverged into distinct nations – about 500 of them. In much the same way as the French and English both inhabited Europe but were utterly unlike each other, so were the nations of North America. This diversity of nationality ensured that while some tribes would resist the European colonialist, others threw in their lot with the newcomers, either to extend their power over their neighbours (the Mohegans), or to defend themselves from hegemonic locals (as did the Crows, who shared the same neck of the Plains as the expansionist Sioux).

It follows that the Native Americans did not share a single

religion. Yet certain generalizations about Native American religion may be hazarded. Running through the religion of Native Peoples was a sense of sacred interconnection between the aboriginal and his environment, a spiritual axis around which myth, morality and aesthetics revolved. To many Native Americans, each tree and animal had its own spirit, with which the individual could commune. If the harmonious relationship with nature was put out of kilter, only bad things could happen until respect, virtuous deeds, beautiful art, dances and prayers harmonized the tribe and their land. Above all, indigenous peoples of the continent sought to preserve balance in their relations with the world by ritual.

Most tribes had shamans, individuals who mixed priest-hood with medicine, who were believed to be able to establish direct contact with the spirit world, as well as ward off evil spirits, ensure good hunting, help the crops grow, bring success in battle. But these good things could only happen if the world and its animals were accorded respect, as well as accessed and honoured with ritual. Animals had the power of reason – and they reasoned that they would only give their life to those who honoured them. The Montagnais above the St Lawrence River, to the incredulity of the Jesuit priests who encountered them in the 1630s, would not allow dogs to eat the bones of animals the Montagnais had trapped. Souls of the beaver, patiently explained the Montagnais to the black-clad priests, visited the home of prospective hunters to see how the bones of dead beaver kin were treated. 'If they [the bones] have been given to the dogs, the other beavers would be warned, and so they would make themselves difficult to catch.' The Dakota Sioux ceremonially buried the bones of elk and beaver after eating the flesh. The Powhatans made offerings of tobacco for their fish traps.

Although generally bound to the Earth, the Amerindian was especially bound to one corner of it. Common to Amerindian religion was the belief that each nation was created for its own land, and it was special to them. In the words of Geronimo, the famed Apache war chief:

> For each tribe of men Usen [God] created he also made a home. In the land for any particular tribe He placed whatever would be best for the welfare of that tribe, the Apaches and their home [were] each created for the other by Usen himself.

And in the words of Luther Standing Bear, who became chief of the Oglala Sioux in 1905:

> The American Indian is of the soil, whether it be the region of forests, plains, pueblos, or mesas. He fits into the landscape, for the hand that fashioned the continent also fashioned the man for his surroundings. He once grew as naturally as the wild flowers; he belongs just as the buffalo belonged.

Just as the Native Americans had no common religion, they had no universal mythology. The multitude of tribes each developed their own stories about the creation of the earth, the coming of the first people, and the lives and doings of deities and heroes.

Before exploring the mythology of North America, it is beneficial to consider the geography and climate of the continent because, as Geronimo and Luther Standing Bear so cogently explained, the link between the Native American (and his and her mythology) and the environment is absolute.

In dealing with the vast mythology of North America contemporary anthropologists, for convenience, organize myths by geography to produce nine or so principal culture areas. These are:

Arctic
A vast desert of ice, tundra, cold seas and rocky beaches, the Arctic culture area extends from Alaska around the northern rim of the continent to eastern Greenland. The two primary

Native peoples are the Inuit and the Aleuts of the Aleutian archipelago off the southwest coast of Alaska. Both groups in the Archaic Period before white contact developed a hunting lifestyle that was nomadic in summer and sedentary in winter, with the key food source being sea mammals and fish, led by seals, salmon, trout, capelin, the narwhal, beluga whales. Inland in summer and in autumn eggs, roots and berries were gathered. Due to nomadism the Eskimo did not evolve political structures; the Aleuts, who lived a more settled existence developed a caste system, which included a slave category.

Subarctic

The Subarctic culture area covers most of Canada, except for the Northwest Coast and the Arctic margin; it also includes the interior of Alaska. The subarctic tundra and forest was home to numerous Native American peoples that can be divided into two major groups: the Algonquian speakers of eastern Canada (including the Cree, Montagnais and Ojibwa) and the Athapascan speakers of western Canada and the Alaskan interior (such as Chipewya and Dogrib). Most tribes were hunters of the caribou, living in easily transportable dwellings of bent poles and caribou skins. Hunting and fishing were supplemented by plant-gathering. To the south of the culture area birch bark was a staple building material, used for everything from wigwams to canoes. The subsistence lifestyle of the subarctic tribes militated against the formation of large political or social groups, and 'villages' were small and based on single autonomous families.

Northwest Coast

Stretching from southern Alaska to northern California, the Pacific Northwest offered a wet but temperate climate, which afforded a comfortable lifestyle based around fishing, predominantly of the salmon that swarmed in the sea and rivers. The forested land behind the shore, which backed onto the

Cascade Range, offered easy and rich pickings, with abundant moose, caribou, deer, mountain sheep, birds, berries, eggs among the firs and redwoods. There was no agriculture. Wood was used for the construction of lodges and canoes, and bark fibres, together with goat and dog wool used to make clothing. (The Salish kept a small breed of dog expressly for the purpose of shearing.) Relative affluence and a sedentary lifestyle, based around permanent large shore-side villages, with up to thirty houses, resulted in a sophisticated culture and highly stratified, hierarchical society based on kinship to the chief. War with rival villages was endemic, with the consequence that heroism was a significant strand in the culture's mythology.

California

The favourable climatic conditions in the culture area of California, approximately the current area of the state absenting the southeast section along the Colorado, provided prolific food and raw materials for housing, cloths and tools. At the time of first contact in 1540, the aboriginal population was estimated to be upwards of 300,000 people. These lived in some 100 tribes and bands, speaking 200 languages. Despite this diversity, almost all native Californians were primarily foragers; only alongside the Colorado River was agriculture practised. Lamas, a type of edible hyacinth, and acorns were major sources of starch. Villages were typically comprised of a small number of families related through the paternal line; the villages were not allied to tribes and rights were extended to all within the curtilage. Indian culture and land holding in California was first eradicated by Spanish missionary activity ('The Mission Period'), then by the gold rush that began in 1848.

Southwest

The Southwest culture area comprises present-day New Mexico and Arizona together with parts of Utah, Colorado, Texas, and northwest Mexico. An arid region of desert and mountains, the Southwest culture area had been home to different people at different times before white contact. Some of the aboriginals were hunter-gatherers and remained so, while others c. 4,000 BC began cultivating maize and squash, probably after contact with cultures from Mesoamerica.

Because farming in the Southwest was labour-intensive (it required irrigation in the form of hundreds of miles of canals), the local society of the Native Peoples ineluctably transformed into a sophisticated, stratified, sedentary village-based civilization – as had all other cultures based around water-control, beginning with the ancient Egyptians. Three complex cultures emerged in the Southwest between AD 200 and 1100 in the form of the Mogollon, Hohokam and the Anasazi, all of which constructed stone and adobe villages (called Pueblos by the Spanish) overseen by a hierarchy of men who combined in their personages the functions of chief and priest. Until 1882, the Anasazi pueblo at Chaco Canyon, New Mexico, with its five-storey building housing maybe 1,500 people was the biggest apartment block in America.

The Anasazi were the probable ancestors of the Acoma, Zuñi and Hopi, while the Hohokam were the ancestors of the Pima and Papago. During the twelfth and thirteenth centuries, Hohokam and Anasazi agriculture experienced a decline due to soil depletion and drought. (The same drought affected the Great Plains; in the mythology of the plains there are stories describing how a giant serpent swallowed all the rivers.) The Hohokam abandoned their villages and reverted to nomadic hunting and gathering; the Anasazi, meanwhile, moved south and east into new pueblos.

Approximately two centuries later, archeologists suggest, the Apache and Navajo migrated to the Southwest from the subarctic (both tribes are Athapascan speakers); the Navajo took to the farming lifestyle of the local tribes, especially sheep-herding, but the Apache remained hunter-gatherers. Generally 'Archaic Period' Indians in the Southwest outside the Pueblos had a loose system of tribal government because the poverty of the environment obliged them to split into small groups. Shamans were known to all tribes. Unusually, Navajo medicine-men often considered themselves to have been magically transgendered and would wear women's clothing.

The popular image of the Native American might be a be-feathered hunter astride a pony on the buffalo Plains, but it is nonetheless the case that 60 per cent of the world's contemporary food comes from plants domesticated by Amerindians such as the Pueblo peoples and their ancestors. These vegetable crops include potatoes, sweet potatoes, tomatoes, tobacco, peppers, pumpkins and maize (or 'corn') plants. Maize derived from a wild grass of Mexico called teosinte, and took approximately 7,000 years of genetic selection to provide large, sustaining cobs. The Indians of the Southwest also domesticated the turkey; this, along with the dog, was the only animal domesticated by Native Americans before white contact.

The move to agriculture enabled population growth. Many have tried to estimate how many 'Indians' inhabited the New World prior to the arrival of the Europeans. While many scholars suggest 5 million aboriginals lived in North America in 1492, the range of population figures spans from 1 million to 10 million. Beyond dispute is that population density was highest in agricultural areas.

Great Basin
A vast area of inhospitable desert and salt flats run through by mountains, the Great Basin largely overlaps with the states of Utah and Nevada, together with parts of Oregon, Idaho, Wyoming, Colorado, California, and includes the Columbia and Fraser River basins. Nearly all of the dominant tribes, which included the Paiute and Bannock, spoke Shoshone. Prior to European contact, the tribes were nomadic foragers, with the exception of some sedentary tribes located along the major rivers and the foothills of the Rockies; the absence of

large game meant that the diet was often vegetarian, supplemented by small animals, reptiles, fish and insects. People generally lived in small family units, only coming together for specific events, principally the pinion harvest in the autumn. As was typical of hunter-gatherers, leadership and social organization were informal; even shamans had no special rights, and the vocation was open to anyone with a calling. Great Basin tribes were pantheistic, believing that a supernatural force, puha, resided in everything. During the eighteenth and early nineteenth centuries, some of the Great Basin tribes became horsed and formed bands of mounted hunters which took on the cultural attributes of the Plains Indians.

The Plains

The almost unbroken ocean of grassland known as the Great Plains, home to great herds of buffalo, extends south from Alberta in Canada to the Gulf of Mexico, from the foothills of the Rockies east to the Mississippi. The original Plains dwellers were small bands of nomads who subsisted on foraging along river bottoms, plus the hunting of buffalo on foot (and stampeding them over cliffs into 'blood kettles') twice a year, in February for robes and in autumn for meat, before taking up part-time farming. Population expansion in the eastern woodlands pushed more people onto the plains c. AD 1300, so that by the mid sixteenth century the grassland supported upwards of 150,000 peoples. However, the tribes which became renowned as *the* Plains Indians – the Sioux, Arapaho, Cheyenne, Blackfeet, Comanche – mostly arrived in the 1700s when the white man's horse had gone native and was available for the taking. These previously pedestrian foragers and farmers took up a mounted, nomadic lifestyle exclusively organized around the hunting of the buffalo. The Sioux found no less than 88 uses for *bos bison Americanus* excluding food.

Plains tribes spent the winter in conical earth lodges; in summer they lived in portable teepees as they followed the buffalo. Fully nomadic tribes lived in teepees made from as many as thirty buffalo hides; until the horse, teepees had been restricted to between six and ten hides in size, because the dog, the aboriginals' original beast of burden, could pull no more. The Sioux liked to decorate the outside of their tents with pictographs, believing that these had supernatural powers to ward off misfortune and sickness; in Blackfeet bands, only high status members were permitted to paint the sacred Morning Star symbol on the top of their teepees.

There was little formal governance on the Great Plains, with bands (extended families sharing a common ancestor) organized into tribes led by a chief, who won his position through bravery or wisdom. Plains society, however, was intricate, and was based on ownership of horses, spiritual power derived from visions, and, above all, from war honours. Most tribes had warrior societies, such as the Kit Fox or Crazy Dogs, that jealously administered war honours, which were recorded on teepees and war bonnets. Warfare was a way of life for Plains Indian males. There were certain differences between the tribes as to what counted as the most daring exploit in war, but generally to 'count coup' – to touch an enemy warrior harmlessly with hand or weapon – was topmost. Scalping had religious purpose, because scalps empowered the taker and ritually transferred mourning to the enemy. Shamans, priestly magicians and healers, were integral to tribal life.

Southeast

A land of mild winters and high rainfall, the Southeast provided abundant and fertile soil, forests filled with game, and rivers teeming with fish. Native society, much influenced by the Mesoamerican tribes to the south, was advanced. Beginning with the Hopewell civilization, which adopted maize-growing c. AD 100, the region saw successive cultures which constructed vast earthen burial mounds, culminating in the Mississippian civilization that flourished c. AD 750 to 1200. The Mississippians were the benefactors of a new strain of corn so productive it became almost the sole crop. As elsewhere, agriculture encouraged more complex social and political structures; the Mississippian capital of Cahokia (across the river from present day St Louis), which contained over 10,000 people, was ruled over by an absolute monarch, the Great Sun chief. Whereas the previous mound cultures had settled for using the mound as a burial site, the Mississippians topped their tumps with temples and palaces. The Great Sun's complex at Cahokia stood on top of a mound 100 feet high and 16 acres in extent. Mississippi culture was unique in North America developing a distinct ruling class. Even with the decline of the classical Mississippian culture, life in the region continued to be based around agriculture and permanent large-scale villages. Often these were governed by a council of elders with a chief (or chieftainess) in a presiding role.

Although they consisted of a large number of tribes, the Indians of the Southeast had in common a complex belief system centred on farming. The most important ritual was the Green Corn Ceremony, a festival of thanksgiving and renewal held to coincide with the ripening of the autumn crop. The Southeast tribes, additionally, all followed a matrilineal clan system.

Northeast
The Northeast culture region stretches south from Canada to Tennessee, west from the Atlantic coast to the Mississippi River. In the heavily wooded Northeast culture region the Indian tribes sustained themselves by hunter-gathering and agriculture. Divided principally into two language groups, Iroquois and Algonquin, the peoples of the Northeast lived in small semi-permanent villages (often fortified) and maize was a staple foodstuff, its culture learned from the horticulturalists of the Southeast. The Algonquian language has added 'toma-hawk' and 'moccasin', among other words, to the English lexicon. Most of the tribes of the Northeastern Woodlands were matrilineal. The Iroquois were intensely politically

sophisticated, and formed a confederation in the sixteenth century to dominate neighbouring tribes. Native land struggles were intensified by European colonization from 1497 onwards, and by the 1700s many Algonquian nations had migrated west to the Great Lakes, where they in turn displaced some of the existing tribes.

The land struggles of the Northeast tribes were not about ownership in the accepted, Western sense. A band or tribe might claim certain land as their territory – which could be vast, as with the Comanche of the southern plains – but it was held communally. Five hundred years of tragedy resulted from the inability of the whites to understand that the Native American's hunting or farming grounds were also his home, and the place to which he was spiritually attached.

But it was not just the tribes and their land that were devastated by European colonization. So was their culture, including their mythologies.

No Native American culture had writing. Consequently, myths, legends and tales were transmitted orally. With the eradication of the tribes, whether through war or the white man's microbes, many myths were lost forever, along with the languages with which they were spoken. About a third of the tongues of native North America were lost for ever.

Although many early European explorers noted the beliefs of the Native Americans they met, Americans and Europeans did not begin recording and collecting Indian myths in earnest until the 1820s, beginning with Henry Rowe Schoolcraft, Indian agent, and spouse of a half-Ojibwa woman. (School-craft's ethnographical studies of the Ojibwa provided Longfellow with much of the source material for his epic poem, *The Song of Hiawatha*.) Another early collector of Indian myths was the artist George Catlin. But the recording and translation of Native American myths reached its zenith between 1887 and 1934, as scholars rushed to record these texts before yet more tribes and their mythological heritage vanished.

One such collector was the Scottish folklorist Lewis Spence (1874–1955), author of *Myths and Legends of the North American Indians*, first published in 1914 and which forms the bulk of the current volume. Spence, rightly, was hugely impressed by the 'conscientious and enterprising' United States Bureau of Ethnology, and relied heavily on their endeavours. In recording Native American myths Spence was sound. However, the interpretation and classification of myth has changed considerably in a century, as has the anthropological understanding of Native Americans in the prehistoric times. Consequently, in order to reflect the state of contemporary research on Native American mythology this volume has omitted Spence's chapter 1 ('Divisions, Customs, and History of the Race') and replaced it with the above survey. Additional information about the tribes, their myths, as well as current folkloric concepts (notably the 'trickster', 'culture hero' and 'transformer') is contained in the commentaries which begin each chapter.

As Spence himself recognized so accurately and sensitively, the reader coming to Native American myth for the first time is stepping into a world wholly unlike the safe and certain belief systems of Western science. It is a world which is often threatening and fantastic, a world where capriciousness, deceit and the inexplicable rule. Welcome to the world of the infamous shape-shifting trickster Coyote.

As is obvious from a mere moment's reflection, myth was the means by which American Indians made sense of an unpredictable universe. Myth was, above all, the method by which the present was explained by the past. Mythology evolved as people sought to answer questions about the world: Who made man? Where did corn – a staple crop of numerous native societies – come from?

Myths have other functions. Another key function of myth is to account for a tribe's religion and lifestyle; in Sioux origin stories, for example, the 'culture hero' (see p 21 for an explanation of the term) White Buffalo gives the Lakota tribes a sacred pipe, the obligation for following seven ceremonies, and the buffalo as their principal food source.

More minor functions of myth are to teach moral values and principles. The recitation of myth plays a role in healing and cultural renewal. The Navajo 'Blessingway' ceremony is simultaneously a telling of the tribe's creation myth and prayer for healing and harmony.

Native myth-making did not stop on contact with the Europeans. Some Native American myths, indeed, were influenced by contact with the first missionaries. This interaction can be detected in the 'First Creator and Lone Man' version of the creation myth of the Mandan, in which the second deity character, Jesus-like, is born as a man then disappears from earth after his good works.

Myths are sacred ancient narratives. Legends and tales, in contrast, while commonly containing a moral kernel, are principally for entertainment rather than religious or social purposes. Both myths and legends were, as already noted, oral narratives; the bare words collected by white scholars would have been complemented in their original telling by the speaker's gestures and illustrative aids, such as stone carvings, shells, or pottery. Speakers in Northeastern tribes used mnemonics to aid their story-telling. The Iroquois had Wampum Belts, while the Ojibwa (Chippewa) recorded the mythical stories of the tribe's heroes in pictographs on birch bark.

The word myth trails an unfortunate connotation of falsehood. In no sense should Native American myths be regarded as being untrue. They are alternative explanations of reality. They address issues germane to those people who developed them. They contain empirical information about history that passes the muster of Western science and law. In one celebrated example of the validity of myth, in 1997 the Supreme Court of Canada recognized the Bear Mother myth of the Gitksan as evidence in support of the tribe's claim to 22,000 square miles of British Columbia.

As the case of the Gitksan demonstrates so dramatically, myth is not dead. For Native Americans it is a source of identity, a mechanism for cultural and political renewal. For everyone else, the myths of Native America are extraordinary gateways into the minds and lives of the continent's original inhabitants.

2

THE MYTHOLOGIES OF THE NORTH AMERICAN INDIANS

Animism

All mythological systems spring from the same fundamental basis. The gods are the children of reverence and necessity. But their genealogy stretches still farther back. Savage man, unable to distinguish between the animate and inanimate, imagines every surrounding object to be, like himself, instinct with life. Trees, the winds, the river (which he names 'the Long Person'), all possess life and consciousness in his eyes. The trees moan and rustle, therefore they speak, or are, perchance, the dwelling-place of powerful spirits. The winds are full of words, sighings, warnings, threats, the noises, without doubt, of wandering powers, friendly or unfriendly beings. The water moves, articulates, prophesies, as, for example, did the Peruvian Rimac and Ipurimac – 'the Oracles', 'the Prophesiers'. Even abstract qualities were supposed to possess the attributes of living things. Light and darkness, heat and cold, were regarded as active and alert agencies. The sky was looked upon as the All-Father from whose co-operation with the Mother Earth all living things had sprung. This condition of belief is known as 'animism'.

Totemism

If inanimate objects and natural phenomena were endowed by savage imagination with the qualities of life and thought, the creatures of the animal world were placed upon a still higher level. The Indian, brought into contact with the denizens of the forest and prairie, conceived a high opinion of their qualities and instinctive abilities. He observed that they possessed greater cunning in forest-craft than himself, that their hunting instinct was much more sure, that they seldom suffered from lack of provisions, that they were more swift of foot. In short, he considered them to be his superiors in those faculties which he most coveted and admired. Various human attributes and characteristics became personified and even exaggerated in some of his neighbours of wood and plain. The fox was proverbial for craft, the wild cat for stealth, the bear for a wrong-headed stupidity, the owl for a cryptic wisdom, the deer for swiftness. In each of these attributes the several animals to whom they belonged appeared to the savage as more gifted than himself, and so deeply was he influenced by this seeming superiority that if he coveted a certain quality he would place himself under the protection of the animal or bird which symbolized it. Again, if a tribe or clan possessed any special characteristic, such as fierceness or cunning, it was usually called by its neighbours after the bird or beast which symbolized its character. A tribe would learn its nickname from captives taken in war; or it might even bestow such an appellation upon itself. After the lapse of a few generations the members of a tribe would regard the animal whose qualities they were supposed to possess as their direct ancestor, and would consider that all the members of his species were their blood-relations. This belief is known as totemism, and its adoption was the means of laying the foundation of a widespread system of tribal rule and custom, by which marriage and many of the affairs of life were and are wholly governed. Probably all European and Asiatic peoples have passed through this stage, and its remains are to be found deeply embedded in our present social system.

Totemic law and custom

Few generations would elapse before the sense of ancestral devotion to the totem or eponymous forefather of the tribe would become so strong as to be exalted into a fully developed system of worship of him as a deity. That the totem develops into the god is proved by the animal likeness and attributes of many deities in lands widely separate. It accounts for the jackal- and ibis-headed gods of Egypt, the bull-like deities of Assyria, the bestial gods of Hindustan – possibly even for the owl which accompanied the Grecian Pallas, for does not Homer speak of her as 'owl-eyed'? May not this goddess have developed from an owl totem, and may not the attendant bird of night which perches on her shoulder have been permitted to remain as a sop to her devotees in her more ancient form, who objected to her portrayal as a human being, and desired that some reminder of her former shape might be preserved? That our British ancestors possessed a totemic system is undoubted. Were not the clan Chattan of the Scottish Highlands the 'sons of the cat'? In the *Dean of Lismore's Book* we read of a tribe included under the 'sons to the king of Rualay' one battalion of whom was 'cat-headed', or wore the totem crest of the cat. The swine-gods and other animal deities possessed by the British Celts assist this theory, as do the remains of many folk-customs in England and Scotland. Our crests are but so many family symbols which have come down to us from the distant days when our forefathers painted them upon their shields or wore them upon their helmets as the badge of their tribe, and thus of its supposed beast-progenitor or protector.

As has been said, a vast and intricate system of tribal law and custom arose from the adoption of totemism. The animal from which the tribe took its name might not be killed or eaten, because of its blood-kinship with the clan. Descent from this ancestor postulated kinship between the various members of the tribe, male and female; therefore the female members were not eligible for marriage with the males, who had perforce to seek for wives elsewhere. This often led to the partial adoption of another tribe or family in the vicinity, and of its totem, in order that a suitable exchange of women might be made as occasion required, and thus to the inclusion of two *gentes* or divisions within the tribe, each with its different totem-name, yet each regarding itself as a division of the tribal family. Thus a member of the 'Fox' *gens* might not marry a woman of his own division, but must seek a bride from the 'Bears', and similarly a 'Bear' tribesman must find a wife from among the 'Foxes'.

Severity of totemic rule

The utmost severity attached to the observation of totemic law and custom, to break which was regarded as a serious crime. Indeed, no one ever thought of infringing it, so powerful are habit and the force of association. It is not necessary to specify here the numerous customs which may be regarded as the outcome of the totemic system, for many of these have little in common with mythology proper. It will suffice to say that they were observed with a rigour beside which the rules of the religions of civilized peoples appear lax and indulgent. As this system exercised such a powerful influence on Indian life and thought, the following passage from the pen of a high authority on Indian totemism may be quoted with advantage:[1]

'The native American Indian, holding peculiar self-centred views as to the unity and continuity of all life and the consequent inevitable interrelations of the several bodies and beings in nature, especially of man to the beings and bodies of his experience and environment, to whom were imputed by

[1] J. R. Swanton, in *Handbook of the North American Indians*.

him various anthropomorphic attributes and functions in addition to those naturally inherent in them, has developed certain fundamentally important cults, based on those views, that deeply affect his social, religious, and civil institutions. One of these doctrines is that persons and organizations of persons are one and all under the protecting and fostering tutelage of some imaginary being or spirit. These tutelary or patron beings may be grouped, by the mode and motive of their acquirement and their functions, into two fairly well defined groups or classes: (1) those which protect individuals only, and (2) those which protect organizations of persons. But with these two classes of tutelary beings is not infrequently confounded another class of protective imaginary beings, commonly called fetishes, which are regarded as powerful spiritual allies of their possessors. Each of these several classes of guardian beings has its own peculiar traditions, beliefs, and appropriate cult. The modes of the acquirement and the motives for the acquisition of these several classes of guardian beings differ in some fundamental and essential respects. The exact method of acquiring the clan or gentile group patrons or tutelaries is still an unsolved problem, although several plausible theories have been advanced by astute students to explain the probable mode of obtaining them. With respect to the personal tutelary and the fetish, the data are sufficiently clear and full to permit a satisfactory description and definition of these two classes of tutelary and auxiliary beings. From the available data bearing on this subject, it would seem that much confusion regarding the use and acquirement of personal and communal tutelaries or patron beings has arisen by regarding certain social, political, and religious activities as due primarily to the influence of these guardian deities, when in fact those features were factors in the social organization on which has been later imposed the cult of the patron or guardian spirit. Exogamy, names and class names, and various taboos exist where "totems" and "totemism", the cults of the guardian spirits, do not exist.

'Some profess to regard the clan or gentile group patron or tutelary as a mere development of the personal guardian, but from the available but insufficient data bearing on the question it appears to be, in some of its aspects, more closely connected in origin, or rather in the method of its acquisition, with the fetish, the Iroquois *otchina' ken'da*, "an effective agency of sorcery", than with any form of the personal tutelary. This patron spirit of course concerns the group regarded as a body, for with regard to each person of the group, the clan or gentile guardian is inherited, or rather acquired by birth, and it may not be changed at will. On the other hand, the personal tutelary is obtained through the rite of vision in a dream or a trance, and it must be preserved at all hazards as one of the most precious possessions. The fetish is acquired by personal choice, by purchase, or by inheritance, or from some chance circumstance or emergency, and it can be sold or discarded at the will of the possessor in most cases; the exception is where a person has entered into a compact with some evil spirit or being that, in consideration of human or other sacrifices in its honour at stated periods, the said spirit undertakes to perform certain obligations to this man or woman, and in default of which the person forfeits his right to live.

'"Totemism" is a purely philosophical term which modern anthropological literature has burdened with a great mass of needless controversial speculation and opinion. The doctrine and use of tutelary or patron guardian spirits by individuals and by organized bodies of persons are defined by Powell as "a method of naming", and as "the doctrine and system of naming". But the motive underlying the acquisition and use of guardian or tutelary spirits, whether by an individual or by an organized body of persons, is always the same – namely, to obtain welfare and to avoid ill-fare. So it appears to be erroneous to define this cult as "the doctrine and system of naming". It is rather the recognition, exploitation, and adjustment of the imaginary mystic relation of the individual or of the body of organized persons to the postulated *orendas*, mystic powers, surrounding each of these units of native society. With but few exceptions, the recognized relation between the clan or *gens* and its patron deity is not one of descent or source, but rather that of protection, guardianship, and support. The relationship as to source between these two classes of superior beings is not yet determined; so to avoid confusion in concepts, it is better to use distinctive names for them, until their connection, if any, has been definitely ascertained: this question must not be prejudged. The hypothetic inclusion of these several classes in a general one, branded with the rubric "totem" or its equivalent, has led to needless confusion. The native tongues have separate names for these objects, and until the native classification can be truthfully shown to be erroneous it would seem to be advisable to designate them by distinctive names. Notwithstanding the great amount of study of the literature of the social features of aboriginal American society, there are many data relative to this subject that have been overlooked or disregarded.'

Fetishism

Side by side with animism and totemism flourishes a third type of primitive belief, known as 'fetishism'. This word is derived from the Portuguese *feitiço*, 'a charm', 'something made by art', and is applied to any object, large or small, natural or artificial, regarded as possessing consciousness, volition, and supernatural qualities, and especially *orenda*, or magic power.

As has been said, the Indian intelligence regards all things, animals, water, the earth, trees, stones, the heavenly bodies, even night and day, and such properties as light and darkness, as possessing animation and the power of volition. It is, however, the general Indian belief that many of these are under some spell or potent enchantment. The rocks and trees are confidently believed by the Indian to be the living tombs of imprisoned spirits, resembling the dryads of Greek folklore, so that it is not difficult for him to conceive an intelligence, more or less potent, in any object, no matter how uncommon – indeed, the more uncommon the greater the probability of its being the abode of some powerful intelligence, incarcerated for revenge or some similar motive by the spell of a mighty enchanter.

The fetish is, in short, a mascot – a luck-bringer. The civilized person who attaches a swastika or small charm to his watch-chain or her bangle is unconsciously following in the footsteps of many pagan ancestors; but with this difference, that the idea that 'luck' resides in the trinket is weak in the civilized mind, whereas in the savage belief the 'luck' resident in the fetish is a powerful and living thing – an intelligence which must be placated with prayer, feast, and sacrifice. Fetishes which lose their reputations as bringers of good-fortune usually degenerate into mere amulets or talismanic ornaments, and their places are taken by others. The fetish differs from the class of tutelary or 'household' gods in that it may be sold or bartered, whereas tutelary or domestic deities are never to be purchased, or even loaned.

Fetish objects
Nearly all the belongings of a *shaman*, or medicine-man, are classed as fetishes by the North American Indians. These usually consist of the skins of beasts, birds, and serpents, roots, bark, powder, and numberless other objects. But the fetish must be altogether divorced from the idea of religion proper, with which it has little or no connection, being found side by side with religious phases of many types. The fetish may be a bone, a feather, an arrow-head, a stick, carved or painted, a fossil, a tuft of hair, a necklace of fingers, a stuffed skin, the hand of an enemy, anything which might be suggested to the original possessor in a dream or a flight of imagination. It is sometimes fastened to the scalp-lock, to the dress, to the bridle, concealed between the layers of a shield, or specially deposited in a shrine in the wigwam. The idea in

the mind of the original maker is usually symbolic, and is revealed only to one formally chosen as heir to the magical possession, and pledged in his turn to a similar secrecy.

Notwithstanding that the cult of fetishism is not, strictly speaking, a department of religious activity, a point exists at which the fetish begins to evolve into a god. This happens when the object survives the test of experience and achieves a more than personal or tribal popularity. Nevertheless the fetish partakes more of the nature of those spirits which are subservient to man (for example, the Arabian *jinn*) than of gods proper, and if it is prayed and sacrificed to on occasion, the 'prayers' are rather of the nature of a magical invocation, and the 'sacrifices' no more than would be accorded to any other assisting agent. Thus sharply must we differentiate between a fetish or captive spirit and a god. But it must be further borne in mind that a fetish is not necessarily a piece of personal property. It may belong collectively to an entire community. It is not necessarily a small article, but may possess all the appearances of a full-blown idol. An idol, however, is the abode of a god – the image into which a deity may materialize. A fetish, on the other hand, is *the place of imprisonment of a subservient spirit*, which cannot escape, and, if it would gain the rank of godhead, must do so by a long series of luck-bringing, or at least by the performance of a number of marvels of a protective or fortune-making nature. It is not unlikely that a belief exists in the Indian mind that there are many wandering spirits who, in return for food and other comforts, are willing to materialize in the shape the savage provides for them, and to assist him in the chase and other pursuits of life.

Apache fetishes

Among the Athapascan Indians the Apaches, both male and female, wear fetishes which they call *tzi-daltai*, manufactured from lightning-riven wood, generally pine or cedar, or fir from the mountains. These are highly valued, and are never sold. They are shaved very thin, rudely carved in the semblance of the human form, and decorated with incised lines representing the lightning. They are small in size, and few of them are painted. Bourke describes one that an Apache chief carried about with him, which was made of a piece of lath, unpainted, having a figure in yellow drawn upon it, with a narrow black band and three snake's heads with white eyes. It was further decorated with pearl buttons and small eagle-down feathers. The reverse and obverse were identical.

Many of the Apaches attached a piece of malachite to their guns and bows to make them shoot accurately. Bourke mentions a class of fetishes which he terms 'phylacteries'. These are pieces of buckskin or other material upon which are inscribed certain characters or symbols of a religious or 'medicine' nature, and they are worn attached to the person who seeks benefit from them. They differ from the ordinary fetish in that they are concealed from the public gaze. These 'phylacteries', Bourke says, 'themselves medicine', may be employed to enwrap other 'medicine', and 'thus augment their own potentialities'. He describes several of these objects. One worn by an Indian named Ta-ul-tzu-je 'was tightly rolled in at least half a mile of saddler's silk, and when brought to light was found to consist of a small piece of buckskin two inches square, upon which were drawn red and yellow crooked lines, which represented the red and yellow snake. Inside were a piece of malachite and a small cross of lightning-riven pine, and two very small perforated shells. The cross they designated "the black mind".' Another 'phylactery' consisted of a tiny bag of hoddentin, holding a small quartz crystal and four feathers of eagle-down. This charm, it was explained by an Indian, contained not merely the 'medicine' of the crystal and the eagle, but also that of the black bear, the white lion, and the yellow snake.

Iroquoian fetishes

Things that seem at all unusual are accepted by the Hurons, a tribe of the Iroquois, as *oky*, or supernatural, and therefore it is accounted lucky to find them. In hunting, if they find a stone or other object in the entrails of an animal they at once make a fetish of it. Any object of a peculiar shape they treasure for the same reason. They greatly fear that demons or evil spirits will purloin their fetishes, which they esteem so highly as to propitiate them in feasts and invoke them in song. The highest type of fetish obtainable by a Huron was a piece of the onniont, or great armoured serpent, a mythological animal revered by many North American tribes.

Fetishism among the Algonquins

Hoffmann states that at the 'medicine' lodges of some Algonquian tribes there are preserved fetishes or amulets worn above the elbows, consisting of strands of bead-work, metal bands, or skunk skins, while bracelets of shells, buckskin, or metal are also worn. A great tribal fetish of the Cheyenne was their 'medicine' arrow, which was taken from them by the Pawnees in battle. The head of this arrow projects from the bag which contains it, and it is covered with delicate waved or spiral lines, which denote its sacred character. It was, indeed, the palladium of the tribe. A peculiar type of fetish consisted of a mantle made from the skin of a deer and covered with feathers mixed with beadings. It was made and used by the medicine-men as a mantle of invisibility, or charmed covering to enable spies to traverse an enemy's country in security. In this instance the fetishistic power depended upon the devices drawn upon the article. The principal fetishes among the Hidatsa tribe of the Sioux are the skins of foxes and wolves, the favourite worn fetish being the stripe from the back of a wolf-skin with the tail hanging down the shoulders. A slit is made in the skin, through which the warrior puts his head, so that the skin of the wolf's head hangs down upon his breast. The most common tribal fetishes of the Sioux are, or were, buffalo heads, the neck-bones of which they preserve in the belief that the buffalo herds will thereby be prevented from removing to too great a distance. At certain periods they perform a ceremony with these bones, which consists in taking a potsherd filled with embers, throwing sweet-smelling grease upon it, and fumigating the bones with the smoke. There are certain trees and stones which are regarded as fetishes. To these offerings of red cloth, red paint, and other articles are made. Each individual has his personal fetish, and it is carried in all hunting and warlike excursions. It usually consists of a head, claws, stuffed skin, or other representative feature of the fetish animal. Even the horses are provided with fetishes, in the shape of a deer's horn, to ensure their swiftness. The rodent teeth of the beaver are regarded as potent charms, and are worn by little girls round their necks to make them industrious.

At Sikyatki, in Arizona, a territorial nucleus of the Hopi Indians, Mr Fewkes had opportunities of inspecting many interesting fetish forms. A number of these discovered in native graves were pebbles with a polished surface, or having a fancied resemblance to some animal shape. Many of the personal fetishes of the Hopi consist of fossils, some of which attain the rank of tribal fetishes and are wrapped up in sacred bundles, which are highly venerated. In one grave was found a single large fetish in the shape of a mountain lion, made of sandstone, in which legs, ears, tail, and eyes are represented, the mouth still showing the red pigment with which it had been coloured. This is almost identical with some fetishes used by the Hopi at the present day.

Totemism and fetishism meet

Fetishism among the Zuñi Indians of the south arose from an idea they entertained that they were kin with animals; in other words, their fetishes were totemistic. Totemism and fetishism were by no means incompatible with one another, but often flourished side by side. Fetishism of the Zuñi description is, indeed, the natural concomitant of a totemic system. Zuñi fetishes are usually concretions of lime or objects in which a natural resemblance to animals has been heightened by artificial means. Ancient fetishes are much valued by these people, and are often found by them in the vicinity of villages inhabited by their ancestors, and as tribal possessions are handed down from one generation to another. The medicine-men believe them to be the actual petrifactions of the animals they represent.

The Sun-Children

The Zuñi philosophy of the fetish is given in the 'Tale of the Two Sun-Children' as follows: 'Now that the surface of the earth was hardened even the animals of prey, powerful and like the fathers [gods] themselves, would have devoured the children of men, and the two thought it was not well that they should all be permitted to live, for, said they, "Alike the children of men and the children of the animals of prey multiply themselves. The animals of prey are provided with talons and teeth; men are but poor, the finished beings of earth, therefore the weaker." Whenever they came across the pathway of one of these animals, were he a great mountain lion or but a mere mole, they struck him with the fire of lightning which they carried on their magic shields. *Thlu!* and instantly he was shrivelled and turned into stone. Then said they to the animals that they had changed into stone, "That ye may not be evil unto man, but that ye may be a great good unto them, have we changed you into rock everlasting. By the magic breath of prey, by the heart that shall endure forever within you, shall ye be made to serve instead of to devour mankind." Thus was the surface of the earth hardened and scorched, and many of all kinds of beings changed to stone. Thus, too, it happens that we find here and there throughout the world their forms, sometimes large, like the beings themselves, sometimes shrivelled and distorted, and we often see among the rocks the forms of many beings that live no longer, which shows us that all was different in the "days of the new". Of these petrifactions, which are, of course, mere concretions or strangely shaped rock-forms, the Zuñi say:

"Whomsoever of us may be met with the light of such great good-fortune may see them, and should treasure them for the sake of the sacred [magic] power which was given them in the days of the new."[2]

The prey-gods

This tradition furnishes additional evidence relative to the preceding statement, and is supposed to enlighten the Zuñi Indian as to wherein lies the power of fetishes. It is thought that the hearts of the great animals of prey are infused with a 'medicinal' or magic influence over the hearts of the animals they prey upon, and that they overcome them with their breath, piercing their hearts and quite numbing them. Moreover, their roar is fatal to the senses of the lower beasts. The mountain lion absorbs the blood of the game animals, therefore he possesses their acute senses. Again, those powers, as derived from his heart, are preserved in his fetish, since his heart still lives, even although his body be changed to stone. It happens, therefore, that the use of these fetishes is chiefly connected with the chase. But there are exceptions. The great animals of the chase, although fetishistic, are also regarded as supernatural beings, the mythological position of which is absolutely defined. In the City of the Mists lives Po-shai-an-K'ia, father of the 'medicine' societies, a culture-hero deity, whose abode is guarded by six beings known as the 'Prey-Gods', and it is their counterfeit presentments that are made use of as fetishes. To the north of the City of the Mists dwells the Mountain Lion prey-god, to the west the Bear, to the south the Badger, to the east the Wolf, above the Eagle, below the Mole. These animals possess not only the guardianship of the six regions, but also the mastership of the 'medicine' or magic powers which emanate from them. They are the mediators between Po-shai-an-K'ia and man. The prey-gods, as 'Makers of the Path of Life', are given high rank among the

[2] Cushing's *Zuñi Fetiches* (1883).

gods, but notwithstanding this their fetishes are 'held as in captivity' by the priests of the various 'medicine' orders, and greatly venerated by them as mediators between themselves and the animals they represent. In this character they are exhorted with elaborate prayers, rituals, and ceremonials, and sometimes placated with sacrifices of the prey-gods of the hunt (*we-ma-a-ha-i*). Their special priests are the members of the Great Coyote People – that is, they consist of eleven members of the Eagle and Coyote clans and of the Prey Brothers priesthood. These prey-gods appear to be almost unique, and may be indicated as an instance of fetishism becoming allied with religious belief. They depict, with two exceptions, the same species of prey animals as those supposed to guard the six regions, the exceptions being the coyote and the wild cat. These six prey animals are subdivided into six varieties. They are, strictly speaking, the property of the priests, and members and priests of the sacred societies are required to deposit their fetishes, when not in use, with the Keeper of the Medicine of the Deer. These 'medicines' or memberships alone can perfect the shape of the fetishes and worship them.

The Council of Fetishes
The Day of the Council of the Fetishes takes place a little before or after the winter solstice or national New Year. The fetishes are taken from their places of deposit, and arranged according to species and colour in the form of a symbolic altar, quadrupeds being placed upright and birds suspended from the roof. The fetishes are prayed to, and prayer-meal is scattered over them. Chants are intoned, and a dance performed in which the cries of the fetish beasts are imitated. A prayer with responses follows. Finally all assemble round the altar and repeat the great invocation,

The fetish in hunting

The use of fetishes in hunting among the Zuñi is extremely curious and involved in its nature. The hunter goes to the house of the Deer Medicine, where the vessel containing the fetish is brought out and placed before him. He sprinkles meal over the sacred vessel in the direction in which he intends to hunt, chooses a fetish from it, and presses it to his lips with an inspiration. He then places the fetish in a buckskin bag over his heart. Proceeding to the hunt, he deposits a spider-knot of yucca leaves where an animal has rested, imitates its cry, and is supposed by this means to confine its movements within a narrow circle. He then inspires deeply from the nostrils of the fetish, as though inhaling the magic breath of the god of prey, and then puffs the breath long and loudly in the direction whence the beast's tracks trend, in the belief that the breath he has borrowed from the prey-god will stiffen the limbs of the animal he hunts. When the beast is caught and killed he inhales its suspiring breath, which he breathes into the nostrils of the fetish. He then dips the fetish in the blood of the slain quarry, sips the blood himself, and devours the liver, in order that he may partake of the animal's qualities. The fetish is then placed in the sun to dry, and lastly replaced in the buckskin pouch with a blessing, afterward being duly returned to the Keeper of the Deer Medicine.

Indian theology

The late Professor Brinton, writing on the Indian attitude toward the eternal verities, says:[3]

'Nature, to the heathen, is no harmonious whole swayed by eternal principles, but a chaos of causeless effects, the meaningless play of capricious ghosts. He investigates not, because he doubts not. All events are to him miracles. Therefore his faith knows no bounds, and those who teach him that doubt is sinful must contemplate him with admiration . . .

---

[3] *Myths of the New World.*

'Natural religions rarely offer more than this negative opposition to reason. They are tolerant to a degree. The savage, void of any clear conception of a supreme deity, sets up no claim that his is the only true church. If he is conquered in battle he imagines that it is owing to the inferiority of his own gods to those of his victor, and he rarely, therefore, requires any other reasons to make him a convert.

'In this view of the relative powers of deities lay a potent corrective to the doctrine that the fate of man was dependent on the caprices of the gods. For no belief was more universal than that which assigned to each individual a guardian spirit. This invisible monitor was an ever-present help in trouble. He suggested expedients, gave advice and warning in dreams, protected in danger, and stood ready to foil the machinations of enemies, divine or human.

'With unlimited faith in this protector, attributing to him the devices suggested by his own quick wits and the fortunate chances of life, the savage escaped the oppressive thought that he was the slave of demoniac forces, and dared the dangers of the forest and the war-path without anxiety.

'By far the darkest side of such a religion is that which it presents to morality. The religious sense is by no means the voice of conscience. The Takahli Indian when sick makes a full and free confession of sins, but a murder, however unnatural and unprovoked, he does not mention, not counting it a crime. Scenes of licentiousness were approved and sustained through-out the continent as acts of worship; maidenhood was in many parts freely offered up or claimed by the priests as a right; in Central America twins were slain for religious motives; human sacrifice was common throughout the tropics, and was not unusual in higher latitudes; cannibalism was often enjoined; and in Peru, Florida, and Central America it was not uncommon for parents to slay their own children at the behest of a priest.

'The philosophical moralist contemplating such spectacles has thought to recognize in them one consoling trait. All history, it has been said, shows man living under an irritated

God, and seeking to appease him by sacrifice of blood; the essence of all religion, it has been added, lies in that of which sacrifice is the symbol – namely, in the offering up of self, in the rendering up of our will to the will of God.

'But sacrifice, when not a token of gratitude, cannot be thus explained. It is not a rendering up, but a *substitution* of our will for God's will. A deity is angered by neglect of his dues; he will revenge, certainly, terribly, we know not how or when. But as punishment is all he desires, if we punish ourselves he will be satisfied; and far better is such self-inflicted torture than a fearful looking-for of judgment to come. Craven fear, not without some dim sense of the implacability of nature's laws, is at its roots.

'Looking only at this side of religion, the ancient philosopher averred that the gods existed solely in the apprehensions of their votaries, and the moderns have asserted that "fear is the father of religion, love her late-born daughter"; that "the first form of religious belief is nothing else but a horror of the unknown", and that "no natural religion appears to have been able to develop from a germ within itself anything whatever of real advantage to civilization".

'Looking around for other standards wherewith to measure the progress of the knowledge of divinity in the New World, *prayer* suggests itself as one of the least deceptive. "Prayer," to quote the words of Novalis, 'is in religion what thought is in philosophy. The religious sense prays, as the reason thinks." Guizot, carrying the analysis farther, thinks that it is prompted by a painful conviction of the inability of our will to conform to the dictates of reason.

'Originally it was connected with the belief that divine caprice, not divine law, governs the universe, and that material benefits rather than spiritual gifts are to be desired. The gradual recognition of its limitations and proper objects marks religious advancement. The Lord's Prayer contains seven petitions, only one of which is for a temporal advantage, and it the least that can be asked for.

'What immeasurable interval between it and the prayer of the Nootka Indian preparing for war:

'"Great Quahootze, let me live, not be sick, find the enemy, not fear him, find him asleep, and kill a great many of him."

'Or, again, between it and a petition of a Huron to a local god, heard by Father Brébeuf:

'"Oki, thou who liveth in this spot, I offer thee tobacco. Help us, save us from shipwreck, defend us from our enemies, give us a good trade and bring us back safe and sound to our villages."

'This is a fair specimen of the supplications of the lowest religions. Another equally authentic is given by Father Allouez. In 1670 he penetrated to an outlying Algonkin village, never before visited by a white man. The inhabitants, startled by his pale face and long black gown, took him for a divinity. They invited him to the council lodge, a circle of old men gathered round him, and one of them, approaching him with a double handful of tobacco, thus addressed him, the others grunting approval:

'"This indeed is well, Blackrobe, that thou dost visit us. Have mercy upon us. Thou art a Manito. We give thee to smoke.

'"The Naudowessies and Iroquois are devouring us. Have mercy upon us.

'"We are often sick; our children die; we are hungry. Have mercy upon us. Hear me, O Manito, I give thee to smoke.

'"Let the earth yield us corn; the rivers give us fish; sickness not slay us; nor hunger so torment us. Hear us, O Manito, we give thee to smoke."

'In this rude but touching petition, wrung from the heart of a miserable people, nothing but their wretchedness is visible. Not the faintest trace of an aspiration for spiritual enlightenment cheers the eye of the philanthropist, not the remotest conception that through suffering we are purified can be detected.'

The Indian idea of God

The mythologies of the several stocks of the Red Race differ widely in conception and detail, and this has led many hasty investigators to form the conclusion that they were therefore of separate origin. But careful study has proved that they accord with all great mythological systems in their fundamental principles, and therefore with each other. The idea of God, often strange and grotesque perhaps, was nevertheless powerfully expressed in the Indian mythologies. Each division of the race possessed its own word to signify 'spirit'. Some of these words meant 'that which is above', the higher one, 'the invisible', and these attributes accorded to deity show that the original Indian conception of it was practically the same as those which obtained among the primitive peoples of Europe and Asia. The idea of God was that of a great prevailing force who resided 'in the sky'. Savage or primitive man observes that all brightness emanates from the firmament above him. His eyes are dazzled by its splendour. Therefore he concludes that it must be the abode of the source of all life, of all spiritual excellence.

'Good' and 'bad'

Before man has discovered the uses of that higher machinery of reason, philosophy, and has learned to marshal his theological ideas by its light, such deities as he worships conform very much to his own ethical standard. They mirror his morality, or lack of it. They are, like himself, savage, cruel, insatiable in their appetites. Very likely, too, the bestial attributes of the totemic gods cling to those deities who have been evolved out of that system. Among savage people ideas of good and evil as we conceive them are non-existent. To them 'good' merely implies everything which is to their advantage, 'evil' that which injures or distresses them. It is only when such a system as totemism, with its intricate taboos and stringent laws bearing on the various relationships of life, comes to be adopted that a 'moral' order arises. Slaughter of the totem animal becomes a 'crime' – sacrilege. Slaughter of a member of the totem clan, of a blood-brother, must be atoned for because he is of the totem blood. Marriage with a woman of the same totem blood becomes an offence. Neglect to pay fitting homage and sacrifice to the gods or totem is regarded with severity, especially when the evolution of a priestly caste has been achieved. As the totem is an ancestor, so all ancestors are looked upon with reverence, and deference to living progenitors becomes a virtue. In such ways a code of 'morality' is slowly but certainly produced.

No 'good' or 'bad' gods

But, oddly enough, the gods are usually exempt from these laws by which their worshippers are bound. We find them murderous, unfilial, immoral, polygamous, and often irreverent. This may be accounted for by the circumstance that their general outlines were filled in before totemism had become a fully developed system, or it may mean that the savage did not believe that divine beings could be fettered by such laws as he felt himself bound to obey. However that may be, we find the American gods neither better nor worse than those of other mythological systems. Some of them are prone to a sort of Puckish trickery and are fond of practical joking: they had not reached the exalted nobility of the pantheon of Olympus. But what is more remarkable – and this applies to the deities of all primitive races – we find that they possess no ideas of good and evil. We find them occasionally worshipping gods of their own – usually the creative deities – and that may perhaps be accounted unto them for righteousness. But they are only 'good' to their worshippers inasmuch as they ensure them abundant crops or game, and only 'bad' when they cease to do so. They are not worshipped because they are the founts of truth and justice, but for the more immediately cogent reason that, unless placated by the steam of sacrifice, they will cease to provide an adequate food-supply to man, and may malevolently send destruction upon their neglectful worshippers.

In the relations between god and man among early peoples a specific contract is implied: 'Sacrifice unto us, provide us with those offerings the steam of which is our food, continue to do so, and we will see to it that you do not lack crops and game and the essentials of life. Fail to observe these customs and you perish.' Under such a system it will readily be granted that such horrors as human sacrifice were only undertaken because they were thought to be absolutely necessary to the existence of the race, as a whole, and were not prompted by any mere wanton delight in bloodshed.

Dealing with this point, the late Professor Brinton says in his *Myths of the New World*:

'The confusion of these distinct ideas [monotheism and polytheism] has led to much misconception of the native creeds. But another and more fatal error was that which distorted them into a dualistic form, ranging on one hand the good spirit with his legion of angels, on the other the evil one with his swarm of fiends, representing the world as the scene of their unending conflict, man as the unlucky football who gets all the blows.

'This notion, which has its historical origin among the Parsees of ancient Iran, is unknown to savage nations. "The Hidatsa," says Dr Matthews, "believe neither in a hell nor a devil." "The idea of the devil," justly observes Jacob Grimm, "is foreign to all primitive religions." Yet Professor Mueller, in his voluminous work on those of America, after approvingly quoting this saying, complacently proceeds to classify the deities as good or bad spirits!

'This view, which has obtained without question in earlier works on the native religions of America, has arisen partly from habits of thought difficult to break, partly from mistranslations of native words, partly from the foolish axiom of the early missionaries, "The gods of the Gentiles are devils." Yet their own writings furnish conclusive proof that no such distinction existed out of their own fancies. The same word (*otkon*) which Father Bruyas employs to translate into

Iroquois the term "devil", in the passage "The devil took upon himself the figure of a serpent", he is obliged to use for "spirit" in the phrase, "At the resurrection we shall be spirits", which is a rather amusing illustration how impossible it was by any native word to convey the idea of the spirit of evil.

'When, in 1570, Father Rogel commenced his labours among the tribes near the Savannah River, he told them that the deity they adored was a demon who loved all evil things, and they must hate him; whereas his auditors replied, that so far from this being the case, he whom he called a wicked being was the power that sent them all good things, and indignantly left the missionary to preach to the winds.

'A passage often quoted in support of this mistaken view is one in Winslow's *Good News from New England*, written in 1622. The author says that the Indians worship a good power called Kiehtan, and another "who, as farre as wee can conceive, is the Devill", named Hobbamock, or Hobbamoqui. The former of these names is merely the word "great", in their dialect of Algonkin, with a final *n*, and is probably an abbreviation of Kittanitowit, the great Manitou, a vague term mentioned by Roger Williams and other early writers, manufactured probably by them and not the appellation of any personified deity. The latter, so far from corresponding to the power of evil, was, according to Winslow's own statement, the kindly god who cured diseases, aided them in the chase, and appeared to them in dreams as their protector. Therefore, with great justice, Dr Jarvis has explained it to mean "the *oke* or tutelary deity which each Indian worships", as the word itself signifies.

'So in many instances it turns out that what has been reported to be the evil divinity of a nation, to whom they pray to the neglect of a better one, is in reality the highest power they recognize.'

Creation-myths

The mythologies of the Red Man are infinitely more rich in creative and deluge myths than those of any other race in the two hemispheres. Tales which deal with the origin of man are exceedingly frequent, and exhibit every phase of the type of creative story. Although many of these are similar to European and Asiatic myths of the same class, others show great originality, and strikingly present to our minds the characteristics of American aboriginal thought.

The creation-myths of the various Indian tribes differ as much from one another as do those of Europe and Asia. In some we find the great gods moulding the universe, in others we find them merely discovering it. Still others lead their people from subterranean depths to the upper earth. In many Indian myths we find the world produced by the All-Father sun, who thickens the clouds into water, which becomes the sea. In the Zuñi record of creation Awonawilona, the creator, fecundates the sea with his own flesh, and hatches it with his own heat. From this green scums are formed, which become the fourfold mother Earth and the all-covering father Sky, from whom sprang all creatures. 'Then from the nethermost of the four caves of the world the seed of men and the creatures took form and grew; even as with eggs in warm places worms quickly form and appear, and, growing, soon burst their shells and there emerge, as may happen, birds, tadpoles, or serpents: so man and all creatures grew manifoldly and multiplied in many kinds. Thus did the lowermost world-cave become overfilled with living things, full of unfinished creatures, crawling like reptiles over one another in black darkness, thickly crowding together and treading one on another, one spitting on another and doing other indecency, in such manner that the murmurings and lamentations became loud, and many amidst the growing confusion sought to escape, growing wiser and more manlike. Then Po-shai-an-K'ia, the foremost and the wisest of men, arising from the nethermost sea, came among men and the living things, and pitying them, obtained egress from that first world-cave through such a dark and narrow path that some seeing somewhat, crowding after, could not follow him, so eager mightily did they strive one with another. Alone then did Po-shai-an-K'ia come from one cave to another into this world, then island-like, lying amidst the world-waters, vast, wet, and unstable. He sought and found the Sun-Father, and besought him to deliver the men and the creatures from that nethermost world.'[4]

Algonquian creation-myth

In many other Indian mythologies we find the wind brooding over the primeval ocean in the form of a bird. In some creation-myths amphibious animals dive into the waters and bring up sufficient mud with them to form a beginning of the new earth. In a number of these tales no actual act of creation is recorded, but a reconstruction of matter only. The Algonquins relate that their great god Michabo, when hunting one day with wolves for dogs, was surprised to see the animals enter a great lake and disappear. He followed them into the waters with the object of rescuing them, but as he did so the lake suddenly overflowed and submerged the entire earth. Michabo despatched a raven with directions to find a piece of earth which might serve as a nucleus for a new world, but the bird returned from its quest unsuccessful. Then the god sent an otter on a like errand, but it too failed to bring back the needful terrestrial germ. At last a musk-rat was sent on the same mission, and it returned with sufficient earth to enable Michabo to recreate the solid land. The trees had become denuded of their branches, so the god discharged arrows at them, which provided them with new boughs. After this Michabo married the musk-rat, and from their union sprang the human race.

The Muskhogean creation-story

The Muskhogean Indians believe that in the beginning the primeval waste of waters alone was visible. Over the dreary

[4] Cushing, *13th Report*, Bureau of American Ethnology.

expanse two pigeons or doves flew hither and thither, and in course of time observed a single blade of grass spring above the surface. The solid earth followed gradually, and the terrestrial sphere took its present shape. A great hill, Nunne Chaha, rose in the midst, and in the centre of this was the house of the deity Esaugetuh Emissee, the 'Master of Breath'. He took the clay which surrounded his abode, and from it moulded the first men, and as the waters still covered the earth he was compelled to build a great wall upon which to dry the folk he had made. Gradually the soft mud became transformed into bone and flesh, and Esaugetuh was successful in directing the waters into their proper channels, reserving the dry land for the men he had created.

This myth closely resembles the story in the Book of Genesis. The pigeons appear analogous to the brooding creative Spirit, and the manufacture of the men out of mud is also striking. So far is the resemblance carried that we are almost forced to conclude that this is one of the instances in which Gospel conceptions have been engrafted on a native legend.

Siouan cosmology

The Mandan tribes of the Sioux possess a type of creation-myth which is common to several American peoples. They suppose that their nation lived in a subterranean village near a vast lake. Hard by the roots of a great grapevine penetrated from the earth above, and, clambering up these, several of them got a sight of the upper world, which they found to be rich and well stocked with both animal and vegetable food. Those of them who had seen the new-found world above returned to their home bringing such glowing accounts of its wealth and pleasantness that the others resolved to forsake their dreary underground dwelling for the delights of the sunny sphere above. The entire population set out, and started to climb up the roots of the vine, but no more than half the tribe had ascended when the plant broke owing to the weight of a corpulent woman. The Mandans imagine that after death they will return to the underground world in which they originally dwelt, the worthy reaching the village by way of the lake, the bad having to abandon the passage by reason of the weight of their sins.

The Minnetarees believed that their original ancestor emerged from the waters of a lake bearing in his hand an ear of corn, and the Mandans possessed a myth very similar to that of the Muskhogees concerning the origin of the world.

Bird- and serpent-worship and symbols

The serpent and the bird appear sometimes separately, sometimes in strange combination, in North American mythology. The bird is always incomprehensible to the savage. Its power of flight, its appearance in the heavens where dwell the gods, and its musical song combine to render it in his sight a being of mystery, possessing capabilities far above his own. From it he conceives the idea of the winged spirit or god, and he frequently regards it as a messenger from the bright regions of the sun or the sky deity. The flight and song of birds have always been carefully observed by primitive people as omens of grave import. These superstitions prevailed among the Red Race no less than among our own early ancestors. Many tribes imagined that birds were the visible spirits of the deceased. Thus the Powhatans of Virginia believed that the feathered race received the souls of their chiefs at death, and they were careful to do them no harm, accordingly. The Algonquins believed that birds caused the phenomenon of wind, that they created water-spouts, and that the clouds were the spreading and agitation of their wings. The Navaho thought that a great white swan sat at each of the four points of the compass and conjured up the blasts which came therefrom, while the Dakotas believed that in the west is the home of the Wakinyjan, 'the Flyers', the breezes that send the storms. The thunder, too, is regarded by some Indian peoples as the flapping of the pinions of a great bird, whose tracks are seen in the lightning, 'like the sparks which the buffalo scatters when he scours over a stony plain'. Many of the tribes of the north-west coast hold the same belief, and imagine the lightning to be the flash of the thunder-bird's eye.

Eagle-worship

The eagle appears to have been regarded with extreme veneration by the Red Man of the north. 'Its feathers composed the war-flag of the Creeks, and its image carved in wood or its stuffed skin surmounted their council lodges. None but an approved warrior dared wear it among the Cherokees, and the Dakotas allowed such an honour only to him who had first touched the corpse of the common foe.'[5] The Natchez and other tribes esteemed it almost as a deity. The Zuñi of New Mexico employed four of its feathers to represent the four winds when invoking the rain-god. Indeed, it was venerated by practically every tribe in North America. The owl, too, was employed as a symbol of wisdom, and sometimes, as by the Algonquins, was represented as the attendant of the Lord of the Dead. The Creek medicine-men carried a stuffed owl-skin as the badge of their fraternity and a symbol of their wisdom, and the Cherokees placed one above the 'medicine' stone in their council lodge. The dove also appears to have been looked upon as sacred by the Hurons and Mandans.

The serpent and the sun

Some Indian tribes adopted the serpent as a symbol of time. They reckoned by 'suns', and as the outline of the sun, a circle, corresponds to nothing in nature so much as a serpent with its tail in its mouth, devouring itself, so to speak, this may have been the origin of the symbol. Some writers think that the serpent symbolized the Indian idea of eternity, but it is unlikely that such a recondite conception would appeal to a primitive folk.

---

[5] Brinton, *Myths of the New World*.

The lightning serpent

Among the Indians the serpent also typified the lightning. The rapidity and sinuosity of its motions, its quick spring and sharp recoil, prove the aptness of the illustration. The brilliancy of the serpent's basilisk glance and the general intelligence of its habits would speedily give it a reputation for wisdom, and therefore as the possessor of *orenda*, or magic power. These two conceptions would shortly become fused. The serpent as the type of the lightning, the symbol of the spear of the war-god, would lead to the idea that that deity also had power over the crops or summer vegetation, for it is at the time of year when lightning is most prevalent that these come to fruition. Again, the serpent would through this association with the war-god attain a significance in the eye of warriors, who would regard it as powerful war-physic. Thus, the horn of the great Prince of Serpents, which was supposed to dwell in the Great Lakes, was thought to be the most potent war-charm obtainable, and priests or medicine-men professed to have in their possession fragments of this mighty talisman.

The Algonquins believed that the lightning was an immense serpent vomited by the Manito, or creator, and said that he leaves serpentine twists and folds on the trees that he strikes. The Pawnees called the thunder 'the hissing of the great snake'.

In snake-charming as a proof of magical proficiency, as typifying the lightning, which, as the serpent-spear of the war-god, brings victory in battle, and in its agricultural connection, lies most of the secret of the potency of the serpent symbol. As the emblem of the fertilizing summer showers the lightning serpent was the god of fruitfulness; but as the forerunner of floods and disastrous rains it was feared and dreaded.

Serpent-worship

Probably more ponderous nonsense has been written about the worship of reptiles ('ophiolatry', as the mythologists of half a century ago termed it) than upon any other allied subject. But, this notwithstanding, there is no question that the serpent still holds a high place in the superstitious regard of many peoples, Asiatic and American. As we have already seen, it frequently represents the orb of day, and this is especially the case among the Zuñi and other tribes of the southern portions of North America, where sun-worship is more usual than in the less genial regions. With the Red Man also it commonly typified water. The sinuous motion of the reptile sufficiently accounts for its adoption as the symbol for this element. And it would be no difficult feat of imagination for the savage to regard the serpent as a water-god, bearing in mind as he would the resemblance between its movement and the winding course of a river. Kennebec, the name of a stream in Maine, means 'snake', and Antietam, a creek in Maryland, has the same significance in the Iroquois dialect. Both Algonquins and Iroquois believed in the mighty serpent of the Great Lakes. The wrath of this deity was greatly to be feared, and it was thought that, unless duly placated, he vented his irascible temper upon the foolhardy adventurers who dared to approach his domain by raising a tempest or breaking the ice beneath their feet and dragging them down to his dismal fastnesses beneath.

The rattlesnake

The rattlesnake was the serpent almost exclusively honoured by the Red Race. It is slow to attack, but venomous in the extreme, and possesses the power of the basilisk to attract within reach of its spring small birds and squirrels. 'It has the same strange susceptibility to the influence of rhythmic sounds as the vipers, in which lies the secret of snake-charming. Most of the Indian magicians were familiar with this singularity. They employed it with telling effect to put beyond question their intercourse with the unseen powers, and to vindicate the potency of their own guardian spirits who thus enabled them to handle with impunity the most venomous of reptiles. The well-known antipathy of these serpents to certain plants, for instance the hazel, which, bound around the ankles, is an alleged protection against their attacks, and perhaps some antidote to their poison used by the magicians, led to their frequent introduction in religious ceremonies. Such exhibitions must have made a profound impression on the spectators and redounded in a corresponding degree to the glory of the performer. 'Who is a *manito*?' asks the mystic Meda Chant of the Algonkins. 'He,' is the reply, 'he who walketh with a serpent, walking on the ground; he is a *manito*.' The intimate alliance of this symbol with the mysteries of religion, the darkest riddles of the Unknown, is reflected in their language, and also in that of their neighbours, the Dakotas, in both of which the same words *manito, wakan*, which express the supernatural in its broadest sense, are also used as terms for this species of animals! The pious founder of the Moravian Brotherhood, the Count of Zinzendorf, owed his life on one occasion to this deeply rooted superstition. He was visiting a missionary station among the Shawnees, in the Wyoming valley. Recent quarrels with the whites had unusually irritated this unruly folk, and they resolved to make him their first victim. After he had retired to his secluded hut, several of the braves crept up on him, and, cautiously lifting the corner of the lodge, peered in. The venerable man was seated before a little fire, a volume of the Scriptures on his knees, lost in the perusal of the sacred words. While they gazed, a huge rattlesnake, unnoticed by him, trailed across his feet, and rolled itself into a coil in the comfortable warmth of the fire. Immediately the would-be murderers forsook their purpose and noiselessly retired, convinced that this was indeed a man of God.'[6]

The sacred origin of smoking
Smoking is, of course, originally an American custom, and with the Indians of North America possesses a sacred origin. Says an authority upon the barbarian use of tobacco:[7]

---

[6] Brinton, *Myths of the New World*, pp. 131–133.
[7] Schoolcraft, *op. cit.*

'Of the sacred origin of tobacco the Indian has no doubt, although scarcely two tribes exactly agree in the details of the way in which the invaluable boon was conferred on man. In substance, however, the legend is the same with all. Ages ago, at the time when spirits considered the world yet good enough for their occasional residence, a very great and powerful spirit lay down by the side of his fire to sleep in the forest. While so lying, his arch-enemy came that way, and thought it would be a good chance for mischief; so, gently approaching the sleeper, he rolled him over toward the fire, till his head rested among the glowing embers, and his hair was set ablaze. The roaring of the fire in his ears roused the good spirit, and, leaping to his feet, he rushed in a fright through the forest, and as he did so the wind caught his singed hair as it flew off, and, carrying it away, sowed it broadcast over the earth, into which it sank and took root, and grew up tobacco.

'If anything exceeds the savage's belief in tobacco, it is that which attaches to his pipe. In life it is his dearest companion, and in death is inseparable; for whatever else may be forgotten at his funeral obsequies, his pipe is laid in the grave with him to solace him on his journey to the "happy hunting-ground". "The first pipe" is among the most sacred of their traditions; as well it may be, when it is sincerely believed that no other than the Great Spirit himself was the original smoker.

'Many years ago the Great Spirit called all his people together, and, standing on the precipice of the Red Pipe-stone Rock, he broke a piece from the wall, and, kneading it in his hands, made a huge pipe, which he smoked over them, and to the north, south, east, and west. He told them that this stone was red, that it was their flesh, that of it they might make their pipes of peace; but it belonged equally to all; and the war-club and the scalping-knife must not be raised on this ground. And he smoked his pipe and talked to them till the last whiff, and then his head disappeared in a cloud; and immediately the whole surface of the rock for several miles was melted and glazed. Two great ovens were opened beneath, and two women (guardian spirits of the place) entered them in a blaze of fire; and they are heard there yet, and answer to the invocation of the priests, or medicine-men, who consult them on their visits to this sacred place.

'The "sacred place" here mentioned is the site of the world-renowned "Pipe-stone Quarry". From this place has the North American Indian ever obtained material for his pipe, and from no other spot. Catlin asserts that in every tribe he has visited (numbering about forty, and extending over thousands of miles of country) the pipes have all been made of this red pipe-stone. Clarke, the great American traveller, relates that in his intercourse with many tribes who as yet had had but little intercourse with the whites he learned that almost every adult had made the pilgrimage to the sacred rock and drawn from thence his pipe-stone. So peculiar is this "quarry" that Catlin has been at the pains to describe it very fully and graphically, and from his account the following is taken:

'"Our approach to it was from the east, and the ascent, for the distance of fifty miles, over a continued succession of slopes and terraces, almost imperceptibly rising one above another, that seemed to lift us to a great height. There is not a tree or bush to be seen from the highest summit of the ridge, though the eye may range east and west, almost to a boundless extent, over a surface covered with a short grass, that is green at one's feet, and about him, but changing to blue in distance, like nothing but the blue and vastness of the ocean.

'"On the very top of this mound or ridge we found the far-famed quarry or fountain of the Red Pipe, which is truly an anomaly in nature. The principal and most striking feature of this place is a perpendicular wall of close-grained, compact quartz, of twenty-five and thirty feet in elevation, running nearly north and south, with its face to the west, exhibiting a front of nearly two miles in length, when it disappears at both ends, by running under the prairie, which becomes there a little more elevated, and probably covers it for many miles, both to the north and south. The depression of the brow of the ridge at this place has been caused by the wash of a little stream, produced by several springs at the top, a little back from the wall, which has gradually carried away the superincumbent earth, and having bared the wall for the distance of two miles, is now left to glide for some distance over a perfectly level surface of quartz rock; and then to leap from the top of the wall into a deep basin below, and thence seek its course to the Missouri, forming the extreme source of a noted and powerful tributary, called the 'Big Sioux'.

'"At the base of this wall there is a level prairie, of half a mile in width, running parallel to it, in any, and in all parts of which, the Indians procure the red stone for their pipes, by digging through the soil and several slaty layers of the red stone to the depth of four or five feet. From the very numerous marks of ancient and modern diggings or excavations, it would appear that this place has been for many centuries resorted to for the red stone; and from the great number of graves and remains of ancient fortifications in the vicinity, it would seem, as well as from their actual traditions, that the Indian tribes have long held this place in high superstitious estimation; and also that it has been the resort of different tribes, who have made their regular pilgrimages here to renew their pipes."

'As far as may be gathered from the various and slightly conflicting accounts of Indian smoking observances, it would seem that to every tribe, or, if it be an extensive one, to every detachment of a tribe, belongs a potent instrument known as "medicine pipe-stem". It is nothing more than a tobacco-pipe, splendidly adorned with savage trappings, yet it is regarded as a sacred thing to be used only on the most solemn occasions, or in the transaction of such important business as among us could only be concluded by the sanction of a Cabinet Council, and affixing the royal signature.'

The gods of the Red Man

Most of the North American stocks possessed a regular pantheon of deities. Of these, having regard to their numbers, it will be impossible to speak in any detail, and it will be sufficient if we confine ourselves to some account of the more outstanding figures. As in all mythologies, godhead is often attached to the conception of the bringer of culture, the sapient being who first instructs mankind in the arts of life, agriculture, and religion. American mythologies possess many such hero-gods, and it is not always easy to say whether they belong to history or mythology. Of course, the circumstances surrounding the conception of some of these beings prove that they can be nothing else than mythological, but without doubt some of them were originally mere mortal heroes.

Michabo

We discover one of the first class in Michabo, the Great Hare, the principal deity of the Algonquins. In the accounts of the older travellers we find him described as the ruler of the winds, the inventor of picture-writing, and even the creator and preserver of the world. Taking a grain of sand from the bed of the ocean, he made from it an island which he launched in the primeval waters. This island speedily grew to a great size; indeed, so extensive did it become that a young wolf which managed to find a footing on it and attempted to cross it died of old age before he completed his journey. A great 'medicine' society, called Meda, was supposed to have been founded by Michabo. Many were his inventions. Observing the spider spread its web, he devised the art of knitting nets to catch fish. He furnished the hunter with many signs and charms for use in the chase. In the autumn, ere he takes his winter sleep, he fills his great pipe and smokes, and the smoke which arises is seen in the clouds which fill the air with the haze of the Indian summer.

Some uncertainty prevailed among the various Algonquian tribes as to where Michabo resided, some of them believing that he dwelt on an island in Lake Superior, others on an iceberg in the Arctic Ocean, and still others in the firmament, but the prevalent idea seems to have been that his home was in the east, where the sun rises on the shores of the great river Ocean that surrounds the dry land.

That a being possessing such qualities should be conceived of as taking the name and form of a timid animal like the hare is indeed curious, and there is little doubt that the original root from which the name Michabo has been formed does not signify 'hare'. In fact, the root *wab*, which is the initial syllable of the Algonquian word for 'hare', means also 'white', and from it are derived the words for 'east', 'dawn', 'light', and 'day'. Their names proceeding from the same root, the idea of the hare and the dawn became confused, and the more tangible object became the symbol of the god. Michabo was therefore the spirit of light, and, as the dawn, the bringer of winds. As lord of light he is also wielder of the lightning. He is in constant strife, nevertheless, with his father the West Wind, and in this combat we can see the diurnal struggle between east and west, light and darkness, common to so many mythologies.

Modern Indian tales concerning Michabo make him a mere tricksy spirit, a malicious buffoon, but in these we can see his character in process of deterioration under the stress of modern conditions impinging upon Indian life. It is in the tales of the old travellers and missionaries that we find him in his true colours as a great culture-hero, Lord of the Day and bringer of light and civilization.

The battle of the twin-gods

Among the Iroquois we find a similar myth. It tells of two brothers, Ioskeha and Tawiscara, or the White One and the Dark One, twins, whose grandmother was the moon. When they grew up they quarrelled violently with one another, and finally came to blows. Ioskeha took as his weapon the horns of a stag, while Tawiscara seized a wild rose to defend himself.

The latter proved but a puny weapon, and, sorely wounded, Tawiscara turned to fly. The drops of blood which fell from him became flint stones. Ioskeha later built for himself a lodge in the far east, and became the father of mankind and principal deity of the Iroquois, slaying the monsters which infested the earth, stocking the woods with game, teaching the Indians how to grow crops and make fires, and instructing them in many of the other arts of life. This myth appears to have been accepted later by the Mohawks and Tuscaroras.

Awonawilona

We have already alluded in the Zuñi creation-myth to the native deity Awonawilona. This god stands out as one of the most perfect examples of deity in its constructive aspect to be found in the mythologies of America. He seems in some measure to be identified with the sun, and from the remote allusions regarding him and the manner in which he is spoken of as an architect of the universe we gather that he was not exactly in close touch with mankind.

Ahsonnutli

Closely resembling him was Ahsonnutli, the principal deity of the Navaho Indians of New Mexico, who was regarded as the creator of the heavens and earth. He was supposed to have placed twelve men at each of the cardinal points to uphold the heavens. He was believed to possess the qualities of both sexes, and is entitled the Turquoise Man-woman.

Atius Tiráwa

Atius Tiráwa was the great god of the Pawnees. He also was a creative deity, and ordered the courses of the sun, moon, and stars. As known today he is regarded as omnipotent and intangible; but how far this conception of him has been coloured by missionary influence it would be difficult to say. We find, however, in other Indian mythologies which we know have not been sophisticated by Christian belief many references to deities who possess such attributes, and there is no reason why we should infer that Atius Tiráwa is any other than a purely aboriginal conception.

Esaugetuh Emissee

The great life-giving god of the Creeks and other Musk-hogeans was Esaugetuh Emissee, whose name signifies 'Master of Breath'. The sound of the name represents the emission of breath from the mouth. He was the god of wind, and, like many another divinity in American mythology, his rule over that element was allied with his power over the breath of life – one of the forms of wind or air. Savage man regards the wind as the great source of breath and life. Indeed, in many tongues the words 'wind', 'soul', and 'breath' have a common origin. We find a like conception in the Aztec wind-god Tezcatlipoca, who was looked upon as the primary source of existence.[8]

The Coyote god

Among the people of the far west, the Californians and Chinooks, an outstanding deity is, strangely enough, the Coyote. But whereas among the Chinooks he was thought to be a benign being, the Maidu and other Californian tribes pictured him as mischievous, cunning, and destructive. Kodoyanpe, the Maidu creator, discovered the world along with Coyote, and with his aid rendered it habitable for mankind. The pair fashioned men out of small wooden images, as the gods of the Kiche of Central America are related to have done in the myth in the *Popol Vuh*. But the mannikins proved unsuitable to their purpose, and they turned them into animals. Kodoyanpe's intentions were beneficent, and as matters appeared to be going but ill, he concluded that Coyote was at the bottom of the mischief. In this he was correct, and on consideration he resolved to destroy Coyote. On the side of the disturber was a formidable array of monsters and other

[8] See the author's *Myths of Mexico and Peru*.

evil agencies. But Kodoyanpe received powerful assistance from a being called the Conqueror, who rid the universe of many monsters and wicked spirits which might have proved unfriendly to the life of man, as yet unborn. The combat raged fiercely over a protracted period, but at last the beneficent Kodoyanpe was defeated by the crafty Coyote. Kodoyanpe had buried many of the wooden mannikins whom he had at first created, and they now sprang from their places and became the Indian race.

This is, of course, a day-and-night or light-and-darkness myth. Kodoyanpe is the sun, the spirit of day, who after a diurnal struggle with the forces of darkness flies toward the west for refuge. Coyote is the spirit of night, typified by an animal of nocturnal habits which slinks forth from its den as the shades of dusk fall on the land. We find a similar conception in Egyptian mythology, where Anubis, the jackal-headed, swallows his father Osiris, the brilliant god of day, as the night swallows up the sun.

Another version of the Coyote myth current in California describes how in the beginning there was only the primeval waste of waters, upon which Kodoyanpe and Coyote dropped in a canoe. Coyote willed that the surf beneath them should become sand.

'Coyote was coming. He came to Got'at. There he met a heavy surf. He was afraid that he might be drifted away, and went up to the spruce-trees. He stayed there a long time. Then he took some sand and threw it upon that surf: "This shall be a prairie and no surf. The future generations shall walk on this prairie!" Thus Clatsop became a prairie. The surf became a prairie.'[9]

But among other tribes as well as among the Chinooks Italapas, the Coyote, is a beneficent deity. Thus in the myths of the Shushwap and Kutenai Indians of British Columbia he figures as the creative agency, and in the folk-tales of the

---

[9] Boas, *Chinook Texts*.

Ashochimi of California he appears after the deluge and plants in the earth the feathers of various birds, which according to their colour become the several Indian tribes.

Blue Jay

Another mischievous deity of the Chinooks and other western peoples is Blue Jay. He is a turbulent braggart, schemer, and mischief-maker. He is the very clown of gods, and invariably in trouble himself if he is not manufacturing it for others. He has the shape of a jay-bird, which was given him by the Supernatural People because he lost to them in an archery contest. They placed a curse upon him, telling him the note he used as a bird would gain an unenviable notoriety as a bad omen. Blue Jay has an elder brother, the Robin, who is continually upbraiding him for his mischievous conduct in sententious phraseology. The story of the many tricks and pranks played by Blue Jay, not only on the long-suffering members of his tribe, but also upon the denizens of the supernatural world, must have afforded intense amusement around many an Indian camp-fire. Even the proverbial gravity of the Red Man could scarcely hold out against the comical adventures of this American Owl-glass.

Thunder-gods

North America is rich in thunder-gods. Of these a typical example is Haokah, the god of the Sioux. The countenance of this divinity was divided into halves, one of which expressed grief and the other cheerfulness – that is, on occasion he could either weep with the rain or smile with the sun. Heat affected him as cold, and cold was to him as heat. He beat the tattoo of the thunder on his great drum, using the wind as a drum-stick. In some phases he is reminiscent of Jupiter, for he hurls the lightning to earth in the shape of thunderbolts. He wears a pair of horns, perhaps to typify his connection with the lightning, or else with the chase, for many American thunder-gods are mighty hunters. This double conception arises from their possession of the lightning-spear, or arrow, which also gives them in some cases the character of a war-god. Strangely enough, such gods of the chase often resembled in appearance the animals they hunted. For example, Tsui 'Kalu (Slanting Eyes), a hunter-god of the Cherokee Indians, seems to resemble a deer. He is of giant proportions, and dwells in a great mountain of the Blue Ridge Range, in Northwestern Virginia. He appears to have possessed all the game in the district as his private property. A Cherokee thunder-god is Asgaya Gigagei (Red Man). The facts that he is described as being of a red colour, thus typifying the lightning, and that the Cherokees were originally a mountain people, leave little room for doubt that he is a thunder-god, for it is around the mountain peaks that the heavy thunder-clouds gather, and the red lightning flashing from their depths looks like the moving limbs of the half-hidden deity. We also find occasionally invoked in the Cherokee religious formulae a pair of twin deities known as the 'Little Men', or 'Thunder-boys'. This reminds us that in Peru twins were always regarded as sacred to the lightning, since they were emblematic of the thunder-and-lightning twins, Apocatequil and Piguerao. All these thunder-gods are analogous to the Aztec Tlaloc, the Kiche Hurakan, and the Otomi Mixcoatl.[10] A well-known instance of the thunder- or hunter-god who possesses animal characteristics will occur to those who are familiar with the old English legend of Herne the Hunter, with his deer's head and antlers.

The Dakota Indians worshipped a deity whom they addressed as Waukheon (Thunder-bird). This being was engaged in constant strife with the water-god, Unktahe, who was a cunning sorcerer, and a controller of dreams and witchcraft. Their conflict probably symbolizes the atmospheric changes which accompany the different seasons.

---

[10] See *Myths of Mexico and Peru*.

Idea of a future life

The idea of a future life was very widely disseminated among the tribes of North America. The general conception of such an existence was that it was merely a shadowy extension of terrestrial life, in which the same round of hunting and kindred pursuits was engaged in. The Indian idea of eternal bliss seems to have been an existence in the Land of the Sun, to which, however, only those famed in war were usually admitted.

That the Indians possessed a firm belief in a future state of existence is proved by their statements to the early Moravian missionaries, to whom they said: 'We Indians shall not forever die. Even the grains of corn we put under the earth grow up and become living things.' The old missionary adds: 'They conceive that when the soul has been awhile with God it can, if it chooses, return to earth and be born again.' This idea of rebirth, however, appears to have meant that the soul would return to the bones, that these would clothe themselves with flesh, and that the man would rejoin his tribe. By what process of reasoning they arrived at such a conclusion it would be difficult to ascertain, but the almost universal practice which obtained among the Indians both of North and South America of preserving the bones of the deceased plainly indicates that they possessed some strong religious reason for this belief. Many tribes which dwelt east of the Mississippi once in every decade collected the bones of those who had died within that period, carefully cleaned them, and placed them in a tomb lined with beautiful flowers, over which they erected a mound of wood, stone, or earth. Nor, indeed, were the ancient Egyptians more considerate of the remains of their fathers.

The hope of resurrection

American funerary ritual and practice throughout the northern sub-continent plainly indicates a strong and vivid belief in the resurrection of the soul after death. Among many tribes the practice prevailed of interring with the deceased such objects as he might be supposed to require in the other world. These included weapons of war and of the chase for men, and household implements and feminine finery in the case of women.

Among primitive peoples the belief is prevalent that inanimate objects possess doubles, or, as spiritualists would say, 'astral bodies', or souls, and some Indian tribes supposed that unless such objects were broken or mutilated – that is to say, 'killed' – their doubles would not accompany the spirit of the deceased on its journey.

Indian burial customs

Many methods of disposing of the corpse were, and are, in use among the American Indians. The most common of these were ordinary burial in the earth or under tumuli, burial in caves, tree-burial, raising the dead on platforms, and the disposal of cremated remains in urns.

Embalming and mummification were practised to a certain extent by some of the extinct tribes of the east coast, and some of the north-west tribes, notably the Chinooks, buried their dead in canoes, which were raised on poles. The rites which accompanied burial, besides the placing of useful articles and food in the grave, generally consisted in a solemn dance, in which the bereaved relatives cut themselves and blackened their faces, after which they wailed night and morning in solitary places. It was generally regarded as unlucky to mention the name of the deceased, and, indeed, the bereaved family often adopted another name to avoid such a contingency.

The soul's journey

Most of the tribes appear to have believed that the soul had to undertake a long journey before it reached its destination. The belief of the Chinooks in this respect is perhaps a typical one. They imagine that after death the spirit of the deceased drinks at a large hole in the ground, after which it shrinks and passes on to the country of the ghosts, where it is fed with spirit food and drink. After this act of communion with the spirit-world it may not return. They also believe that everyone is possessed of two spirits, a greater and a less. During illness the lesser soul is spirited away by the denizens of Ghost-land. The Navahos possess a similar belief, and say that the soul has none of the vital force which animates the body, nor any of the faculties of the mind, but a kind of third quality, or personality, like the *ka* of the ancient Egyptians, which may leave its owner and become lost, much to his danger and discomfort. The Hurons and Iroquois believe that after death the soul must cross a deep and swift stream, by a bridge formed by a single slender tree, upon which it has to combat the attacks of a fierce dog. The Athapascans imagine that the soul must be ferried over a great water in a stone canoe, and the Algonquins and Dakotas believe that departed spirits must cross a stream bridged by an enormous snake.

Paradise and the supernatural people

The Red Man appears to have possessed two wholly different conceptions of supernatural life. We find in Indian myth allusions both to a 'Country of the Ghosts' and to a 'Land of the Supernatural People'. The first appears to be the destination of human beings after death, but the second is apparently the dwelling-place of a spiritual race some degrees higher than mankind. Both these regions are within the reach of mortals, and seem to be mere extensions of the terrestrial sphere. Their inhabitants eat, drink, hunt, and amuse themselves in the same manner as earthly folk, and are by no means invulnerable or immortal. The instinctive dread of the supernatural which primitive man possesses is well exemplified in the myths in which he is brought into contact with the denizens of Ghost-land or the Spirit-world. These myths were undoubtedly framed for the same purpose as the old Welsh poem on the harrying of hell, or the story of the Tourney of the twin brothers to Xibalba in the Central American *Popol Vuh*. That is to say, the desire was felt for some assurance that man, on entering the spiritual sphere, would only be treading in the footsteps of heroic beings who had preceded him, who had vanquished the forces of death and hell and had stripped them of their terrors.

The mythologies of the North American Indians possess no place of punishment, any more than they possess any deities who are frankly malevolent toward humanity. Should a place of torment be discernible in any Indian mythology at the present day it may unhesitatingly be classed as the product of missionary sophistication. Father Brébeuf, an early French missionary, could only find that the souls of suicides and those killed in war were supposed to dwell apart from the others. 'But as to the souls of scoundrels,' he adds, 'so far from being shut out, they are welcome guests; though for that matter, if it were not so their paradise would be a total desert, as "Indian" and "scoundrel" are one and the same.'

The sacred number four
Over the length and breadth of the American continent a peculiar sanctity is attached by the aborigines to the four points of the compass. This arises from the circumstance that from these quarters come the winds which carry the fertilizing rains. The Red Man, a dweller in vast undulating plains where landmarks are few, recognized the necessity of such guidance in his wanderings as could alone be received from a strict adherence to the position of the four cardinal points. These he began to regard with veneration as his personal safeguards, and recognized in them the dwelling-places of powerful beings, under whose care he was. Most of his festivals and celebrations had symbolical or direct allusions to the four points of the compass. The ceremony of smoking, without which no treaty could be commenced or ratified, was usually begun by the chief of the tribe exhaling tobacco-smoke toward the four quarters of the earth. Among some tribes other points were also recognized, as, for example, one in the

sky and one in the earth. All these points had their symbolical colours, and were presided over by various animal or other divinities. Thus the Apaches took black for the east, white for the south, yellow for the west, and blue for the north, the Cherokees red, white, black, and blue for the same points, and the Navahos white, blue, yellow, and black, with white and black for the lower regions and blue for the upper or ethereal world.

Indian time and festivals

The North American tribes have various ways of computing time. Some of them rely merely upon the changes in season and the growth of crops for guidance as to when their annual festivals and seasonal celebrations should take place. Others fix their system of festivals on the changes of the moon and the habits of animals and birds. It was, however, upon the moon that most of these peoples depended for information regarding the passage of time. Most of them assigned twelve moons to the year, while others considered thirteen a more correct number. The Kiowa reckoned the year to consist of twelve and a half moons, the other half being carried over to the year following.

The Zuñi of New Mexico allude to the year as a 'passage of time', and call the seasons the 'steps of the year'. The first six months of the Zuñi year possess names which have an agricultural or natural significance, while the last six have ritualistic names. Captain Jonathan Carver, who travelled among the Sioux at the end of the eighteenth century, says that some tribes among them reckoned their years by moons, and made them consist of twelve lunar months, observing when thirty moons had waned to add a supernumerary one, which they termed the 'lost moon'. They gave a name to each month as follows, the year beginning at the first new moon after the spring equinox: March, Worm Moon; April, Moon of Plants; May, Moon of Flowers; June, Hot Moon; July, Buck Moon; August, Sturgeon Moon; September, Corn Moon; October,

Travelling Moon; November, Beaver Moon; December, Hunting Moon; January, Cold Moon; February, Snow Moon. These people had no division into weeks, but counted days by 'sleeps', half-days by pointing to the sun at noon, and quarter-days by the rising and setting of the sun, for all of which they possessed symbolic signs. Many tribes kept records of events by means of such signs, as has already been indicated. The eastern Sioux measure time by knotted leather thongs, similar to the *quipos* of the ancient Peruvians. Other tribes have even more primitive methods. The Hupa of California tell a person's age by examining his teeth. The Maidu divide the seasons into Rain Season, Leaf Season, Dry Season, and Falling-leaf Season. The Pima of Southern Arizona record events by means of notched sticks, which no one but the persons who mark them can understand.

The chief reason for the computation of time among savage peoples is the correct observance of religious festivals. With the rude methods at their command they are not always able to hit upon the exact date on which these should occur. These festivals are often of a highly elaborate nature, and occupy many days in their celebration, the most minute attention being paid to the proper performance of the various rites connected with them. They consist for the most part of a preliminary fast, followed by symbolic dances or magical ceremonies, and concluding with a gluttonous orgy. Most of these observances possess great similarity one to another, and visible differences may be accounted for by circumstances of environment or seasonal variations.

When the white man first came into contact with the Algonquian race it was observed that they held regularly recurring festivals to celebrate the ripening of fruits and grain, and more irregular feasts to mark the return of wildfowl and the hunting season in general. Dances were engaged in, and heroic songs chanted. Indeed, the entire observance appears to have been identical in its general features with the festival of today.

One of the most remarkable of these celebrations is that of the Creeks called the 'Busk', a contraction for its native name, Pushkita. Commencing with a rigorous fast which lasts three days, the entire tribe assembles on the fourth day to watch the high-priest produce a new fire by means of friction. From this flame the members of the tribe are supplied, and feasting and dancing are then engaged in for three days. Four logs are arranged in the form of a cross pointing to the four quarters of the earth, and burnt as an offering to the four winds.

The Buffalo Dance

The Mandans, a Dakota tribe, each year celebrate as their principal festival the Buffalo Dance, a feast which marks the return of the buffalo-hunting season. Eight men wearing buffalo-skins on their backs, and painted black, red, or white, imitate the actions of buffaloes. Each of them holds a rattle in his right hand and a slender rod six feet long in his left, and carries a bunch of green willow boughs on his back. The ceremony is held at the season of the year when the willow is in full leaf. The dancers take up their positions at four different points of a canoe to represent the four cardinal points of the compass. Two men dressed as grizzly bears stand beside the canoe, growling and threatening to spring upon anyone who interferes with the ceremony. The bystanders throw them pieces of food, which are at once pounced upon by two other men, and carried off by them to the prairie. During the ceremony the old men of the tribe beat upon sacks, chanting prayers for the success of the buffalo-hunt. On the fourth day a man enters the camp in the guise of an evil spirit, and is driven from the vicinity with stones and curses.

The elucidation of this ceremony may perhaps be as follows: From some one of the four points of the compass the buffalo must come; therefore all are requested to send goodly supplies. The men dressed as bears symbolize the wild beasts which might deflect the progress of the herds of buffalo toward the territory of the tribe, and therefore must be placated. The demon who visits the camp after the ceremony is, of course, famine.

Dance-festivals of the Hopi

The most highly developed North American festival system is that of the Hopi or Moqui of Arizona, the observances of which are almost of a theatrical nature. All the Pueblo Indians, of whom the Hopi are a division, possess similar festivals, which recur at various seasons or under the auspices of different totem clans or secret societies. Most of these 'dances' are arranged by the Katcina clan, and take place in dance-houses known as *kivas*. These ceremonies have their origin in the universal reverence shown to the serpent in America – a reverence based on the idea that the symbol of the serpent, tail in mouth, represented the round, full sun of August. In the summer 'dances' snake-charming feats are performed, but in the Katcina ceremony serpents are never employed.

Devil-dances are by no means uncommon among the Indians. The purpose of these is to drive evil spirits from the vicinity of the tribe.

Medicine-men

The native American priesthood, whether known as medicine-men, *shamans*, or wizards, were in most tribes a caste apart, exercising not only the priestly function, but those of physician and prophet as well. The name 'medicine-men', therefore, is scarcely a misnomer. They were skilled in the handling of occult forces such as hypnotism, and thus exercised unlimited sway over the rank and file of the tribe. But we shall first consider them in their religious aspect. In many of the Indian tribes the priesthood was a hereditary office; in others it was obtained through natural fitness or revelation in dreams. With the Cherokees, for example, the seventh son of a family was usually marked out as a suitable person for the priesthood. As a rule the religious body did not share in the general life of the tribe, from which to a great degree it isolated itself. For example, Bartram in his *Travels in the Carolinas* describes the younger priests of the Creeks as being arrayed in white robes, and carrying on their heads or arms 'a great owl-skin stuffed very ingeniously as an insignia of wisdom and divination. These bachelors are also distinguishable from the other people by their taciturnity, grave and solemn countenance, dignified step, and singing to themselves songs or hymns in a low, sweet voice as they stroll about the towns.' To add to the feeling of awe which they inspired among the laymen of the tribe, the priests conversed with one another in a secret tongue. Thus the magical formulae of some of the Algonquin priests were not in the ordinary language, but in a dialect of their own invention. The Choctaws, Cherokees, and Zuñi employed similar esoteric dialects, all of which are now known to be merely modifications of their several tribal languages, fortified with obsolete words, or else mere borrowings from the idioms of other tribes.

Medicine-men as healers

It was, however, as healers that the medicine-men were pre-eminent. The Indian assigns all illness or bodily discomfort to supernatural agency. He cannot comprehend that indisposition may arise within his own system, but believes that it must necessarily proceed from some external source. Some supernatural being whom he has offended, the soul of an animal which he has slain, or perhaps a malevolent sorcerer, torments him. If the bodies of mankind were not afflicted in this mysterious manner their owners would endure forever. When the Indian falls sick he betakes himself to a medicine-man, to whom he relates his symptoms, at the same time acquainting him with any circumstances which he may suspect of having brought about his condition. If he has slain a deer and omitted the usual formula of placation afterward he suspects that the spirit of the beast is actively harming him. Should he have shot a bird and have subsequently observed any of the same species near his dwelling, he will almost invariably conclude that they were bent on a mission of vengeance and have by some means injured him. The medicine-man, in the first instance, may give his patient some simple native remedy. If this treatment does not avail he will arrange to go to the sufferer's lodge for the purpose of making a more thorough examination. Having located the seat of the pain, he will blow upon it several times, and then proceed to massage it vigorously, invoking the while the aid of the natural enemy of the spirit which he suspects is tormenting the sick man. Thus if a deer's spirit be suspected he will call upon the mountain lion or the Great Dog to drive it away, but if a bird of any of the smaller varieties he will invoke the Great Eagle who dwells in the zenith to slay or devour it. Upon the supposed approach of these potent beings he will become more excited, and, vigorously slapping the patient, will chant incantations in a loud and sonorous voice, which are supposed to hasten the advent of the friendly beings whom he has summoned. At last, producing by sleight of hand an image of the disturbing spirit worked in bone, he calls for a vessel of boiling water, into which he promptly plunges the supposed cause of his patient's illness. The bone figure is withdrawn from the boiling water after a space, and on being examined may be found to have one or more scores on its surface. Each of these shows that it has already slain its man, and the patient is assured that had the native Aesculapius not adopted severe measures the malign spirit would have added him to the number of its victims.

Should these methods not result in a cure, others are resorted to. The patient is regaled with the choicest food and drink, while incantations are chanted and music performed to frighten away the malign influences.

Professional etiquette

The priestly class is not given to levying exorbitant fees upon its patients. As a rule the Indian medicine-man strongly resents any allusion to a fee. Should the payment be of a perishable nature, such as food, he usually shares it with his relatives, brother-priests, or even his patients, but should it consist of something that may be retained, such as cloth, teeth necklaces, or skins, he will carefully hoard it to afford provision for his old age. The Indian practitioner is strongly of opinion that white doctors are of little service in the cure of native illnesses. White medicine, he says, is good only for white men, and Indian medicine for the red man; in which conclusion he is probably justified.

Journeys in spirit-land

In many Indian myths we read how the *shamans*, singly or in companies, seek the Spirit-land, either to search for the souls of those who are ill, but not yet dead, or to seek advice from supernatural beings. These thaumaturgical practices were usually undertaken by three medicine-men acting in concert. Falling into a trance, in which their souls were supposed to become temporarily disunited from their bodies, they would follow the track of the sick man's spirit into the spirit-world. The order in which they travelled was determined by the relative strength of their guardian spirits, those with the strongest being first and last, and he who had the weakest being placed in the middle. If the sick man's track turned to the left they said he would die, but if to the right, he would recover. From the trail they could also divine whether any supernatural danger was near, and the foremost priest would utter a magic chant to avert such evils if they came from the front, while if the danger came from the rear the incantation was sung by the priest who came last. Generally their sojourn occupied one or two nights, and, having rescued the soul of the patient, they returned to place it in his body.

Not only was the *shaman* endowed with the power of projecting his own 'astral body' into the Land of Spirits. By placing cedar-wood charms in the hands of persons who had not yet received a guardian spirit he could impart to them his clairvoyant gifts, enabling them to visit the Spirit-land and make any observations required by him.

The souls of chiefs, instead of following the usual route, went directly to the sea-shore, where only the most gifted *shamans* could follow their trail. The sea was regarded as the highway to the supernatural regions. A sick man was in the greatest peril at high water, but when the tide was low the danger was less.

The means adopted by the medicine-men to lure ghosts away from their pursuit of a soul was to create an 'astral' deer. The ghosts would turn from hunting the man's soul to follow that of the beast.

The savage and religion
It cannot be said that the religious sense was exceptionally strong in the mind of the North American Indian. But this was due principally to the stage of culture at which he stood, and in some cases still stands. In man in his savage or barbarian condition the sense of reverence as we conceive it is small, and its place is largely filled by fear and superstition. It is only at a later stage, when civilizing influences have to some extent banished the grosser terrors of animism and fetishism, that the gods reveal themselves in a more spiritual aspect.

*   *   *

Native American creation myths fall into two broad categories, of which the primeval flood myth is the most widespread, being found everywhere but Alaska and parts of the Southwest. In this, standardly myth a water creature – such as the Algonquin's Muskrat – plunges to the depths of the sea and returns with a mouthful of mud that becomes the earth, this often supported on the back of a Giant Turtle. Since 'the Earth Diver' myth also exists in Asia, it can be hypothesized that the Native American versions are echoes of the ancient Asian originals.

Meanwhile, some Plains tribes, as well as the Navajo and Pueblo peoples of the Southwest have a concept of creation in which life emerges from the earth, not unlike a plant sprouting from the ground. In the Navajo emergence story it is related how insects climbed up from the Red World to the Blue World, where the birds lived. When this world became too crowded, the insects and birds flew up to the Yellow World, where they found people and animals. When food became scarce, the people, animals, birds, and insects flew up into the Black and White World of night and day. There they found people already created by the gods, and these people taught the newcomers how to farm and to survive. Meanwhile, in the Hopi emergence myth Spider-Woman, a powerful earth goddess, sang a duet with Tawa, the sun-god; Spider-Woman was able to weave the Tawa's thoughts into solid form, creating fish, birds and other animals, including humans. Spider-Woman then divided the humans into groups, and led them to their homelands, after which she disappeared back into the earth, down through a whirlpool of sand. Among the people of Acoma Pueblo, it is told that the sisters Iatiku and Nautsiti emerged from a hole in the ground, Sipapu, and when Nautsiti was tempted away by the evil Snake, Iatiku bore many children, each of which became an Acoma clan. In the religion of the Pueblo tribes, the emergence myth is physically reincarnated in the construction of the kiva, a sacred underground chamber for worship.

The absence of a primeval flood in the cosmology of the Hopi and Navajo is not difficult to account for. Little about the arid Southwest would ever suggest that a deluge could swamp the earth. Equally, the inclusion of a diluvian motif in the creation myths of the Apache – the Jicarilla, for instance, believed humans emerged from underground on to an earth almost wholly covered by water – despite sharing the same desiccated environment as the Pueblo peoples is easily explained. The Apache were Athapaskan-speakers who had only moved to the Southwest from Canada in the 1500s.

It is important to register that, because it cannot be reconciled with their creation myths, many Native Americans deny the Bering Strait migration theory.

Several Native American mythologies, that of the Apache included, have a high deity, who is creator of the world. Where such a creator 'Great Spirit' exists he/she rarely, however, does the full work of creation alone, but disappears to heaven, and allows lesser gods to complete the project and supervise the workings of the planet. These secondary gods are often personifications of natural forces and elements, such as the wind. In the mythology of the Iroquois people, for example, the thunder-god Hunin is a warrior who shoots arrows of fire.

The creator is not always separate from his creation. The Lakota (Sioux) people are pantheists, believing that the sun, earth, sky, wind, fire and other elements of the natural, spiritual and human worlds are all aspects of one, single supreme being, Wakan Tanka, 'The Great Spirit' (or, in a more accurate translation of the Lakota, 'the Great Mystery').

It is notable that the concept of the creation of the world out of the imagination of God or out of nothingness is practically unknown in Native American mythology. In short, there is no Creator in North American mythology. The creator almost always moulds or rearranges what already exists into a new earth. Many contemporary folklorists define the maker deities in Amerindian myths as being 'transformers'. Transformers do not create the world; they bring order from chaos.

The Sioux were fortunate in having a benevolent creator god. Their Blackfeet (Siksika) neighbours were made by Na'pi, the 'Old Man' – who was also an archetypal trickster, capable of malevolence, violence and black humour. The trickster is a common character throughout Native American mythology, but generally has a greater place in the folklore of hunter-gatherer peoples than of sedentary agricultural groups, largely because people who lived on wild things were more horribly aware of the vagaries of nature. The trickster, who is always male, is the representation of uncertainty. Sometimes the trickster's acts are simply practical jokes, but he can be a cruel destroyer. Invariably his actions stem from an uncontrollable appetite, frequently sexual, often transgressive, such as when he shape-shifts to marry his own daughters. The trickster appears in various guises in Amerindian mythologies, sometimes as an animal, sometimes as a human. To paint with a broad brush, the trickster appears as Coyote almost everywhere but most often west of the

Mississippi, as Raven and Blue Jay in the Northwest, as Nanabush the Great Hare (and variants such as Manabozho and Winabojo) in the Northeast, as Rabbit in the Southeast and Southwest, as Spider and Hare amongst the Sioux, and Na'pi in the Great Basin. (See Michael P. Carroll, 'The Trickster as Selfish-Buffoon and Culture Hero', *Ethos* 12, no. 2. Summer 1984.)

As a trickster Rabbit obtained a currency outside Native America. He is the ancestor of Brer Rabbit in the Uncle Remus tales. Brer Rabbit's ancestral DNA is to be clearly observed in the tale of 'Fox and Rabbit' from the Jicarilla Apache:

Fox one day met a Rabbit who was sewing a sack. 'What do you intend to do with that sack?' asked he. 'I am making this coat to protect myself from being killed by the hard hail which we are going to have today,' replied Rabbit. 'My friend, you know how to make them; give me this coat and make another for yourself.' Rabbit agreed to this, and Fox put the sack over his head. Rabbit then hung him on a [tree] limb and pelted him with stones, while Fox, thinking it was hail striking him, endured the punishment as long as he could, but finally fell nearly dead from the tree, and looked out, to see no signs of hail, but discovered Rabbit had run away. Fox wished to avenge himself by killing Rabbit, and set off in pursuit of him. When overtaken Rabbit was chewing soft gum with which to make spectacles. Fox's curiosity was stronger than his passion for revenge. 'What are you making those for?' said he. 'It is going to be very hot, and I am making them to protect my eyes,' answered Rabbit. 'Let me have this pair, you know how to make them and can make yourself another pair.' 'Very well,' said Rabbit, and he put the eye-shields on Fox, who could then see nothing, as the gum was soft and filled his eyes. Rabbit set fire to the brush all around Fox, who was badly singed in running through it. The gum melted in the fire, and yet remained as dark rings around his eyes. Fox again started on the trail of Rabbit, with the determination of eating him as soon as he saw him. He found Rabbit sitting beside the opening of a beehive. 'I am going to eat you,' said Fox; 'you have tried to kill me.' 'You must not kill me,' replied Rabbit. 'I am teaching these children,' and he closed the opening of the hive, so that Fox could not see inside. Fox desired very much to see what was in the hive making such a noise. 'If you wish to see, stay here and teach them while I rest. When it is dinner time strike them with a club,' said Rabbit, who then ran away. Fox patiently awaited the dinner hour, and then struck the hive with such force that he broke into it. The bees poured out and stung him until he rolled in agony. 'When I see you again, I will kill you before you can say a word!' declared he, as he started after Rabbit again. Fox tracked the Rabbit to a small hole in the fence around a field of watermelons belonging to a Mexican. The Rabbit had entered to steal, and was angered by the gum figure of a man which the owner of the field had placed beside the path. 'What do you desire from me?' he cried, as he struck at the figure with his forefoot, which stuck fast in the soft gum. He struck at the gum with every foot, and even his head was soon stuck in the gum. Thus Fox found him. 'What are you doing here?' he asked. 'They put me here because I would not eat chicken for them,' said Rabbit. 'I will take your place,' said Fox, 'I know how to eat chicken.' The Mexican found him in the morning and skinned him, and then let him go – still on the trail of the Rabbit who had so frequently outwitted him.

('Myths of the Jicarilla Apache,' Frank Russell,
The Journal of American Folklore, Vol. XI, No. XLIII, 1898)

Frequently the trickster is a transformer. Coyote, Old Man, and Raven are all transformers as well as tricksters.

Native American myths contain another common agent, the culture hero, someone or more usually something responsible for creating a distinctive benefit or aspect of the tribe's life. Native American mythology contains hundreds of culture heroes, a diverse array that reflects Amerindian respect for and connection with nature. The Seminole culture hero Breath Maker (Hisagita) creates both the Milky Way and the pumpkin. For the Haida Raven is the culture hero who steals light from the Old Man and makes the sun, moon and stars. As is the case with this Haida myth, the culture hero is sometimes combined in Native American mythology with the transformer, and also the trickster. The Raven in the mythology of the Pacific Coast tribes is such a tripartite being. Raven, it might be added, is therefore a prime example of how aboriginal American religion defies rigid boundaries and easy categorization. A god may act as a creator, transformer, trickster or cultural hero, while a cultural hero may be an animal or natural element, while a Rabbit (say) may be a deity creator with a mind for destruction. Or for helping humanity.

Duality, or the coupling of opposites, as in the Iroquian 'The Battle of the Twin-gods', occurs in numerous Amerindian myths and legends. Duality does not necessarily entail destruction; on the contrary, it can result, by the process of dialectics, in a positive synthesis. In Navajo myth, Monster Slayer is associated with light, while his twin brother is Child of Water with rain clouds. While journeying to see Sun, the warrior twins see smoke rising from a hole in the earth. Climbing down, they find themselves in the cave of Spider-Woman. She gives them magic feathers for their protection. After many adventures, the twins reach the house of Sun, who tests them by attempting to spear them, boil them, and poison them. With the aid of their magic feathers (and their own togetherness) they survive the ordeals, and the Sun recognizes them as his sons. The proud solar father gives them weapons to protect the Navajos.

An important myth, such as that of the Navajo warrior twins and their search for their Sun-Father, is not to be told lightly. It will form the basis of a sacred ritual, including ceremonies in which the participants act out the story. An important myth told at the wrong time can bring calamity upon the teller, such as attack by a swarm of snakes.

3

ALGONQUIAN MYTHS AND LEGENDS

Glooskap and Malsum

The Algonquin Indians have perhaps a more extensive mythology than the majority of Indian peoples, and as they have been known to civilization for several centuries their myths have the advantage of having been thoroughly examined.

One of the most interesting figures in their pantheon is Glooskap, which means 'The Liar'; but so far from an affront being intended to the deity by this appellation, it was bestowed as a compliment to his craftiness, cunning being regarded as one of the virtues by all savage peoples.

Glooskap and his brother Malsum, the Wolf, were twins, and from this we may infer that they were the opposites of a dualistic system, Glooskap standing for what seems 'good' to the savage, and Malsum for all that was 'bad'.[1] Their mother

---

[1] This 'goodness' and 'badness', however, is purely relative and of modern origin, such deities, as already explained, being figures in a light-and-darkness myth.

died at their birth, and out of her body Glooskap formed the
sun and moon, animals, fishes, and the human race, while the
malicious Malsum made mountains, valleys, serpents, and
every manner of thing which he considered would inconven-
ience the race of men.

Each of the brothers possessed a secret as to what would kill
him, as do many other beings in myth and fairy story, notably
Llew Llaw Gyffes in Welsh romance.

Malsum asked Glooskap in what manner he could be killed,
and Glooskap, to try his sincerity, replied that the only way
in which his life could be taken was by the touch of an owl's
feather – or, as some variants of the myth say, by that of a
flowering rush. Malsum in his turn confided to Glooskap that
he could only perish by a blow from a fern-root. The
malicious Wolf, taking his bow, brought down an owl, and
while Glooskap slept struck him with a feather plucked from
its wing. Glooskap immediately expired, but to Malsum's
chagrin came to life again. This tale is surprisingly reminiscent
of the Scandinavian myth of Balder, who would only die if
struck by a sprig of mistletoe by his brother Hodur. Like
Balder, Glooskap is a sun-god, as is well proved by the
circumstance that when he dies he does not fail to revive.

But Malsum resolved to learn his brother's secret and to
destroy him at the first opportunity. Glooskap had told him
subsequently to his first attempt that only a pine-root could
kill him, and with this Malsum struck him while he slept as
before, but Glooskap, rising up and laughing, drove Malsum
into the forest, and seated himself by a stream, where he
murmured, as if musing to himself: 'Only a flowering rush can
kill me.' Now he said this because he knew that Quah-beet,
the Great Beaver, was hidden among the rushes on the bank
of the stream and would hear every word he uttered. The
Beaver went at once to Malsum and told him what he regarded
as his brother's vital secret. The wicked Malsum was so glad
that he promised to give the Beaver whatever he might ask for.
But when the beast asked for wings like a pigeon Malsum

burst into mocking laughter and cried: 'Ho, you with the tail like a file, what need have you of wings?' At this the Beaver was wroth, and, going to Glooskap, made a clean breast of what he had done. Glooskap, now thoroughly infuriated, dug up a fern-root, and, rushing into the recesses of the forest, sought out his treacherous brother and with a blow of the fatal plant struck him dead.

Scandinavian analogies

But although Malsum was slain he subsequently appears in Algonquian myth as Lox, or Loki, the chief of the wolves, a mischievous and restless spirit. In his account of the Algonquian mythology Charles Godfrey Leland appears to think that the entire system has been sophisticated by Norse mythology filtering through the Eskimo. Although the probabilities are against such a theory, there are many points in common between the two systems, as we shall see later, and among them few are more striking than the fact that the Scandinavian and Algonquian evil influences possess one and the same name.

When Glooskap had completed the world he made man and the smaller supernatural beings, such as fairies and dwarfs. He formed man from the trunk of an ash-tree, and the elves from its bark. Like Odin, he trained two birds to bring him the news of the world, but their absences were so prolonged that he selected a black and a white wolf as his attendants. He waged a strenuous and exterminating warfare on the evil monsters which then infested the world, and on the sorcerers and witches who were harmful to man. He levelled the hills and restrained the forces of nature in his mighty struggles, in which he towered to giant stature, his head and shoulders rising high above the clouds. Yet in his dealings with men he was gentle and quietly humorous, not to say ingenuous.

On one occasion he sought out a giant sorcerer named Win-pe, one of the most powerful of the evil influences then dwelling upon the earth. Win-pe shot upward till his head was above the tallest pine of the forest, but Glooskap, with a god-like laugh, grew till his head reached the stars, and tapped the wizard gently with the butt of his bow, so that he fell dead at his feet.

But although he exterminated many monsters and placed a check upon the advance of the forces of evil, Glooskap did not find that the race of men grew any better or wiser. In fact, the more he accomplished on their behalf the worse they became, until at last they reached such a pitch of evil conduct that the god resolved to quit the world altogether. But, with a feeling of consideration still for the beings he had created, he announced that within the next seven years he would grant to all and sundry any request they might make. A great many people were desirous of profiting by this offer, but it was with the utmost difficulty that they could discover where Glooskap was. Those who did find him and who chose injudiciously were severely punished, while those whose desires were reasonable were substantially rewarded.

Glooskap's gifts

Four Indians who won to Glooskap's abode found it a place of magical delights, a land fairer than the mind could conceive. Asked by the god what had brought them thither, one replied that his heart was evil and that anger had made him its slave, but that he wished to be meek and pious. The second, a poor man, desired to be rich, and the third, who was of low estate and despised by the folk of his tribe, wished to be universally honoured and respected. The fourth was a vain man, conscious of his good looks, whose appearance was eloquent of conceit. Although he was tall, he had stuffed fur into his moccasins to make him appear still taller, and his wish was that he might become bigger than any man of his tribe and that he might live for ages.

Glooskap drew four small boxes from his medicine-bag and gave one to each, desiring that they should not open them until they reached home. When the first three arrived at their respective lodges each opened his box, and found therein an unguent of great fragrance and richness, with which he rubbed himself. The wicked man became meek and patient, the poor man speedily grew wealthy, and the despised man became stately and respected. But the conceited man had stopped on his way home in a clearing in the woods, and, taking out his box, had anointed himself with the ointment it contained. His wish also was granted, but not exactly in the manner he expected, for he was changed into a pine-tree, the first of the species, and the tallest tree of the forest at that.

Glooskap and the baby

Glooskap, having conquered the Kewawkqu', a race of giants and magicians, and the Medecolin, who were cunning sorcerers, and Pamola, a wicked spirit of the night, besides hosts of fiends, goblins, cannibals, and witches, felt himself great indeed, and boasted to a certain woman that there was nothing left for him to subdue.

But the woman laughed and said: 'Are you quite sure, Master? There is still one who remains unconquered, and nothing can overcome him.'

In some surprise Glooskap inquired the name of this mighty individual.

'He is called Wasis,' replied the woman; 'but I strongly advise you to have no dealings with him.'

Wasis was only the baby, who sat on the floor sucking a piece of maple-sugar and crooning a little song to himself. Now Glooskap had never married and was quite ignorant of how children are managed, but with perfect confidence he smiled to the baby and asked it to come to him. The baby smiled back to him, but never moved, whereupon Glooskap imitated the beautiful song of a certain bird. Wasis, however, paid no heed to him, but went on sucking his maple-sugar. Glooskap, unaccustomed to such treatment, lashed himself into a furious rage, and in terrible and threatening accents ordered Wasis to come crawling to him at once. But Wasis burst into direful howling, which quite drowned the god's thunderous accents, and for all the threatenings of the deity he would not budge. Glooskap, now thoroughly aroused, brought all his magical resources to his aid. He recited the most terrible spells, the most dreadful incantations. He sang the songs which raise the dead, and which sent the devil scurrying to the nethermost depths of the pit. But Wasis evidently seemed to think this was all some sort of a game, for he merely smiled wearily and looked a trifle bored. At last Glooskap in despair rushed from the hut, while Wasis, sitting on the floor, cried, 'Goo, goo', and crowed triumphantly. And to this day the Indians say that when a baby cries 'Goo' he remembers the time when he conquered the mighty Glooskap.

Glooskap's farewell

At length the day on which Glooskap was to leave the earth arrived, and to celebrate the event he caused a great feast to be made on the shores of Lake Minas. It was attended by all the animals, and when it drew to a close Glooskap entered his great canoe and slowly drifted out of sight. When they could see him no longer they still heard his beautiful singing growing fainter and fainter in the distance, until at last it died away altogether. Then a strange thing happened. The beasts, who up to this time had spoken but one language, could no longer understand each other, and in confusion fled away, never again to meet in friendly converse until Glooskap shall return and revive the halcyon days of the Golden Age.

This tradition of Glooskap strikingly recalls that of the Mexican god Quetzalcoatl, who drifted from the shores of Mexico eastward toward the fabled land of Tlapallan, whence he had originally come. Glooskap, like the Mexican deity alluded to, is, as has already been indicated, a sun-god, or, more properly speaking, a son of the sun, who has come to earth on a mission of enlightenment and civilization, to render the world habitable for mankind and to sow the seeds of the arts, domestic and agricultural. Quetzalcoatl disappeared toward the east because it was the original home of his father, the sun, and not toward the west, which is merely the sun's resting-place for the night. But Glooskap drifted westward, as most sun-children do.

How Glooskap caught the summer

A very beautiful myth tells how Glooskap captured the summer. The form in which it is preserved is a kind of poetry possessing something in the nature of metre, which until a few generations ago was recited by many Algonquian firesides. A long time ago Glooskap wandered very far north to the Ice-country, and, feeling tired and cold, sought shelter at a wigwam where dwelt a great giant – the giant Winter. Winter received the god hospitably, filled a pipe of tobacco for him, and entertained him with charming stories of the old time as he smoked. All the time Winter was casting his spell over Glooskap, for as he talked drowsily and monotonously he gave forth a freezing atmosphere, so that Glooskap first dozed and then fell into a deep sleep – the heavy slumber of the winter season. For six whole months he slept; then the spell of the frost arose from his brain and he awoke. He took his way homeward and southward, and the farther south he fared the warmer it felt, and the flowers began to spring up around his steps.

At length he came to a vast, trackless forest, where, under primeval trees, many little people were dancing. The queen of these folk was Summer, a most exquisitely beautiful, if very tiny, creature. Glooskap caught the queen up in his great hand, and, cutting a long lasso from the hide of a moose, secured it round her tiny frame. Then he ran away, letting the cord trail loosely behind him.

The Elves of Light

The tiny people, who were the Elves of Light, came clamouring shrilly after him, pulling frantically at the lasso. But as Glooskap ran the cord ran out, and pull as they might they were left far behind.

Northward he journeyed once more, and came to the wigwam of Winter. The giant again received him hospitably, and began to tell the old stories whose vague charm had exercised such a fascination upon the god. But Glooskap in his turn began to speak. Summer was lying in his bosom, and her strength and heat sent forth such powerful magic that at length Winter began to show signs of distress. The sweat poured profusely down his face, and gradually he commenced to melt, as did his dwelling. Then slowly nature awoke, the song of birds was heard, first faintly, then more clearly and joyously. The thin green shoots of the young grass appeared, and the dead leaves of last autumn were carried down to the river by the melting snow. Lastly the fairies came out, and Glooskap, leaving Summer with them, once more bent his steps southward.

This is obviously a nature-myth conceived by a people dwelling in a climate where the rigours of winter gave way for a more or less brief space only to the blandishments of summer. To them winter was a giant, and summer an elf of pigmy proportions. The stories told during the winter season are eloquent of the life led by people dwelling in a sub-arctic climate, where the traditional tale, the father of epic poetry, whiles away the long dark hours, while the winter tempest roars furiously without and the heaped-up snow renders the daily occupation of the hunter impossible.

Glooskap's wigwam

The Indians say that Glooskap lives far away, no one knows where, in a very great wigwam. His chief occupation is making arrows, and it would appear that each of these stands for a day. One side of his wigwam is covered with arrows, and when his lodge shall be filled with them the last great day will arrive. Then he will call upon his army of good spirits and go forth to attack Malsum in a wonderful canoe, which by magical means can be made to expand so as to hold an army or contract so that it may be carried in the palm of the hand. The war with his evil brother will be one of extermination, and not one single individual on either side will be left. But the good will go to Glooskap's beautiful abode, and all will be well at last.

The snow-lodge

Chill breezes had long forewarned the geese of the coming cold season, and the constant cry from above of 'Honk, honk', told the Indians that the birds' migration was in progress.

The buffalo-hunters of the Blackfeet, an Algonquian tribe, were abroad with the object of procuring the thick robes and the rich meat which would keep them warm and provide good fare through the desolate winter moons. Sacred Otter had been lucky. Many buffaloes had fallen to him, and he was busily occupied in skinning them. But while the braves plied the knife quickly and deftly they heeded not the dun, lowering clouds heavy with tempest hanging like a black curtain over the northern horizon. Suddenly the clouds swooped down from their place in the heavens like a flight of black eagles, and with a roar the blizzard was upon them.

Sacred Otter and his son crouched beneath the carcass of a dead buffalo for shelter. But the air was frore as water in which the ice is floating, and he knew that they would quickly perish unless they could find some better protection from the bitter wind. So he made a small *tepee*, or tent, out of the buffalo's hide, and both crawled inside. Against this crazy shelter the snow quickly gathered and drifted, so that soon the inmates of the tiny lodge sank into a comfortable drowse induced by the gentle warmth. As Sacred Otter slept he dreamed. Away in the distance he descried a great *tepee*, crowned with a colour like the gold of sunlight, and painted with a cluster of stars symbolic of the North. The ruddy disc of the sun was pictured at the back, and to this was affixed the tail of the Sacred Buffalo. The skirts of the *tepee* were painted to represent ice, and on its side had been drawn four yellow legs with green claws, typical of the Thunder-bird. A buffalo in glaring red frowned above the door, and bunches of crow-feathers, with small bells attached, swung and tinkled in the breeze.

Sacred Otter, surprised at the unusual nature of the paintings, stood before the *tepee* lost in admiration of its decorations, when he was startled to hear a voice say: 'Who walks round my *tepee*? Come in – come in!'

The Lord of Cold Weather

Sacred Otter entered, and beheld a tall, white-haired man, clothed all in white, sitting at the back of the lodge, of which he was the sole occupant. Sacred Otter took a seat, but the owner of the *tepee* never looked his way, smoking on in stolid silence. Before him was an earthen altar, on which was laid juniper, as in the Sun ceremonial. His face was painted yellow, with a red line in the region of the mouth, and another across the eyes to the ears. Across his breast he wore a mink-skin, and round his waist small strips of otter skin, to all of which bells were attached. For a long time he kept silence, but at length he laid down his black stone pipe and addressed Sacred Otter as follows:

'I am Es-tonea-pesta, the Lord of Cold Weather, and this, my dwelling, is the Snow-tepee, or Yellow Paint Lodge. I control and send the driving snow and biting winds from the Northland. You are here because I have taken pity upon you, and on your son who was caught in the blizzard with you. Take this Snow-tepee with its symbols and medicines. Take also this mink-skin tobacco-pouch, this black stone pipe, and my supernatural power. You must make a *tepee* similar to this on your return to camp.'

The Lord of Cold Weather then minutely explained to Sacred Otter the symbols of which he must make use in painting the lodge, and gave him the songs and ceremonial connected with it. At this juncture Sacred Otter awoke. He observed that the storm had abated somewhat, and as soon as it grew fair enough he and his son crawled from their shelter and tramped home waist-high through the soft snow. Sacred Otter spent the long, cold nights in making a model of the Snow-tepee and painting it as he had been directed in his dream. He also collected the 'medicines' necessary for the ceremonial, and in the spring, when new lodges were made, he built and painted the Snow-tepee.

The power of Sacred Otter waxed great because of his possession of the Snow-lodge which the Lord of Cold had vouchsafed to him in dream. Soon was it proved. Once more while hunting buffalo he and several companions were caught in a blizzard when many a weary mile from camp. They appealed to Sacred Otter to utilize the 'medicine' of the Lord of Cold. Directing that several women and children who were with the party should be placed on sledges, and that the men should go in advance and break a passage through the snow for the horses, he took the mink tobacco-pouch and the black stone pipe he had received from the Cold-maker and commenced to smoke. He blew the smoke in the direction whence the storm came and prayed to the Lord of Cold to have pity on the people. Gradually the storm-clouds broke and cleared and on every side the blue sky was seen. The people hastened on, as they knew the blizzard was only being held back for a space. But their camp was at hand, and they soon reached it in safety.

Never again, however, would Sacred Otter use his mystic power. For he dreaded that he might offend the Lord of Cold. And who could afford to do that?

The Star-maiden

A pretty legend of the Chippeways, an Algonquian tribe, tells how Algon, a hunter, won for his bride the daughter of a star. While walking over the prairies he discovered a circular pathway, worn as if by the tread of many feet, though there were no foot-marks visible outside its bounds. The young hunter, who had never before encountered one of these 'fairy rings', was filled with surprise at the discovery, and hid himself in the long grass to see whether an explanation might not be forthcoming. He had not long to wait. In a little while he heard the sound of music, so faint and sweet that it surpassed anything he had ever dreamed of. The strains grew fuller and richer, and as they seemed to come from above he turned his eyes toward the sky. Far in the blue he could see a tiny white speck like a floating cloud. Nearer and nearer it came, and the astonished hunter saw that it was no cloud, but a dainty osier car, in which were seated twelve beautiful maidens. The music he had heard was the sound of their voices as they sang strange and magical songs. Descending into the charmed ring, they danced round and round with such exquisite grace and abandon that it was a sheer delight to watch them. But after the first moments of dazzled surprise Algon had eyes only for the youngest of the group, a slight, vivacious creature, so fragile and delicate that it seemed to the stalwart hunter that a breath would blow her away.

He was, indeed, seized with a fierce passion for the dainty sprite, and he speedily decided to spring from the grass and carry her off. But the pretty creatures were too quick for him. The fairy of his choice skilfully eluded his grasp and rushed to the car. The others followed, and in a moment they were soaring up in the air, singing a sweet, unearthly song. The disconsolate hunter returned to his lodge, but try as he might he could not get the thought of the Star-maiden out of his head, and next day, long before the hour of the fairies' arrival, he lay in the grass awaiting the sweet sounds that would herald their approach. At length the car appeared. The twelve ethereal beings danced as before. Again Algon made a desperate attempt to seize the youngest, and again he was unsuccessful.

'Let us stay,' said one of the Star-maidens. 'Perhaps the mortal wishes to teach us his earthly dances.' But the youngest sister would not hear of it, and they all rose out of sight in their osier basket.

Algon's strategy

Poor Algon returned home more unhappy than ever. All night he lay awake dreaming of the pretty, elusive creature who had wound a chain of gossamer round his heart and brain, and early in the morning he repaired to the enchanted spot. Casting about for some means of gaining his end, he came upon the hollow trunk of a tree in which a number of mice gambolled. With the aid of the charms in his 'medicine'-bag he turned himself into one of these little animals, thinking the fair sisters would never pierce his disguise.

That day when the osier car descended its occupants alighted and danced merrily as they were wont in the magic circle, till the youngest saw the hollow tree-trunk (which had not been there on the previous day) and turned to fly. Her sisters laughed at her fears, and tried to reassure her by overturning the tree-trunk. The mice scampered in all directions, and were quickly pursued by the Star-maidens, who killed them all except Algon. The latter regained his own shape just as the youngest fairy raised her hand to strike him. Clasping her in his arms, he bore her to his village, while her frightened sisters ascended to their Star-country.

Arrived at his home, Algon married the maiden, and by his kindness and gentleness soon won her affection. However, her thoughts still dwelt on her own people, and though she indulged her sorrow only in secret, lest it should trouble her husband, she never ceased to lament her lost home.

The Star-maiden's escape

One day while she was out with her little son she made a basket of osiers, like the one in which she had first come to earth. Gathering together some flowers and gifts for the Star-people, she took the child with her into the basket, sang the magical songs she still remembered, and soon floated up to her own country, where she was welcomed by the king, her father.

Algon's grief was bitter indeed when he found that his wife and child had left him. But he had no means of following them. Every day he would go to the magic circle on the prairie and give vent to his sorrow, but the years went past and there was no sign of his dear ones returning.

Meanwhile the woman and her son had almost forgotten Algon and the Earth-country. However, when the boy grew old enough to hear the story he wished to go and see his father. His mother consented, and arranged to go with him. While they were preparing to descend the Star-people said:

'Bring Algon with you when you return, and ask him to bring some feature from every beast and bird he has killed in the chase.'

Algon, who had latterly spent almost all his time at the charmed circle, was overjoyed to see his wife and son come back to him, and willingly agreed to go with them to the Star-country. He worked very hard to obtain a specimen of all the rare and curious birds and beasts in his land, and when at last he had gathered the relics – a claw of one, a feather of another, and so on – he piled them in the osier car, climbed in himself with his wife and boy, and set off to the Star-country.

The people there were delighted with the curious gifts Algon had brought them, and, being permitted by their king to take one apiece, they did so. Those who took a tail or a claw of any beast at once became the quadruped represented by the fragment, and those who took the wings of birds became birds themselves. Algon and his wife and son took the feathers of a white falcon and flew down to the prairies, where their descendants may still be seen.

Cloud-carrier and the Star-folk

A handsome youth once dwelt with his parents on the banks of Lake Huron. The old people were very proud of their boy, and intended that he should become a great warrior. When he grew old enough to prepare his 'medicine'-bag he set off into the forest for that purpose. As he journeyed he grew weary, and lay down to sleep, and while he slept he heard a gentle voice whisper:

'Cloud-carrier, I have come to fetch you. Follow me.'

The young man started to his feet.

'I am dreaming. It is but an illusion', he muttered to himself, as he gazed at the owner of the soft voice, who was a damsel of such marvellous beauty that the sleepy eyes of Cloud-carrier were quite dazzled.

'Follow me,' she said again, and rose softly from the ground like thistledown. To his surprise the youth rose along with her, as lightly and as easily. Higher they went, and still higher, far above the tree-tops, and into the sky, till they passed at length through an opening in the spreading vault, and Cloud-carrier saw that he was in the country of the Star-people, and that his beautiful guide was no mortal maiden, but a supernatural being. So fascinated was he by her sweetness and gentleness that he followed her without question till they came to a large lodge. Entering it at the invitation of the Star-maiden, Cloud-carrier found it filled with weapons and ornaments of silver, worked in strange and grotesque designs. For a time he wandered through the lodge admiring and praising all he saw, his warrior-blood stirring at the sight of the rare weapons. Suddenly the lady cried:

'Hush! My brother approaches! Let me hide you. Quick!'

The young man crouched in a corner, and the damsel threw a richly coloured scarf over him. Scarcely had she done so when a grave and dignified warrior stalked into the lodge.

'Nemissa, my dear sister,' he said, after a moment's pause, 'have you not been forbidden to speak to the Earth-people? Perhaps you imagine you have hidden the young man, but you have not.' Then, turning from the blushing Nemissa to Cloud-carrier, he added, good-naturedly:

'If you stay long there you will be very hungry. Come out and let us have a talk.'

The youth did as he was bid, and the brother of Nemissa gave him a pipe and a bow and arrows. He gave him also Nemissa for his wife, and for a long time they lived together very happily.

The Star-country

Now the young man observed that his brother-in-law was in the habit of going away every day by himself, and feeling curious to know what his business might be, he asked one morning whether he might accompany him.

The brother-in-law consented readily, and the two set off. Travelling in the Star-country was very pleasant. The foliage was richer than that of the earth, the flowers more delicately coloured, the air softer and more fragrant, and the birds and beasts more graceful and harmless. As the day wore on to noon Cloud-carrier became very hungry.

'When can we get something to eat?' he asked his brother-in-law.

'Very soon,' was the reassuring reply. 'We are just going to make a repast.' As he spoke they came to a large opening, through which they could see the lodges and lakes and forests of the earth. At one place some hunters were preparing for the chase. By the banks of a river some women were gathering reeds, and down in a village a number of children were playing happily.

'Do you see that boy down there in the centre of the group?' said the brother of Nemissa, and as he spoke he threw something at the child. The poor boy fell down instantly, and was carried, more dead than alive, to the nearest hut.

The sacrifice

Cloud-carrier was much perplexed at the act of his supernatural relative. He saw the medicine-men gather round the child and chant prayers for his recovery.

'It is the will of Manitou,' said one priest, 'that we offer a white dog as a sacrifice.'

So they procured a white dog, skinned and roasted it, and put it on a plate. It flew up in the air and provided a meal for the hungry Cloud-carrier and his companion. The child recovered and returned to his play.

'Your medicine-men,' said Nemissa's brother, 'get a great

reputation for wisdom simply because they direct the people to me. You think they are very clever, but all they do is to advise you to sacrifice to me. It is I who recover the sick.'

Cloud-carrier found in this spot a new source of interest, but at length the delights of the celestial regions began to pall. He longed for the companionship of his own kin, for the old commonplace pastimes of the Earth-country. He became, in short, very homesick, and begged his wife's permission to return to earth. Very reluctantly she consented.

'Remember,' she said, 'that I shall have the power to recall you when I please, for you will still be my husband. And above all do not marry an Earth-woman, or you will taste of my vengeance.'

The young man readily promised to respect her injunctions. So he went to sleep, and awoke a little later to find himself lying on the grass close by his father's lodge. His parents greeted him joyfully. He had been absent, they told him, for more than a year, and they had not hoped to see him again.

The remembrance of his sojourn among the Star-people faded gradually to a dim recollection. By and by, forgetting the wife he had left there, he married a young and handsome woman belonging to his own village. Four days after the wedding she died, but Cloud-carrier failed to draw a lesson from this unfortunate occurrence. He married a third wife. But one day he was missing, and was never again heard of. His Star-wife had recalled him to the sky.

The Snow-man husband

In a northern village of the Algonquins dwelt a young girl so exquisitely beautiful that she attracted hosts of admirers. The fame of her beauty spread far and wide, and warriors and hunters thronged to her father's lodge in order to behold her. By universal consent she received the name of 'Handsome'. One of the braves who was most assiduous in paying her his addresses was surnamed 'Elegant', because of the richness of his costume and the nobility of his features. Desiring to know his fate, the young man confided the secret of his love for Handsome to another of her suitors, and proposed that they two should that day approach her and ask her hand in marriage. But the coquettish maiden dismissed the young braves disdainfully, and, to add to the indignity of her refusal, repeated it in public outside her father's lodge. Elegant, who was extremely sensitive, was so humiliated and mortified that he fell into ill-health. A deep melancholy settled on his mind. He refused all nourishment, and for hours he would sit with his eyes fixed on the ground in moody contemplation. A profound sense of disgrace seized upon him, and notwithstanding the arguments of his relations and comrades he sank deeper into lethargy. Finally he took to his bed, and even when his family were preparing for the annual migration customary with the tribe he refused to rise from it, although they removed the tent from above his head and packed it up for transport.

The lover's revenge

After his family had gone Elegant appealed to his guardian spirit or totem to revenge him on the maiden who had thus cast him into despondency. Going from lodge to lodge, he collected all the rags that he could find, and, kneading snow over a framework of animals' bones, he moulded it into the shape of a man, which he attired in the tatters he had gathered, finally covering the whole with brilliant beads and gaudy feathers so that it presented a very imposing appearance. By magic art he animated this singular figure, placed a bow and arrows into its hands, and bestowed on it the name of Moowis.

Together the pair set out for the new encampment of the tribe. The brilliant appearance of Moowis caused him to be received by all with the most marked distinction. The chieftain of the tribe begged him to enter his lodge, and entertained him as an honoured guest. But none was so struck by the bearing of the noble-looking stranger as Handsome. Her mother requested him to accept the hospitality of her lodge, which he duly graced with his presence, but being unable to approach too closely to the hearth, on which a great fire was burning, he placed a boy between him and the blaze, in order that he should run no risk of melting. Soon the news that Moowis was to wed Handsome ran through the encampment, and the nuptials were celebrated. On the following day Moowis announced his intention of undertaking a long journey. Handsome pleaded for leave to accompany him, but he refused on the ground that the distance was too great and that the fatigues and dangers of the route would prove too much for her strength. Finally, however, she overcame his resistance, and the two set out.

A strange transformation
A rough and rugged road had to be traversed by the newly wedded pair. On every hand they encountered obstacles, and the unfortunate Handsome, whose feet were cut and bleeding, found the greatest difficulty in keeping up with her more active husband. At first it was bitterly cold, but at length the sun came out and shone in all his strength, so that the girl forgot her woes and began to sing gaily. But on the appearance of the luminary a strange transformation had slowly overtaken her spouse. At first he attempted to keep in the shade, to avoid the golden beams that he knew meant death to him, but all to no purpose. The air became gradually warmer, and slowly he dissolved and fell to pieces, so that his frenzied wife now only beheld his garments, the bones that had composed his framework, and the gaudy plumes and beads with which he had been bedecked. Long she sought his real self, thinking that some trick had been played upon her; but at length, exhausted with fatigue and sorrow, she cast herself on the ground, and with his name on her lips breathed her last. So was Elegant avenged.

The Spirit-bride
A story is told of a young Algonquin brave whose bride died on the day fixed for their wedding. Before this sad event he

had been the most courageous and high-spirited of warriors and the most skilful of hunters, but afterward his pride and his bravery seemed to desert him. In vain his friends urged him to seek the chase and begged him to take a greater interest in life. The more they pressed him the more melancholy he became, till at length he passed most of his time by the grave of his bride.

He was roused from his state of apathy one day, however, by hearing some old men discussing the existence of a path to the Spirit-world, which they supposed lay to the south. A gleam of hope shone in the young brave's breast, and, worn with sorrow as he was, he armed himself and set off southward. For a long time he saw no appreciable change in his surroundings – rivers, mountains, lakes, and forests similar to those of his own country environed him. But after a weary journey of many days he fancied he saw a difference. The sky was more blue, the prairie more fertile, the scenery more gloriously beautiful. From the conversation he had overheard before he set out, the young brave judged that he was nearing the Spirit-world. Just as he emerged from a spreading forest he saw before him a little lodge set high on a hill. Thinking its occupants might be able to direct him to his destination, he climbed to the lodge and accosted an aged man who stood in the doorway.

'Can you tell me the way to the Spirit-world?' he inquired.

The Island of the Blessed

'Yes,' said the old man gravely, throwing aside his cloak of swan's skin. 'Only a few days ago she whom you seek rested in my lodge. If you will leave your body here you may follow her. To reach the Island of the Blessed you must cross yonder gulf you see in the distance. But I warn you the crossing will be no easy matter. Do you still wish to go?'

'Oh, yes, yes,' cried the warrior eagerly, and as the words were uttered he felt himself grow suddenly lighter. The whole aspect, too, of the scene was changed. Everything looked brighter and more ethereal. He found himself in a moment walking through thickets which offered no resistance to his passage, and he knew that he was a spirit, travelling in the Spirit-world. When he reached the gulf which the old man had indicated he found to his delight a wonderful canoe ready on the shore. It was cut from a single white stone, and shone and sparkled in the sun like a jewel. The warrior lost no time in embarking, and as he put off from the shore he saw his pretty bride enter just such another canoe as his and imitate all his movements. Side by side they made for the Island of the Blessed, a charming woody islet set in the middle of the water, like an emerald in silver. When they were about half-way across a sudden storm arose, and the huge waves threatened to engulf them. Many other people had embarked on the perilous waters by this time, some of whom perished in the furious tempest. But the youth and maiden still battled on bravely, never losing sight of one another. Because they were good and innocent, the Master of Life had decreed that they should arrive safely at the fair island, and after a weary struggle they felt their canoes grate on the shore.

Hand in hand the lovers walked among the beautiful sights and sounds that greeted their eyes and ears from every quarter. There was no trace of the recent storm. The sea was as smooth as glass and the sky as clear as crystal. The youth and his bride felt that they could wander on thus forever. But at length a faint, sweet voice bade the former return to his home in the Earth-country.

The Master of Life

'You must finish your mortal course,' it whispered softly. 'You will become a great chief among your own people. Rule wisely and well, and when your earthly career is over you shall return to your bride, who will retain her youth and beauty forever.'

The young man recognized the voice as that of the Master of Life, and sadly bade farewell to the woman. He was not without hope now, however, but looked forward to another and more lasting reunion.

Returning to the old man's lodge, he regained his body, went home as the gentle voice on the island had commanded him, and became a father to his people for many years. By his just and kindly rule he won the hearts of all who knew him, and ensured for himself a safe passage to the Island of the Blessed, where he arrived at last to partake of everlasting happiness with his beautiful bride.

Otter-heart

In the heart of a great forest lay a nameless little lake, and by its side dwelt two children. Wicked magicians had slain their parents while they were yet of tender years, and the little orphans were obliged to fend for themselves. The younger of the two, a boy, learned to shoot with bow and arrow, and he soon acquired such skill that he rarely returned from a hunting expedition without a specimen of his prowess in the shape of a bird or a hare, which his elder sister would dress and cook.

When the boy grew older he naturally felt the need of some companionship other than that of his sister. During his long, solitary journeys in search of food he thought a good deal about the great world outside the barrier of the still, silent forest. He longed for the sound of human voices to replace the murmuring of the trees and the cries of the birds.

'Are there no Indians but ourselves in the whole world?' he would ask wistfully.

'I do not know,' his sister invariably replied. Busying herself cheerfully about her household tasks, she knew nothing of the strange thoughts that were stirring in the mind of her brother.

But one day he returned from the chase in so discontented a mood that his unrest could no longer pass unnoticed. In response to solicitous inquiries from his sister, he said abruptly:

'Make me ten pairs of moccasins. Tomorrow I am going to travel into the great world.'

The girl was much disturbed by this communication, but like a good Indian maiden she did as he requested her and kept a respectful silence.

Early on the following morning the youth, whose name was Otter-heart, set out on his quest. He soon came to a clearing in the forest, but to his disappointment he found that the tree-stumps were old and rotten.

'It is a long, long time,' he said mournfully, 'since there were Indians here.'

In order that he might find his way back, he suspended a pair of moccasins from the branch of a tree, and continued his journey. Other clearings he reached in due time, each showing traces of a more recent occupation than the last, but still it seemed to him that a long time must have elapsed since the trees were cut down, so he hung up a pair of moccasins at each stage of his journey, and pursued his course in search of human beings.

At last he saw before him an Indian village, which he approached with mingled feelings of pleasure and trepidation, natural enough when it is remembered that since his early childhood he had spoken to no one but his sister.

The ball-players

On the outskirts of the village some youths of about his own age were engaged in a game of ball, in which they courteously invited the stranger to join. Very soon he had forgotten his natural shyness so far as to enter into the sport with whole-hearted zest and enjoyment. His new companions, for their part, were filled with astonishment at his skill and agility, and, wishing to do him honour, led him to the great lodge and introduced him to their chief.

Now the chief had two daughters, one of whom was surnamed 'The Good' and the other 'The Wicked'. To the guest the names sounded rather suggestive, and he was not a little embarrassed when the chief begged him to marry the maidens.

'I will marry "The Good",' he declared.

But the chief would not agree to that.

'You must marry both,' he said firmly.

Here was a dilemma for our hero, who had no wish to wed the cross, ugly sister. He tried hard to think of a way of escape.

'I am going to visit So-and-so', he said at last, mentioning the name of one of his companions at ball, and he dressed himself carefully as though he were about to pay a ceremonious visit.

Directly he was out of sight of the chief's lodge, however, he took to his heels and ran into the forest as hard as he could. Meanwhile the maidens sat waiting their intended bridegroom. When some hours passed without there being any signs of his coming they became alarmed, and set off to look for him.

Toward nightfall the young Otter-heart relaxed his speed. 'I am quite safe now,' he thought. He did not know that the sisters had the resources of magic at their command. Suddenly he heard wild laughter behind him. Recognizing the shrill voice of The Wicked, he knew that he was discovered, and cast about for a refuge. The only likely place was in the branches of a dense fir-tree, and almost as soon as the thought entered his mind he was at the top. His satisfaction was short-lived. In a moment the laughter of the women broke out anew, and they commenced to hew down the tree. But Otter-heart himself was not without some acquaintance with magic art. Plucking a small fir-cone from the tree-top, he threw it into the air, jumped astride it, and rode down the wind for half a mile or more. The sisters, absorbed in their task of cutting down the tree, did not notice that their bird was flown. When at last the great fir crashed to the ground and the youth was nowhere to be seen the pursuers tore their hair in rage and disappointment.

Otter-heart's stratagem

Only on the following evening did they overtake Otter-heart again. This time he had entered a hollow cedar-tree, the hard wood of which he thought would defy their axes. But he had underestimated the energy of the sisters. In a short time the tree showed the effect of their blows, and Otter-heart called on his guardian spirit to break one of the axes.

His wish was promptly gratified, but the other sister continued her labours with increased energy. Otter-heart now wished that the other axe might break, and again his desire was fulfilled. The sisters were at a loss to know what to do.

'We cannot take him by force,' said one; 'we must take him by subtlety. Let each do her best, and the one who gets him can keep him.'

So they departed, and Otter-heart was free to emerge from his prison. He travelled another day's journey from the spot, and at last, reaching a place where he thought he would be safe, he laid down his blanket and went in search of food. Fortune favoured the hunter, and he shortly returned with a fine beaver. What was his amazement when he beheld a handsome lodge where he had left his blanket!

'It must be those women again,' he muttered, preparing to fly. But the light shone so warmly from the lodge, and he was so tired and hungry, that he conquered his fears and entered. Within he found a tall, thin woman, pale and hungry-eyed, but rather pretty. Taking the beaver, she proceeded to cook it. As she did so Otter-heart noticed that she ate all the best parts herself, and when the meal was set out only the poorest pieces remained for him. This was so unlike an Indian housewife that he cast reproaches at her and accused her of greediness. As he spoke a curious change came over her. Her features grew longer and thinner. In a moment she had turned into a wolf and slunk into the forest. It was The Wicked, who had made herself pretty by means of magic, but could not conceal her voracious nature.

Otter-heart was glad to have found her out. He journeyed on still farther, laid down his blanket, and went to look for game. This time several beavers rewarded his skill, and he carried them to the place where he had left his blanket.

Another handsome lodge had been erected there! More than ever he wanted to run away, but once more his hunger and fatigue detained him.

'Perhaps it is The Good,' he said. 'I shall go inside, and if she has laid my blanket near her couch I shall take it for a sign and she shall become my wife.'

The Beaver-woman

He entered the lodge, and found a small, pretty woman busily engaged in household duties. Sure enough she had laid his blanket near her couch. When she had dressed and cooked the beavers she gave the finest morsels to her husband, who was thoroughly pleased with his wife.

Hearing a sound in the night, Otter-heart awoke, and fancied he saw his wife chewing birch-bark. When he told her of the dream in the morning she did not laugh, but looked very serious.

'Tell me,' asked Otter-heart, 'why did you examine the beavers so closely yesterday?'

'They were my relatives,' she replied; 'my cousin, my aunt, and my great-uncle.'

Otter-heart was more than ever delighted, for the otters, his totem-kin, and the beavers had always been on very good terms. He promised never to kill any more beavers, but only deer and birds, and he and his wife, The Good, lived together very happily for a long time.

The fairy wives

Once upon a time there dwelt in the forest two braves, one of whom was called the Moose and the other the Marten. Moose was a great hunter, and never returned from the chase without a fine deer or buffalo, which he would give to his old grandmother to prepare for cooking. Marten, on the other hand, was an idler, and never hunted at all if he could obtain food by any other means. When Moose brought home a trophy of his skill in the hunt Marten would repair to his friend's lodge and beg for a portion of the meat. Being a good-natured fellow, Moose generally gave him what he asked for, to the indignation of the old grandmother, who declared that the lazy creature had much better learn to work for himself.

'Do not encourage his idle habits,' said she to her grandson. 'If you stop giving him food he will go and hunt for himself.'

Moose agreed with the old woman, and having on his next expedition killed a bear, he told the grandmother to hide it, so that Marten might know nothing of it.

When the time came to cook the bear-meat, however, the grandmother found that her kettle would not hold water, and remembering that Marten had just got a nice new kettle, she went to borrow his.

'I will clean it well before I return it,' she thought. 'He will never know what I want it for.'

But Marten made a very good guess, so he laid a spell on the kettle before lending it, and afterward set out for Moose's lodge. Looking in, he beheld a great quantity of bear-meat.

'I shall have a fine feast tomorrow,' said he, laughing, as he stole quietly away without being seen.

On the following day the old grandmother of Moose took the borrowed kettle, cleaned it carefully, and carried it to its owner. She never dreamed that he would suspect anything.

'Oh,' said Marten, 'what a fine kettleful of bear-meat you have brought me!'

'I have brought you nothing,' the old woman began in astonishment, but a glance at her kettle showed her that it was full of steaming bear-meat. She was much confused, and knew that Marten had discovered her plot by magic art.

Moose demands a wife

Though Marten was by no means so brave or so industrious as Moose, he nevertheless had two very beautiful wives, while his companion had not even one. Moose thought this rather unfair, so he ventured to ask Marten for one of his wives. To this Marten would not agree, nor would either of the women consent to be handed over to Moose, so there was nothing for it but that the braves should fight for the wives, who, all unknown to their husband, were fairies. And fight they did, that day and the next and the next, till it grew to be a habit with them, and they fought as regularly as they slept.

In the morning Moose would say: 'Give me one of your wives.' 'Paddle your own canoe,' Marten would retort, and the fight would begin. Next morning Moose would say again: 'Give me one of your wives.' 'Fish for your own minnows,' the reply would come, and the quarrel would be continued with tomahawks for arguments.

'Give me one of your wives,' Moose persisted.

'Skin your own rabbits!'

Meanwhile the wives of Marten had grown tired of the perpetual skirmishing. So they made up their minds to run away. Moose and Marten never missed them: they were too busy fighting.

All day the fairy wives, whose name was Weasel, travelled as fast as they could, for they did not want to be caught. But when night came they lay down on the banks of a stream and watched the stars shining through the pine-branches.

'If you were a Star-maiden,' said one, 'and wished to marry a star, which one would you choose?'

'I would marry that bright little red one,' said the other. 'I am sure he must be a merry little fellow.'

'I,' said her companion, 'should like to marry that big yellow one. I think he must be a great warrior.' And so saying she fell asleep.

The Red Star and the Yellow Star

When they awoke in the morning the fairies found that their wishes were fulfilled. One was the wife of the great yellow star, and the other the wife of the little red one.

This was the work of an Indian spirit, whose duty it is to punish unfaithful wives, and who had overheard their remarks on the previous night. Knowing that the fulfilment of their wishes would be the best punishment, he transported them to the Star-country, where they were wedded to the stars of their choice. And punishment it was, for the Yellow Star was a fierce warrior who frightened his wife nearly out of her wits, and the Red Star was an irritable old man, and his wife was obliged to wait on him hand and foot. Before very long the fairies found their life in the Star-country exceedingly irksome, and they wished they had never quitted their home.

Not far from their lodges was a large white stone, which their husbands had forbidden them to touch, but which their curiosity one day tempted them to remove. Far below they saw the Earth-country, and they became sadder and more homesick than ever. The Star-husbands, whose magic powers told them that their wives had been disobedient, were not really cruel or unkind at heart, so they decided to let the fairies return to earth.

'We do not want wives who will not obey,' they said, 'so you may go to your own country if you will be obedient once.'

The fairies joyfully promised to do whatever was required of them if they might return home.

'Very well,' the stars replied. 'You must sleep tonight, and in the morning you will wake and hear the song of the chickadee, but do not open your eyes. Then you will hear the voice of the ground-squirrel; still you must not rise. The red squirrel also you shall hear, but the success of our scheme depends on your remaining quiet. Only when you hear the striped squirrel you may get up.'

The return to earth
The fairies went to their couch and slept, but their sleep was broken by impatience. In the morning the chickadee woke them with its song. The younger fairy eagerly started up, but the other drew her back.

'Let us wait till we hear the striped squirrel,' said she.

When the red squirrel's note was heard the younger fairy could no longer curb her impatience. She sprang to her feet, dragging her companion with her. They had indeed reached the Earth-country, but in a way that helped them but little, for they found themselves in the topmost branches of the highest tree in the forest, with no prospect of getting down. In vain they called to the birds and animals to help them; all the creatures were too busy to pay any attention to their plight. At last Lox, the wolverine, passed under the tree, and though he was the wickedest of the animals the Weasels cried to him for help.

'If you will promise to come to my lodge,' said Lox, 'I will help you.'

'We will build lodges for you,' cried the elder fairy, who had been thinking of a way of escape.

'That is well,' said Lox; 'I will take you down.'

While he was descending the tree with the younger of the fairies the elder one wound her magic hair-string in the branches, knotting it skilfully, so that the task of undoing it would be no light one. When she in her turn had been carried to the ground she begged Lox to return for her hair-string, which, she said, had become entangled among the branches.

'Pray do not break it,' she added, 'for if you do I shall have no good fortune.'

The escape from Lox

Once more Lox ascended the tall pine, and strove with the knots which the cunning fairy had tied. Meanwhile the Weasels built him a wigwam. They filled it with thorns and briers and all sorts of prickly things, and induced their friends the ants and hornets to make their nests inside. So long did Lox take to untie the knotted hair-string that when he came down it was quite dark. He was in a very bad temper, and pushed his way angrily into the new lodge. All the little creatures attacked him instantly, the ants bit him, the thorns pricked him, so that he cried out with anger and pain.

The fairies ran away as fast as they could, and by and by found themselves on the brink of a wide river. The younger sat down and began to weep, thinking that Lox would certainly overtake them. But the elder was more resourceful. She saw the Crane, who was ferryman, standing close by, and sang a very sweet song in praise of his long legs and soft feathers.

'Will you carry us over the river?' she asked at length.

'Willingly,' replied the Crane, who was very susceptible to flattery, and he ferried them across the river.

They were just in time. Scarcely had they reached the opposite bank when Lox appeared on the scene, very angry and out of breath.

'Ferry me across, Old Crooked-legs,' said he, and added other still more uncomplimentary remarks.

The Crane was furious, but he said nothing, and bore Lox out on the river.

'I see you,' cried Lox to the trembling fairies. 'I shall have you soon!'

'You shall not, wicked one,' said the Crane, and he threw Lox into the deepest part of the stream.

The fairies turned their faces homeward and saw him no more.

The malicious mother-in-law

An Ojibway or Chippeway legend tells of a hunter who was greatly devoted to his wife. As a proof of his affection he presented her with the most delicate morsels from the game he killed. This aroused the jealousy and envy of his mother, who lived with them, and who imagined that these little attentions should be paid to her, and not to the younger woman. The latter, quite unaware of her mother-in-law's attitude, cooked and ate the gifts her husband brought her. Being a woman of a gentle and agreeable disposition, who spent most of her time attending to her household duties and watching over her child and a little orphan boy whom she had adopted, she tried to make friends with the old dame, and was grieved and disappointed when the latter would not respond to her advances.

The mother-in-law nursed her grievance until it seemed of gigantic proportions. Her heart grew blacker and blacker against her son's wife, and at last she determined to kill her. For a time she could think of no way to put her evil intent into action, but finally she hit upon a plan.

One day she disappeared from the lodge, and returned after a space looking very happy and good-tempered. The younger woman was surprised and delighted at the alteration. This was an agreeably different person from the nagging, cross-grained old creature who had made her life a burden! The old woman repeatedly absented herself from her home after this, returning on each occasion with a pleased and contented smile on her wrinkled face. By and by the wife allowed her curiosity to get the better of her, and she asked the meaning of her mother-in-law's happiness.

The death-swing

'If you must know,' replied the old woman, 'I have made a beautiful swing down by the lake, and always when I swing on it I feel so well and happy that I cannot help smiling.'

The young woman begged that she too might be allowed to enjoy the swing.

'Tomorrow you may accompany me,' was the reply. But next day the old woman had some excuse, and so on, day after day, till the curiosity of her son's wife was very keen. Thus when the elder woman said one day, 'Come with me, and I will take you to the swing. Tie up your baby and leave him in charge of the orphan,' the other complied eagerly, and was ready in a moment to go with her mother-in-law.

When they reached the shores of the lake they found a lithe sapling which hung over the water.

'Here is my swing,' said the old creature, and she cast aside her robe, fastened a thong to her waist and to the sapling, and swung far over the lake. She laughed so much and seemed to find the pastime so pleasant that her daughter-in-law was more anxious than ever to try it for herself.

'Let me tie the thong for you,' said the old woman, when she had tired of swinging. Her companion threw off her robe and allowed the leather thong to be fastened round her waist. When all was ready she was commanded to swing. Out over the water she went fearlessly, but as she did so the jealous old mother-in-law cut the thong, and she fell into the lake.

The old creature, exulting over the success of her cruel scheme, dressed herself in her victim's clothes and returned to the lodge. But the baby cried and refused to be fed by her, and the orphan boy cried too, for the young woman had been almost a mother to him since his parents had died.

'Where is the baby's mother?' he asked, when some hours had passed and she did not return.

'At the swing,' replied the old woman roughly.

When the hunter returned from the chase he brought with him, as usual, some morsels of game for his wife, and, never dreaming that the woman bending over the child might not be she, he gave them to her. The lodge was dark, for it was evening, and his mother wore the clothes of his wife and imitated her voice and movements, so that his error was not surprising. Greedily she seized the tender pieces of meat, and cooked and ate them.

The heart of the little orphan was so sore that he could not sleep. In the middle of the night he rose and went to look for his foster-mother. Down by the lake he found the swing with the thong cut, and he knew that she had been killed. Crying bitterly, he crept home to his couch, and in the morning told the hunter all that he had seen.

'Say nothing,' said the chief, 'but come with me to hunt, and in the evening return to the shores of the lake with the child, while I pray to Manitou that he may send me back my wife.'

The silver girdle

So they went off in search of game without a word to the old
woman; nor did they stay to eat, but set out directly it was
light. At sunset they made their way to the lake-side, the little
orphan carrying the baby. Here the hunter blackened his face
and prayed earnestly that the Great Manitou might send back
his wife. While he prayed the orphan amused the child by
singing quaint little songs; but at last the baby grew weary and
hungry and began to cry.

Far in the lake his mother heard the sound, and skimmed
over the water in the shape of a great white gull. When she
touched the shore she became a woman again, and hugged the
child to her heart's content. The orphan boy besought her to
return to them.

'Alas!' said she, 'I have fallen into the hands of the Water
Manitou, and he has wound his silver tail about me, so that I
never can escape.'

As she spoke the little lad saw that her waist was encircled
by a band of gleaming silver, one end of which was in the
water. At length she declared that it was time for her to return
to the home of the water-god, and after having exacted a
promise from the boy that he would bring her baby there
every day, she became a gull again and flew away. The hunter
was informed of all that had passed, and straightaway
determined that he would be present on the following evening.
All next day he fasted and besought the goodwill of Manitou,
and when the night began to fall he hid himself on the shore
till his wife appeared. Hastily emerging from his concealment,
the hunter poised his spear and struck the girdle with all his
force. The silver band parted, and the woman was free to
return home with her husband.

Overjoyed at her restoration, he led her gently to the lodge,
where his mother was sitting by the fire. At the sight of her
daughter-in-law, whom she thought she had drowned in the
lake, she started up in such fear and astonishment that she
tripped, overbalanced, and fell into the fire. Before they could

pull her out the flames had risen to the smoke-hole, and when the fire died down no woman was there, but a great black bird, which rose slowly from the smoking embers, flew out of the lodge, and was never seen again.

As for the others, they lived long and happily, undisturbed by the jealousy and hatred of the malicious crone.

The maize spirit

The Chippeways tell a charming story concerning the origin of the zea maize, which runs as follows:

A lad of fourteen or fifteen dwelt with his parents, brothers, and sisters in a beautifully situated little lodge. The family, though poor, were very happy and contented. The father was a hunter who was not lacking in courage and skill, but there were times when he could scarcely supply the wants of his family, and as none of his children was old enough to help him things went hardly with them then. The lad was of a cheerful and contented disposition, like his father, and his great desire was to benefit his people. The time had come for him to observe the initial fast prescribed for all Indian boys of his age, and his mother made him a little fasting-lodge in a remote spot where he might not suffer interruption during his ordeal.

Thither the boy repaired, meditating on the goodness of the Great Spirit, who had made all things beautiful in the fields and forests for the enjoyment of man. The desire to help his fellows was strong upon him, and he prayed that some means to that end might be revealed to him in a dream.

On the third day of his fast he was too weak to ramble through the forest, and as he lay in a state between sleeping and waking there came toward him a beautiful youth, richly dressed in green robes, and wearing on his head wonderful green plumes.

'The Great Spirit has heard your prayers,' said the youth, and his voice was like the sound of the wind sighing through the grass. 'Hearken to me and you shall have your desire fulfilled. Arise and wrestle with me.'

The struggle

The lad obeyed. Though his limbs were weak his brain was clear and active, and he felt he could not but obey the soft-voiced stranger. After a long, silent struggle the latter said:

'That will do for today. Tomorrow I shall come again.'

The lad lay back exhausted, but on the morrow the green-clad stranger reappeared, and the conflict was renewed. As the struggle went on the youth felt himself grow stronger and more confident, and before leaving him for the second time the supernatural visitor offered him some words of praise and encouragement.

On the third day the youth, pale and feeble, was again summoned to the contest. As he grasped his opponent the very contact seemed to give him new strength, and he fought more and more bravely, till his lithe companion was forced to cry out that he had had enough. Ere he took his departure the visitor told the lad that the following day would put an end to his trials.

'Tomorrow,' said he, 'your father will bring you food, and that will help you. In the evening I shall come and wrestle with you. I know that you are destined to succeed and to obtain your heart's desire. When you have thrown me, strip off my garments and plumes, bury me where I fall, and keep the earth above me moist and clean. Once a month let my remains be covered with fresh earth, and you shall see me again, clothed in my green garments and plumes.' So saying, he vanished.

The final contest

Next day the lad's father brought him food; the youth, however, begged that it might be set aside till evening. Once again the stranger appeared. Though he had eaten nothing, the hero's strength, as before, seemed to increase as he struggled, and at length he threw his opponent. Then he stripped off his garments and plumes, and buried him in the earth, not without sorrow in his heart for the slaying of such a beautiful youth.

His task done, he returned to his parents, and soon

recovered his full strength. But he never forgot the grave of his friend. Not a weed was allowed to grow on it, and finally he was rewarded by seeing the green plumes rise above the earth and broaden out into graceful leaves. When the autumn came he requested his father to accompany him to the place. By this time the plant was at its full height, tall and beautiful, with waving leaves and golden tassels. The elder man was filled with surprise and admiration.

'It is my friend,' murmured the youth, 'the friend of my dreams.'

'It is Mon-da-min,' said his father, 'the spirit's grain, the gift of the Great Spirit.'

And in this manner was maize given to the Indians.

The seven brothers

The Blackfeet have a curious legend in explanation of the constellation known as the Plough or Great Bear. Once there dwelt together nine children, seven boys and two girls. While the six older brothers were away on the war-path the elder daughter, whose name was Bearskin-woman, married a grizzly bear. Her father was so enraged that he collected his friends and ordered them to surround the grizzly's cave and slay him. When the girl heard that her spouse had been killed she took a piece of his skin and wore it as an amulet. Through the agency of her husband's supernatural power, one dark night she was changed into a grizzly bear, and rushed through the camp, killing and rending the people, even her own father and mother, sparing only her youngest brother and her sister, Okinai and Sinopa. She then took her former shape, and returned to the lodge occupied by the two orphans, who were greatly terrified when they heard her muttering to herself, planning their deaths.

Sinopa had gone to the river one day, when she met her six brothers returning from the war-path. She told them what had happened in their absence. They reassured her, and bade her gather a large number of prickly pears. These she was to strew in front of the lodge, leaving only a small path uncovered by them. In the dead of night Okinai and Sinopa crept out of the lodge, picking their way down the little path that was free from the prickly pears, and meeting their six brothers, who were awaiting them. The Bearskin-woman heard them leaving the lodge, and rushed out into the open, only to tread on the prickly pears. Roaring with pain and anger, she immediately assumed her bear shape and rushed furiously at her brothers. But Okinai rose to the occasion. He shot an arrow into the air, and so far as it flew the brothers and sister found themselves just that distance in front of the savage animal behind them.

The chase

The beast gained on them, however; but Okinai waved a magic feather, and thick underbrush rose in its path. Again Bearskin-woman made headway. Okinai caused a lake to spring up before her. Yet again she neared the brothers and sister, and this time Okinai raised a great tree, into which the refugees climbed. The Grizzly-woman, however, succeeded in dragging four of the brothers from the tree, when Okinai shot an arrow into the air. Immediately his little sister sailed into the sky. Six times more he shot an arrow, and each time a brother went up, Okinai himself following them as the last arrow soared into the blue. Thus the orphans became stars; and one can see that they took the same position in the sky as they had occupied in the tree, for the small star at one side of the bunch is Sinopa, while the four who huddle together at the bottom are those who had been dragged from the branches by Bearskin-woman.

The Beaver Medicine legend[2]

Two brothers dwelt together in the old time. The elder, who was named Nopatsis, was married to a woman who was

---

[2] The first portion of this legend has its exact counterpart in Egyptian story. See Wiedemann, *Popular Literature of Ancient Egypt*, p. 45.

wholly evil, and who hated his younger brother, Akaiyan. Daily the wife pestered her husband to be rid of Akaiyan, but he would not agree to part with his only brother, for they had been together through long years of privation – indeed, since their parents had left them together as little helpless orphans – and they were all in all to each other. So the wife of Nopatsis had resort to a ruse well known to women whose hearts are evil. One day when her husband returned from the chase he found her lamenting with torn clothes and disordered appearance. She told him that Akaiyan had treated her brutally. The lie entered into the heart of Nopatsis and made it heavy, so that in time he conceived a hatred of his innocent brother, and debated with himself how he should rid himself of Akaiyan.

Summer arrived, and with it the moulting season when the wild water-fowl shed their feathers, with which the Indians fledge their arrows. Near Nopatsis's lodge there was a great lake, to which these birds resorted in large numbers, and to this place the brothers went to collect feathers with which to plume their darts. They built a raft to enable them to reach an island in the middle of the lake, making it of logs bound securely with buffalo-hide. Embarking, they sailed to the little island, along the shores of which they walked, looking for suitable feathers. They parted in the quest, and after some time Akaiyan, who had wandered far along the strand, suddenly looked up to see his brother on the raft sailing toward the mainland. He called loudly to him to return, but Nopatsis replied that he deserved to perish there because of the brutal manner in which he had treated his sister-in-law. Akaiyan solemnly swore that he had not injured her in any way, but Nopatsis only jeered at him, and rowed away. Soon he was lost to sight, and Akaiyan sat down and wept bitterly. He prayed earnestly to the nature spirits and to the sun and moon, after which he felt greatly uplifted. Then he improvised a shelter of branches, and made a bed of feathers of the most comfortable description. He lived well on the ducks and geese which frequented the island, and made a warm robe against the winter season from their skins. He was careful also to preserve many of the tame birds for his winter food.

One day he encountered the lodge of a beaver, and while he looked at it curiously he became aware of the presence of a little beaver.

'My father desires that you will enter his dwelling,' said the animal. So Akaiyan accepted the invitation and entered the lodge, where the Great Beaver, attended by his wife and family, received him. He was, indeed, the chief of all the beavers, and white with the snows of countless winters. Akaiyan told the Beaver how cruelly he had been treated, and the wise animal condoled with him, and invited him to spend the winter in his lodge, when he would learn many wonderful and useful things. Akaiyan gratefully accepted the invitation, and when the beavers closed up their lodge for the winter he remained with them. They kept him warm by placing their thick, soft tails on his body, and taught him the secret of the healing art, the use of tobacco, and various ceremonial dances, songs, and prayers belonging to the great mystery of 'medicine'.

The summer returned, and on parting the Beaver asked Akaiyan to choose a gift. He chose the Beaver's youngest child, with whom he had contracted a strong friendship; but the father prized his little one greatly, and would not at first permit him to go. At length, however, Great Beaver gave way to Akaiyan's entreaties and allowed him to take Little Beaver with him, counselling him to construct a sacred Beaver Bundle when he arrived at his native village.

In due time Nopatsis came to the island on his raft, and, making sure that his brother was dead, began to search for his remains. But while he searched, Akaiyan caught up Little Beaver in his arms and, embarking on the raft, made for the mainland, espied by Nopatsis. When Akaiyan arrived at his native village he told his story to the chief, gathered a Beaver Bundle, and commenced to teach the people the mystery of 'medicine', with its accompanying songs and dances. Then he invited the chiefs of the animal tribes to contribute their knowledge to the Beaver Medicine, which many of them did.

Having accomplished his task of instruction, which occupied him all the winter, Akaiyan returned to the island with Little Beaver, who had been of immense service to him in teaching the Indians the 'medicine' songs and dances. He returned Little Beaver to his parents, and received in exchange for him a sacred pipe, being also instructed in its accompanying songs and ceremonial dances. On the island he found the bones of his credulous and vengeful brother, who had met with the fate he had purposed for the innocent Akaiyan. Every spring Akaiyan visited the beavers, and as regularly he received something to add to the Beaver Medicine Bundle, until it reached the great size it now has. And he married and founded a race of medicine-men who have handed down the traditions and ceremonials of the Beaver Medicine to the present day.

The sacred Bear-spear
An interesting Blackfoot myth relates how that tribe obtained its sacred Bear-spear. Many generations ago, even before the Blackfeet used horses as beasts of burden, the tribe was undertaking its autumn migration, when one evening before striking camp for the night it was reported that a dog-sledge or cart belonging to the chief was missing. To make matters worse, the chief's ermine robe and his wife's buckskin dress, with her sacred elk-skin robe, had been packed in the little cart. Strangely enough, no one could recollect having noticed the dog during the march. Messengers were dispatched to the camping-site of the night before, but to no avail. At last the chief's son, Sokumapi, a boy about twelve years of age, begged to be allowed to search for the missing dog, a proposal to which his father, after some demur, consented. Sokumapi set out alone for the last camping-ground, which was under the shadows of the Rocky Mountains, and carefully examined the site. Soon he found a single dog-sledge track leading into a deep gulch, near the entrance to which he discovered a large

cave. A heap of freshly turned earth stood in front of the cave, beside which was the missing cart. As he stood looking at it, wondering what had become of the dog which had drawn it, an immense grizzly bear suddenly dashed out. So rapid was its attack that Sokumapi had no chance either to defend himself or to take refuge in flight. The bear, giving vent to the most terrific roars, dragged him into the cave, hugging him with such force that he fainted. When he regained consciousness it was to find the bear's great head within a foot of his own, and he thought that he saw a kindly and almost human expression in its big brown eyes. For a long time he lay still, until at last, to his intense surprise, the Bear broke the silence by addressing him in human speech.

'Have no fear,' said the grizzly. 'I am the Great Bear, and my power is extensive. I know the circumstances of your search, and I have drawn you to this cavern because I desired to assist you. Winter is upon us, and you had better remain with me during the cold season, in the course of which I will reveal to you the secret of my supernatural power.'

Bear magic
It will be observed that the circumstances of this tale are almost identical with those that relate to the manner in which the Beaver Medicine was revealed to mankind. The hero of both stories remains during the winter with the animal, the chief of its species, who in the period of hibernation instructs him in certain potent mysteries.

The Bear, having reassured Sokumapi, showed him how to transform various substances into food. His strange host slept during most of the winter; but when the warm winds of spring returned and the snows melted from the hills the grizzly became restless, and told Sokumapi that it was time to leave the cave. Before they quitted it, however, he taught the lad the secret of his supernatural power. Among other things, he showed him how to make a Bear-spear. He instructed him to take a long stick, to one end of which he must secure a sharp point, to symbolize the bear's tusks. To the staff must be attached a bear's nose and teeth, while the rest of the spear was to be covered with bear's skin, painted the sacred colour, red. The Bear also told him to decorate the handle with eagle's feathers and grizzly claws, and in war-time to wear a grizzly claw in his hair, so that the strength of the Great Bear might go with him in battle, and to imitate the noise a grizzly makes when it charges. The Bear furthermore instructed him what songs should be used in order to heal the sick, and how to paint his face and body so that he would be invulnerable in battle, and, lastly, told him of the sacred nature of the spear, which was only to be employed in warfare and for curing disease. Thus if a person was sick unto death, and a relative purchased the Bear-spear, its supernatural power would restore the ailing man to health. Equipped with this knowledge, Sokumapi returned to his people, who had long mourned him as dead. After a feast had been given to celebrate his homecoming he began to manufacture the Bear-spear as directed by his friend.

How the magic worked
Shortly after his return the Crows made war upon the Blackfeet, and on the meeting of the two tribes in battle Sokumapi appeared in front of his people carrying the Bear-spear on his back. His face and body were painted as the Great Bear had instructed him, and he sang the battle-songs that the grizzly had taught him. After these ceremonies he impetuously charged the enemy, followed by all his braves in a solid phalanx, and such was the efficacy of the Bear magic that the Crows immediately took to flight. The victorious Blackfeet brought back Sokumapi to their camp in triumph, to the accompaniment of the Bear songs. He was made a war-chief, and ever afterward the spear which he had used was regarded as the palladium of the Blackfoot Indians. In the spring the Bear-spear is unrolled from its covering and produced when the first thunder is heard, and when the Bear

begins to quit his winter quarters; but when the Bear returns to his den to hibernate the spear is once more rolled up and put away. The greatest care is taken to protect it against injury. It has a special guardian, and no woman is permitted to touch it.

The Young Dog Dance

A dance resembling the Sun Dance was formerly known to the Pawnee Indians, who called it the Young Dog Dance. It was, they said, borrowed from the Crees, who produced the following myth to account for it.

One day a young brave of the Cree tribe had gone out from his village to catch eagles, in order to provide himself with feathers for a war-bonnet, or to tie in his hair. Now the Crees caught eagles in this fashion. On the top of a hill frequented by these birds they would dig a pit and cover it over with a roof of poles, cunningly concealing the structure with grass. A piece of meat was fastened to the poles, so that the eagles could not carry it off. Then the Indian, taking off his clothes, would descend into the pit, and remain there for hours, or days, as the case might be, until an eagle was attracted by the bait, when he would put his hand between the poles, seize the bird by the feet, and quickly dispatch it.

The young brave whose fortune it was to discover the Young Dog Dance had prepared the trap in this wise, and was lying in the pit praying that an eagle might come and bring his uncomfortable vigil to an end. Suddenly he heard a sound of drumming, distant but quite distinct, though he could not tell from what direction it proceeded. All night the mysterious noise continued. Next night as he lay in the same position he heard it again, and resolved to find out its origin, so he clambered out of his pit and went off in the direction from which the drum-beating seemed to proceed. At last, when dawn was near, he reached the shores of a great lake. Here he stopped, for the sounds quite evidently came from the lake. All that day he sat by the water bemoaning his ill-luck and praying for better fortune. When night fell the drumming began anew, and the young man saw countless animals and birds swimming in the lake. Four days he remained on the lake-shore, till at length, worn out by fatigue and hunger (for many days had elapsed since he had eaten), he fell asleep.

The lodge of animals

When he awoke he found himself in a large lodge, surrounded by many people, some of whom were dancing, while others sat round the walls. All these people wore robes made from the skins of various animals or birds. They were, in fact, the animals the young Indian had seen swimming in the water, who had changed themselves into human shape. A chief at the back of the lodge stood up and addressed him thus:

'My friend, we have heard your prayers, and our desire is to help you. You see these people? They represent the animals. I am the Dog. The Great Spirit is very fond of dogs. I have much power, and my power I shall give to you, so that you may be like me, and my spirit will always protect you. Take this dance home to your people, and it will make them lucky in war.' And he imparted the nature of the rite to the Indian by action.

The Dog turned from the Cree brave and his eye swept the company.

The gift

'Brothers,' he said, 'I have given him my power. Will you not pity him and give him the power you have?'

For a time there was silence. No one seemed disposed to respond to the chief's appeal. At last the Owl rose.

'I will help you,' he said to the young man. 'I have power to see in the dark wherever I may go. When you go out at night I will be near you, and you shall see as well as I do. Take these feathers and tie them in your hair.' And, giving him a bunch of feathers, the Owl sat down.

There was a pause, and the next to rise was the Buffalo Bull, who gave to the young Indian his strength and endurance and the power to trample his enemies underfoot. As a token he gave him a shoulder-belt of tanned buffalo-hide, bidding him wear it when he went on the war-path.

By and by the Porcupine stood up and addressed the guest. Giving him some of his quills with which to ornament the leather belt, he said:

'I also will help you. I can make my enemies as weak as women, so that they fly before me. When you fight your foes shall flee and you shall overcome them.'

Another long silence ensued, and when at last the Eagle rose everyone listened to hear what he had to say.

'I also,' he said majestically, 'will be with you wherever you go, and will give you my prowess in war, so that you may kill your foes as I do.' As he spoke he handed to the brave some eagle feathers to tie in his hair.

The Whooping Crane followed, and gave him a bone from its wing for a war-whistle to frighten his enemies away.

The Deer and the Bear came next, the one giving him swiftness, with a rattle as token, and the other hardiness, and a strip of fur for his belt.

After he had received these gifts from the animals the brave lay down and fell asleep again. When he awoke he found himself on the shores of the lake once more.

Returning home, he taught the Crees the Young Dog Dance, which was to make them skilful in war, and showed them the articles he had received. So the young men formed a Society of Young Dogs, which practised the dance and obtained the benefits.

The medicine wolf

A quaint story of a 'medicine' wolf is told among the Blackfoot Indians. On one occasion when the Blackfeet were moving camp they were attacked by a number of Crow Indians who had been lying in wait for them. The Blackfeet were travelling slowly in a long, straggling line, with the old men and the women and children in the middle, and a band of warriors in front and in the rear. The Crows, as has been said, made an ambush for their enemies, and rushed out on the middle portion of the line. Before either party of the Blackfoot warriors could reach the scene of the struggle many of the women and children had perished, and others were taken captive by the attacking force. Among the prisoners was a young woman called Sits-by-the-door. Many weary miles lay between them and the Crow camp on the Yellowstone River, but at length the tired captives, mounted with their captors on jaded horses, arrived at their destination. The warrior who had taken Sits-by-the-door prisoner now presented her to a friend of his, who in turn gave her into the keeping of his wife, who was somewhat older than her charge. The young Blackfoot woman was cruelly treated by the Crow into whose possession she had passed. Every night he tied her feet together so that she might not escape, and also tied a rope round her waist, the other end of which he fastened to his wife. The Crow woman, however, was not unmoved by the wretchedness of her prisoner. While her husband was out she managed to converse with her and to show her that she pitied her misfortunes. One day she informed Sits-by-the-door that she had overheard her husband and his companions plotting to kill her, but she added that when darkness fell she would help her to escape. When night came the Crow woman waited until the deep breathing of her husband told her that he was sound asleep; then, rising cautiously, she loosened the ropes that bound her captive, and, giving her a pair of moccasins, a flint, and a small sack of pemmican, bade her make haste and escape from the fate that would surely befall her if she remained where she was. The trembling woman obeyed, and travelled at a good pace all night. At dawn she hid in the dense undergrowth, hoping to escape observation should her captors pursue her. They, meanwhile, had discovered her absence, and were searching high and low, but no tracks were visible, and at last, wearied with their unprofitable search, they gave up the chase and returned to their homes.

The friendly wolf

When the woman had journeyed on for four nights she stopped concealing herself in the daytime and travelled straight on. She was not yet out of danger, however, for her supply of pemmican was soon exhausted, and she found herself face to face with the miseries of starvation. Her moccasins, besides, were worn to holes and her feet were cut and bleeding, while, to add to her misfortunes, a huge wolf dogged her every movement. In vain she tried to run away; her strength was exhausted and she sank to the ground. Nearer and nearer came the great wolf, and at last he lay down at her feet. Whenever the woman walked on her way the wolf followed, and when she lay down to rest he lay down also.

At length she begged her strange companion to help her, for she knew that unless she obtained food very soon she must die. The animal trotted away, and returned shortly with a buffalo calf which it had killed, and laid it at the woman's feet. With the aid of the flint – one of the gifts with which the Crow woman had sped her unhappy guest – she built a fire and cooked some of the buffalo meat. Thus refreshed, she proceeded on her way. Again and again the wolf provided food in a similar manner, until at length they reached the Blackfoot camp. The woman led the animal into her lodge, and related to her friends all that had befallen her in the Crow camp, and the manner of her escape. She also told them how the wolf had befriended her, and begged them to treat it kindly. But soon afterward she fell ill, and the poor wolf was driven out of the village by the Indian dogs. Every evening he would come to the top of a hill overlooking the camp and watch the lodge where Sits-by-the-door dwelt. Though he was still fed by her friends, after a time he disappeared and was seen no more.[3]

---

[3] The reader cannot fail to discern the striking resemblance between this episode and that of Una and the lion in Spenser's *Faerie Queene*.

The story of Scar-face

Scar-face was brave but poor. His parents had died while he was yet a boy, and he had no near relations. But his heart was high, and he was a mighty hunter. The old men said that Scar-face had a future before him, but the young braves twitted him because of a mark across his face, left by the rending claw of a great grizzly which he had slain in close fight.

The chief of his tribe possessed a beautiful daughter, whom all the young men desired in marriage. Scar-face also had fallen in love with her, but he felt ashamed to declare his passion because of his poverty. The maiden had already repulsed half the braves of his tribe. Why, he argued, should she accept him, poor and disfigured as he was?

One day he passed her as she sat outside her lodge. He cast a penetrating glance at her – a glance which was observed by one of her unsuccessful suitors, who sneeringly remarked:

'Scar-face would marry our chief's daughter! She does not desire a man without a blemish. Ha, Scar-face, now is your chance!'

Scar-face turned upon the jeerer, and in his quiet yet dignified manner remarked that it was his intention to ask the chief's daughter to be his wife. His announcement met with ridicule, but he took no notice of it and sought the girl.

He found her by the river, pulling rushes to make baskets. Approaching, he respectfully addressed her.

'I am poor,' he said, 'but my heart is rich in love for you. I have no wealth of furs or pemmican. I live by my bow and spear. I love you. Will you dwell with me in my lodge and be my wife?'

The Sun-god's decree

The girl regarded him with bright, shy eyes peering up through lashes as the morning sun peers through the branches.

'My husband would not be poor,' she faltered, 'for my father, the chief, is wealthy and has abundance in his lodge.

But it has been laid upon me by the Sun-god that I may not marry.'

'These are heavy words,' said Scar-face sadly. 'May they not be recalled?'

'On one condition only,' replied the girl. 'Seek the Sun-god and ask him to release me from my promise. If he consents to do so, request him to remove the scar from your face as a sign that I may know that he gives me to you.'

Scar-face was sad at heart, for he could not believe that the Sun-god, having chosen such a beautiful maiden for himself, would renounce her. But he gave the chief's daughter his promise that he would seek out the god in his own bright country and ask him to grant his request.

For many moons Scar-face sought the home of the Sun-god. He traversed wide plains and dense forests, crossed rivers and lofty mountains, yet never a trace of the golden gates of the dwelling of the God of Light could he see.

Many inquiries did he make from the wild denizens of the forest – the wolf, the bear, the badger. But none was aware of the way to the home of the Sun-god. He asked the birds, but though they flew far they were likewise in ignorance of the road thither. At last he met a wolverine who told him that he had been there himself, and promised to set him on the way. For a long and weary season they marched onward, until at length they came to a great water, too broad and too deep to cross.

As Scar-face sat despondent on the bank bemoaning his case two beautiful swans advanced from the water, and, requesting him to sit on their backs, bore him across in safety. Landing him on the other side, they showed him which way to take and left him. He had not walked far when he saw a bow and arrows lying before him. But Scar-face was punctilious and would not pick them up because they did not belong to him. Not long afterward he encountered a beautiful youth of handsome form and smiling aspect.

'I have lost a bow and arrows,' he said to Scar-face. 'Have you seen them?'

Scar-face told him that he had seen them a little way back, and the handsome youth praised him for his honesty in not appropriating them. He further asked him where he was bound for.

'I am seeking the Sun in his home,' replied the Indian, 'and I believe that I am not far from my destination.'

'You are right,' replied the youth. 'I am the son of the Sun, Apisirahts, the Morning Star, and I will lead you to the presence of my august father.'

They walked onward for a little space, and then Apisirahts pointed out a great lodge, glorious with golden light and decorated with an art more curious than any that Scar-face had ever beheld. At the entrance stood a beautiful woman, the mother of Morning Star, Kokomikis, the Moon-goddess, who welcomed the footsore Indian kindly and joyously.

The chase of the savage birds

Then the great Sun-god appeared, wondrous in his strength and beauty as the mighty planet over which he ruled. He too greeted Scar-face kindly, and requested him to be his guest and to hunt with his son. Scar-face and the youth gladly set out for the chase. But on departing the Sun-god warned them not to venture near the Great Water, as there dwelt savage birds which might slay Morning Star.

Scar-face tarried with the Sun, his wife and child, fearful of asking his boon too speedily, and desiring to make as sure as possible of its being granted.

One day he and Morning Star hunted as usual, and the youth stole away, for he wished to slay the savage birds of which his father had spoken. But Scar-face followed, rescued the lad in imminent peril, and killed the monsters. The Sun was grateful to him for having saved his son from a terrible death, and asked him for what reason he had sought his lodge. Scar-face acquainted him with the circumstances of his love for the chief's daughter and of his quest. At once the Sun-god granted his desire.

'Return to the woman you love so much,' he said, 'return and make her yours. And as a sign that it is my will that she should be your wife, I make you whole.'

With a motion of his bright hand the deity removed the unsightly scar. On quitting the Sun-country the god, his wife and son presented Scar-face with many good gifts, and showed him a short route by which to return to Earth-land once more.

Scar-face soon reached his home. When he sought his chief's daughter she did not know him at first, so rich was the gleaming attire he had obtained in the Sun-country. But when she at last recognized him she fell upon his breast with a glad cry. That same day she was made his wife. The happy pair raised a 'medicine' lodge to the Sun-god, and henceforth Scar-face was called Smooth-face.

The legend of Poïa
A variant of this beautiful story is as follows:

One summer morning a beautiful girl called Feather-woman, who had been sleeping outside her lodge among the long prairie grass, awoke just as the Morning Star was rising above the horizon. She gazed intently at it, and so beautiful did it seem that she fell deeply in love with it. She awakened her sister, who was lying beside her, and declared to her that she would marry nobody but the Morning Star. The people of her tribe ridiculed her because of what they considered her absurd preference; so she avoided them as much as possible, and wandered alone, eating her heart out in secret for love of the Morning Star, who seemed to her unapproachable.

One day she went alone to the river for water, and as she returned she beheld a young man standing before her. At first she took him for one of the young men of the tribe, and would have avoided him, but he said:

'I am the Morning Star. I beheld you gazing upward at me, and knew that you loved me. I returned your love, and have descended to ask you to go with me to my dwelling in the sky.'

Feather-woman trembled violently, for she knew that he who spoke to her was a god, and replied hesitatingly that she must bid farewell to her father and mother. But this Morning Star would not permit. He took a rich yellow plume from his hair and directed her to hold this in one hand, while she held a juniper branch in the other. Then he commanded her to close her eyes, and when she opened them again she was in the Sky-country, standing before a great and shining lodge. Morning Star told her that this was the home of his parents, the Sun and Moon, and requested her to enter. It was daytime, so that the Sun was away on his diurnal round, but the Moon was at home. She welcomed Feather-woman as the wife of her son, as did the Sun himself when he returned. The Moon clothed her in a soft robe of buckskin, trimmed with elks' teeth. Feather-woman was very happy, and dwelt contentedly in the lodge of Morning Star. They had a little son, whom they called Star-boy. The Moon gave Feather-woman a root-digger, and told her that she could dig up all kinds of roots, but warned her on no account to dig up the large turnip which grew near the home of the Spider Man, telling her that it would bring unhappiness to all of them if she did so.

The great turnip

Feather-woman often saw the large turnip, but always avoided touching it. One day, however, her curiosity got the better of her, and she was tempted to see what might be underneath it. She laid her little son on the ground and dug until her root-digger stuck fast. Two large cranes came flying overhead. She begged these to help her. They did so, and sang a magic song which enabled them to uproot the turnip.

Now, although she was unaware of it, this very turnip filled up the hole through which Morning Star had brought her into the Sky-country. Gazing downward, she saw the camp of the Blackfeet where she had lived. The smoke was ascending from the lodges, she could hear the song of the women as they went about their work. The sight made her homesick and lonely, and as she went back to her lodge she cried softly to herself. When she arrived Morning Star gazed earnestly at her, and said with a sorrowful expression of countenance: 'You have dug up the sacred turnip.'

The Moon and Sun were also troubled, and asked her the meaning of her sadness, and when she had told them they said that as she had disobeyed their injunction she must return to earth. Morning Star took her to the Spider Man, who let her down to earth by a web, and the people beheld her coming to earth like a falling star.

The return to earth

She was welcomed by her parents, and returned with her child, whom she had brought with her from the Sky-country, to the home of her youth. But happiness never came back to her. She mourned ceaselessly for her husband, and one morning, climbing to the summit of a high mound, she watched the beautiful Morning Star rise above the horizon, just as on the day when she had first loved him. Stretching out her arms to the eastern sky, she besought him passionately to take her back. At length he spoke to her.

'It is because of your own sin,' he said, 'that you are forever shut out from the Sky-country. Your disobedience has brought sorrow upon yourself and upon all your people.'

Her pleadings were in vain, and in despair she returned to her lodge, where her unhappy life soon came to a close. Her little son, Star-boy, was now an orphan, and the death of his grandparents deprived him of all his earthly kindred. He was a shy, retiring, timid boy, living in the deepest poverty, notwithstanding his exalted station as grandchild of the Sun. But the most noticeable thing about him was a scar which disfigured his face, because of which he was given the name of Poïa (Scar-face) by the wits of the tribe. As he grew older the scar became more pronounced, and ridicule and abuse were heaped upon him. When he became a man he fell in love with a maiden of surpassing beauty, the daughter of a great chief, of his tribe. She, however, laughed him to scorn, and told him that she would marry him when he removed the scar from his face. Poïa, greatly saddened by her unkindness, consulted an old medicine-woman, to see whether the scar might not be removed. She could only tell him that the mark had been placed on his face by the Sun, and that the Sun alone could remove it. This was melancholy news for Poïa. How could he reach the abode of the Sun? Nevertheless, encouraged by the old woman, he resolved to make the attempt. Gratefully accepting her parting gift of pemmican and moccasins, he set off on a journey that was to last for many days.

The Big Water

After climbing mountains and traversing forests and wandering over trackless prairies he arrived at the Big Water (that is to say, the Pacific Ocean), on the shores of which he sat down, praying and fasting for three days. On the third day, when the Sun was sinking behind the rim of the ocean, he saw a bright pathway leading straight to the abode of the Sun. He resolved to follow the shining trail, though he knew not what might lie before him in the great Sky-country. He arrived quite safely, however, at the wonderful lodge of the Sun. All night he hid himself outside the lodge, and in the morning the Sun, who was about to begin his daily journey, saw a ragged wayfarer lying by his door. He did not know that the intruder was his grandson, but, seeing that he had come from the Earth-country, he determined to kill him, and said so to his wife, the Moon. But she begged that the stranger's life should be spared, and Morning Star, who at that moment issued from the lodge, also gave Poïa his protection. Poïa lived very happily in the lodge of the Sun, and having on one occasion killed seven birds who were about to destroy Morning Star, he earned the gratitude of his grandparents. At the request of Morning Star the Sun removed the scar on Poïa's face, and bade him return with a message to the Blackfeet. If they would honour him once a year in a Sun Dance he would consent to heal their sick.

The secrets of the Sun Dance were taught to Poïa, two raven's feathers were placed in his hair, and he was given a robe of elk-skin. The latter, he was told, must only be worn by a virtuous woman, who should then dance the Sun Dance, so that the sick might be restored to health. From his father Poïa received an enchanted flute and a magic song, which would win the heart of the maid he loved.

Poïa came to earth by the Milky Way, or, as the Indians call it, the Wolf-trail, and communicated to the Blackfeet all that he had learned in the Sky-country. When they were thoroughly conversant with the Sun Dance he returned to the Sky-country, the home of his father, accompanied by his beautiful bride. Here they dwelt together happily, and Poïa and the Morning Star travelled together through the sky.

A Blackfoot day-and-night myth

Many stories are told by the Blackfoot Indians of their creator, Nápi, and these chiefly relate to the manner in which he made the world and its inhabitants.

One myth connected with this deity tells how a poor Indian who had a wife and two children lived in the greatest indigence on roots and berries. This man had a dream in which he heard a voice command him to procure a large spider-web, which he was to hang on the trail of the animals where they passed through the forest, by which means he would obtain plenty of food. This he did, and on returning to the place in which he had hung the web he found deer and rabbits entangled in its magical meshes. These he killed for food, for which he was now never at a loss.

Returning with his game on his shoulders one morning, he discovered his wife perfuming herself with sweet pine, which she burned over the fire. He suspected that she was thus making herself attractive for the benefit of someone else, but, preserving silence, he told her that on the following day he would set his spider-web at a greater distance, as the game in the neighbouring forest was beginning to know the trap too well. Accordingly he went farther afield, and caught a deer, which he cut up, carrying part of its meat back with him to his lodge. He told his wife where the remainder of the carcass was to be found, and asked her to go and fetch it.

His wife, however, was not without her own suspicions, and, concluding that she was being watched by her husband, she halted at the top of the nearest hill and looked back to see if he was following her. But he was sitting where she had left him, so she proceeded on her way. When she was quite out of sight the Indian himself climbed the hill, and, seeing that she was not in the vicinity, returned to the camp. He inquired of his children where their mother went to gather firewood, and they pointed to a large patch of dead timber. Proceeding to the clump of leafless trees, the man instituted a thorough search, and after a while discovered a den of rattlesnakes. Now it was one of these reptiles with which his wife was in love, so the Indian in his wrath gathered fragments of dry wood and set the whole plantation in a blaze. Then he returned to his lodge and told his children what he had done, at the same time warning them that their mother would be very wrathful, and would probably attempt to kill them all. He further said that he would wait for her return, but that they had better run away, and that he would provide them with three things which they would find of use. He then handed to the children a stick, a stone, and a bunch of moss, which they were to throw behind them should their mother pursue them. The children at once ran away, and their father hung the spider-web over the door of the lodge. Meanwhile the woman had seen the blaze made by the dry timber-patch from a considerable distance, and in great anger turned and ran back to the lodge. Attempting to enter it, she was at once entangled in the meshes of the spider-web.

The pursuing head
She struggled violently, however, and succeeded in getting her head through the opening, whereupon her husband severed it

from her shoulders with his stone axe. He then ran out of the lodge and down the valley, hotly pursued by the woman's body, while her head rolled along the ground in chase of the children. The latter soon descried the grisly object rolling along in their tracks at a great speed, and one of them quickly threw the stick behind him as he had been told to do. Instantly a dense forest sprang up in their rear, which for a space retarded their horrible pursuer. The children made considerable headway, but once more the severed head made its appearance, gnashing its teeth in a frenzy of rage and rolling its eyes horribly, while it shrieked out threats which caused the children's blood to turn to water.

Then another of the boys threw the stone which he had been given behind him, and instantly a great mountain sprang up which occupied the land from sea to sea, so that the progress of the head was quite barred. It could perceive no means of overcoming this immense barrier, until it encountered two rams feeding, which it asked to make a way for it through the mountain, telling them that if they would do so it would marry the chief of the sheep. The rams made a valiant effort to meet this request, and again and again fiercely rushed at the mountain, till their horns were split and broken and they could butt no longer. The head, growing impatient, called upon a colony of ants which dwelt in the neighbourhood to tunnel a passage through the obstacle, and offered, if they were successful, to marry the chief ant as a recompense for their labours. The insects at once took up the task, and toiled incessantly until they had made a tunnel through which the head could roll.

The fate of the head
The children were still running, but felt that the head had not abandoned pursuit. At last, after a long interval, they observed it rolling after them, evidently as fresh as ever. The child who had the bunch of moss now wet it and wrung out the water over their trail, and immediately an immense strait separated

them from the land where they had been but a moment before. The head, unable to stop, fell into this great water and was drowned.

The children, seeing that their danger was past, made a raft and sailed back to the land from which they had come. Arrived there, they journeyed eastward through many countries, peopled by many different tribes of Indians, in order to reach their own territory. When they arrived there they found it occupied by tribes unknown to them, so they resolved to separate, one going north and the other south. One of them was shrewd and clever, and the other simple and ingenious. The shrewd boy is he who made the white people and instructed them in their arts. The other, the simple boy, made the Blackfeet, but, being very stupid, was unable to teach them anything. He it was who was called Nápi. As for the mother's body, it continued to chase her husband, and is still following him, for she is the Moon and he is the Sun. If she succeeds in catching him she will slay him, and night will reign for evermore, but as long as he is able to evade her day and night will continue to follow one another.

Nápi and the Buffalo-stealer

There was once a great famine among the Blackfeet. For months no buffaloes were killed, and the weaker members of the tribe dropped off one by one, while even the strong braves and hunters began to sink under the privation. The chief in despair prayed that the creator, Nápi, would send them food. Nápi, meanwhile, was far away in the south, painting the plumage of the birds in gorgeous tints. Nevertheless he heard the voice of the chief over all the distance, and hastened northward.

'Who has summoned me?' he demanded.

'It was I,' said the chief humbly. 'My people are starving, and unless relief comes soon I fear we must all perish.'

'You shall have food,' answered Nápi. 'I will provide game for you.'

Taking with him the chief's son, Nápi travelled toward the west. As they went the youth prayed earnestly to the Sun, the Moon, and the Morning Star, but his companion rebuked his impatience and bade him hold his peace. They crossed the Sweet Grass Hills, which Nápi had made from huge handfuls of herbage, and where he loved to rest. Still there was no sign of game. At length they reached a little lodge by the side of a river, and Nápi called a halt.

'There dwells the cause of your misfortunes,' said he. 'He who lives in that lodge is the Buffalo-stealer. He it is who has taken all the herds from the prairies, so that there is none left.'

To further his design, Nápi took the shape of a dog, and turned the youth into a stick. Not long afterward the little son of Buffalo-stealer was passing that way, and immediately desired to take the little dog home with him.

'Very well,' said his mother; 'take that stick and drive it to the lodge.'

But the boy's father frowned angrily.

'I do not like the look of the beast,' he said. 'Send it away.'

The boy refused to part with the dog, and his mother wanted the stick to gather roots with, so the father was obliged to give way. Still he did not show any goodwill to the dog. The following day he went out of the lodge, and in a short time returned with a buffalo, which he skinned and prepared for cooking. His wife, who was in the woods gathering berries, came home toward evening, and at her husband's bidding cooked part of the buffalo-meat. The little boy incurred his father's anger again by giving a piece of meat to the dog.

'Have I not told you,' cried Buffalo-stealer irately, 'that he is an evil thing? Do not touch him.'

That night when all was silent Nápi and the chief's son resumed their human form and supped off the buffalo-meat.

'It is Buffalo-stealer who keeps the herds from coming near the Blackfoot camp,' said Nápi. 'Wait till morning and see.'

The herds of Buffalo-stealer

In the morning they were once more dog and stick. When the woman and her child awoke they set off for the woods again, the former taking the stick to dig for roots, the latter calling for his little dog to accompany him. Alas! when they reached the spot they had fixed upon for root-gathering operations both dog and stick had vanished! And this was the reason for their disappearance. As the dog was trotting through the wood he had observed an opening like the mouth of a cavern, all but concealed by the thick undergrowth, and in the aperture he perceived a buffalo. His short, sharp barking attracted the attention of the stick, which promptly wriggled snake-wise after him. Within the cavern were great herds of deer and buffalo, enough to provide the Blackfeet with food for years and years. Nápi ran among them, barking, and they were driven out to the prairie.

When Buffalo-stealer returned and discovered his loss his wrath knew no bounds. He questioned his wife and son, but they denied all knowledge of the affair.

'Then,' said he, 'it is that wretched little dog of yours. Where is he now?'

But the child could not tell him.

'We lost him in the woods,' said he.

'I shall kill him,' shouted the man, 'and I shall break the stick as well!'

Nápi overheard the threat, and clung to the long hair of an old buffalo. He advised the stick to conceal itself in the buffalo's hair also, and so the twain escaped unnoticed from the cave, much as did Ulysses from the Cyclops' cavern. Once again they took the form of men, and drove a herd of buffalo to the Blackfoot camp, while Buffalo-stealer and his family sought them in vain.

The people met them with delighted acclamations, and the famine was at an end. Yet there were still some difficulties in the way, for when they tried to get the herd into the enclosure a large grey bird so frightened the animals with its dismal note that they refused to enter. This occurred so often that Nápi suspected that the grey bird was no other than Buffalo-stealer. Changing himself into an otter, he lay by the side of a river and pretended to be dead. The greedy bird saw what he thought to be a dead otter, and pounced upon it, whereupon Nápi seized him by the leg and bore him off to the camp. By way of punishment he was tied over the smoke-hole of the wigwam, where his grey feathers soon became black and his life a burden to him.

'Spare me!' he cried. 'Let me return to my wife and child. They will surely starve.'

His piteous appeals moved the heart of Nápi, and he let him go, but not without an admonition.

'Go,' said he, 'and hunt for food, that you may support your wife and child. But do not take more than you need, or you shall die.'

The bird did as he was bidden. But to this day the feathers of the raven are black, and not grey.

The story of Kutoyis

There once lived on the banks of the Missouri an old couple who had one daughter, their only child. When she grew to be a woman she had a suitor who was cruel and over-bearing, but as she loved him her parents offered no opposition to their marriage. Indeed, they gave the bride the best part of their possessions for a dowry, so that she and her husband were rich, while her father and mother lived in a poor lodge and had very little to eat. The wicked son-in-law took advantage of their kindness in every way. He forced the old man to accompany him on his hunting expeditions, and then refused to share the game with him. Sometimes one would kill a buffalo and sometimes the other, but always it was the younger man who got the best of the meat and who made himself robes and moccasins from the hide.

Thus the aged couple were nearly perishing from cold and

hunger. Only when her husband was out hunting would the daughter venture to carry a morsel of meat to her parents.

On one occasion the younger man called in his overbearing way to his father-in-law, bidding him help in a buffalo-hunt. The old man, reduced by want almost to a skeleton, was too much afraid of the tyrant to venture to disobey him, so he accompanied him in the chase. Ere long they encountered a fine buffalo, whereupon both drew their bows and fired. But it was the arrow of the elder man which pierced the animal and brought it to the ground. The old man set himself to skin the buffalo, for his son-in-law never shared in these tasks, but left them to his companion. While he was thus engaged the latter observed a drop of blood on one of his arrows which had fallen to the ground.

Thinking that even a drop of blood was better than nothing, he replaced the arrow in its quiver and set off home. As it happened, no more of the buffalo than that fell to his share, the rest being appropriated by his son-in-law.

On his return the old man called to his wife to heap fuel on the fire and put on the kettle. She, thinking he had brought home some buffalo-meat, hastened to do his bidding. She waited curiously till the water in the kettle had boiled; then to her surprise she saw him place in it an arrow with a drop of blood on it.

How Kutoyis was born

'Why do you do that?' she asked.

'Something will come of it,' he replied. 'My spirit tells me so.'

They waited in silence.

Then a strange sound was heard in their lonely little lodge – the crying of a child. Half fearfully, half curiously, the old couple lifted the lid of the kettle, and there within was a little baby boy.

'He shall bring us good luck,' said the old Indian.

They called the child Kutoyis – that is, 'Drop of Blood' – and wrapped him up as is customary with Indian babies.

'Let us tell our son-in-law,' said the old man, 'that it is a little girl, and he will let it live. If we say it is a boy he will surely kill it.'

Kutoyis became a great favourite in the little lodge to which he had come. He was always laughing, and his merriment won the hearts of the old people. One day, while they thought him much too young to speak, they were astonished to hear his voice.

'Lash me up and hang me from the lodge pole,' said he, 'and I shall become a man.'

When they had recovered from their astonishment they lashed him to the lodge pole. In a moment he had burst the lashings and grown before their eyes into a tall, strong man. Looking round the lodge, which seemed scarcely large enough to hold him, Kutoyis perceived that there was no food about.

'Give me some arrows,' said he, 'and I will bring you food.'

'We have no arrows,' replied the old man, 'only four arrow-heads.'

Kutoyis fetched some wood, from which he cut a fine bow, and shafts to fit the flint arrow-heads. He begged the old Indian to lead him to a good hunting-ground, and when he had done so they quickly killed a magnificent buffalo.

Meanwhile the old Indian had told Kutoyis how badly his son-in-law had treated him, and as they were skinning the buffalo who should pass by but the subject of their conversation. Kutoyis hid behind the dead animal to see what would happen, and a moment later the angry voice of the son-in-law was heard.

Getting no reply, the cowardly hunter fitted an arrow to his bow and shot it at his father-in-law. Enraged at the cruel act, Kutoyis rose from his hiding-place behind the dead buffalo and fired all his arrows at the young man, whom he slew. He afterward gave food in plenty to the old man and his wife, and bade them return to their home. They were delighted to find themselves once more free from persecution, but their daughter wept so much that finally Kutoyis asked her whether she would have another husband or whether she wished to follow her first spouse to the Land of Shadows, as she must do if she persisted in lamenting him.

The lady chose the former alternative as the lesser evil, and Kutoyis found her an excellent husband, with whom she lived happily for a long time.

Kutoyis on his travels

At length Kutoyis tired of his monotonous life, and desired to see more of the world. So his host directed him to a distant village, where he was welcomed by two old women. They set before their handsome guest the best fare at their disposal, which was buffalo-meat of a rather unattractive appearance.

'Is there no good meat?' queried Kutoyis.

The old women explained that one of the lodges was occupied by a fierce bear, who seized upon all the good meat and left only the dry, poor sort for his neighbours. Without hesitation Kutoyis went out and killed a buffalo calf, which he presented to the women, desiring them to place the best parts of the meat in a prominent position outside the lodge, where the big bear could not fail to see it.

This they did, and sure enough one of the bear-cubs shortly passed by and seized the meat. Kutoyis, who had been lying in wait, rushed out and hit the animal as hard as he could. The cub carried his tale of woe to his father, and the big bear, growling threats of vengeance, gathered his whole family round him and rushed to the lodge of the old women, intending to kill the bold hunter.

However, Kutoyis was more than a match for all of them, and very soon the bears were slain. Still he was unsatisfied, and longed for further adventures.

'Tell me,' said he, 'where shall I find another village?'

The wrestling woman

'There is a village by the Big River,' said the old women, 'but you must not go there, for a wicked woman dwells in it who wrestles with and slays all who approach.'

No sooner did Kutoyis hear this than he determined to seek the village, for his mission was to destroy evil beings who were a danger to his fellow-men. So in spite of the dissuasions of the old women he departed.

As he had been warned, the woman came out of her lodge on the approach of the stranger and invited him to wrestle with her.

'I cannot,' said he, pretending to be frightened.

The woman mocked and jeered at him, while he made various excuses, but all the time he was observing how the land lay. When he drew nearer he saw that she had covered the ground with sharp flints, over which she had strewn grass. At last he said: 'Very well, I will wrestle with you.'

It was no wonder that she had killed many braves, for she was very strong. But Kutoyis was still stronger. With all her skill she could not throw him, and at last she grew tired, and was herself thrown on the sharp flints, on which she bled to death. The people rejoiced greatly when they heard of her death, and Kutoyis was universally acclaimed as a hero.

Kutoyis did many other high deeds before he departed to the Shadow-land, and when he went he left sorrow in many lodges.

* * *

There is a distinction to be made between the Algonquin tribe and the Algonquian language group: historically the former were a people of the eastern woodlands based on the River Ottawa and Hudson Bay, while the language group to which they give their name was spread far and wide across North America, from the Atlantic to the Rockies, and included, *inter alia*, the Algonquin themselves, the Arapaho, Blackfoot, Cheyenne, Chippewa (Ojibwa), Ottawa, Fox, Kickapoo, Powhatan, Sauk, Wampanoag, and Cree. It is the language group Spence generally refers to in the phrase 'Algonquin Indians'. The diversity in lifestyle of the Algonquian tribes was almost absolute, from the nomadic buffalo-hunting Blackfeet on the Plains of Montana to the horticulturalist Wampanoags on the East Coast, via the rice-gathering Ottawa on the Great Lakes. Genetically, the Algonquian tribes of the East Coast were closely linked, whereas the Algonquian tribes of the central and western areas of the language groups were largely Algonquian in language only. While scholars largely agree that the Algonquian language derives from a single source spoken around 3,000 years ago ('Proto-Algonquian') there is substantial disagreement over the *urheimat* or homeland of the language, which is variously suggested as being near Lake Ontario or west of Lake Superior.

Given the miscellaneous nature of the Algonquian-language group, it should be no surprise that it produced trickster-culture heroes/transformers aside from Glooskap and Michabo, the Great Hare. The Cree tell of Wisgatcak, who tried to trap the Giant Beaver by breaking down his dam, only to flood the world. Swiftly making a raft, Wisgatcak collected as many of the animals swimming in the rising waters as he could. After two weeks, Wisgatcak made magic and called upon the Wolf to help. With a ball of moss in his mouth, Wolf ran round and round the rafts until the moss grew and earth formed on it. Putting the earth-ball down, Wolf sang songs and the earth grew. And grew and grew until it created the whole world.

Nanabozho is the Ojibwa's version of the trickster-culture hero. In the Ojibwa version of the origins of man:

Long ago there lived an old man named Nana-bo-zhoo in a big wigwam with his brother, who was a great hunter, and those animals he did not shoot with his bow he ran down and killed with his club. The animals, in great fear, held a council to consider the means of preventing N.'s brother from killing them all. The white deer, who was able to outrun all the rest, was chosen to decoy him out on the ice of a lake, so that when the 'sea-lion' made a loud noise the ice would break and the hunter be drowned. One day N. being out for a walk saw the white deer, came back and asked his brother to get the animal for him and to be sure to run him down and club him, so as not to spoil his skin, for N. was a skilful dresser of furs and skins. So the brother set out and ran after the deer all day without reaching him. About sunset they came to a lake and the deer ran out upon the ice. When they got near the middle of the lake the hunter seemed to be gaining upon the deer, who appeared to be somewhat tired; he was just raising his arm to strike him down, when there was a loud noise, the ice cracked and the hunter sank to the bottom, while the animal escaped.

N., finding that his brother did not return, was somewhat anxious when nightfall came on, but supposed his brother had wandered a long way and would be back next day. Three days passed and the hunter did not return. Then N. took his brother's bow and arrows and followed his tracks to the lake, but when he got there a snow-storm covered them up.

In the spring the ice melted and N. could not find the tracks. One day, however, he saw the kingfisher seated on a tree looking into the water. By telling the bird that he would paint its feathers and give it pretty colours, N. induced it to say that it was watching the 'sea-lions' playing with N.'s brother. N. again bribed the bird, by promising to give it a tuft of feathers on its head, to tell him how to get his brother away from the 'sea-lions'.

So N. walked along the lake shore until he came to a nice sandy beach. The day was calm and as he looked at the water he saw it begin to boil. N. changed himself into an old tree-stump and waited to see how things would turn out. Very soon the 'sea-lions' came out and began to sport about on the beach. By and by one of them noticed the stump and said it must be N., for it had not been there before. The 'sea-lions' discussed the matter for some time; at last the one who had first seen the stump suggested that they should try to pull it up, which they could not do if it were a real stump. So they tugged away, and N. had to exert all his power and magic to prevent his being pulled up. The 'sea-lions' then gave up the attempt, and, lying down in the sun, were soon fast asleep. N. then changed himself into a man and shot the biggest 'white sea-lion', who made a great noise, whereupon they disappeared beneath the waters of the lake.

N. then walked along the lake shore and soon met a big toad with a club in his hand and a bag thrown over his shoulder. The toad was singing, and, when N. spoke to him, said that he was going to cure the white 'sea-lion' that had been wounded by N. Then N. killed the toad, took up the club and bag, and changing himself into a toad, went along singing. Going into the lake he dived down and walked along the bottom until he came to a door through which he saw the 'sea-lions' sporting about. He went in singing, and when asked what he wanted, said that he had come to cure their chief who had been wounded by N.

As the door opened he saw his brother hanging across the door-way. When all the 'sea-lions' came into the room, N. told them that he could do nothing unless he were left alone. When they had gone he killed the 'sea-lion' and, taking down his brother, made for the shore with him. The 'sea-lions' chased him, and when they got to the edge of the lake they made the waters rise and follow N. and his brother, who kept running farther inland, pursued by the 'sea-lions' and the waters, and accompanied by all the birds and beasts.

At length they reached the summit of the highest mountain, closely followed by the waters. N. then built a raft and got on it with his brother and all the animals, and when the waters covered the mountain the raft floated away. After some time N. called to him the best divers to see which of them could find the bottom. After the beaver, the otter, and the loon had gone down, and after a long time risen up to the surface dead, Nanabozhoo breathed life into them again. The muskrat tried, and after a very long time came up dead. But N., upon examining him, found that his fore-paws were clasped together, and in them he discovered a little bit of mud. Then N. made him alive again, petted and praised him, but would not let him go down again as he desired to do. Taking the little bit of mud, N. rolled it between his hands until it was very fine and then threw it in the air, when it spread out over the water and covered it. Then with his fingers he drew upon it the lakes, rivers, islands, mountains, hills, etc., and the world was made.

(A. F. Chamberlain, 'Nanibozhu amongst the Otchipwe, Mississagas and Other Algonkian Tribes' *The Journal of American Folk-Lore*, Vol. IV, July–September 1891)

'The Song of Hiawatha', the epic 1855 poem by Henry Wadsworth Longfellow, is based on the Nanabozho stories. He bears a strong resemblance to Na'pi, 'the Old Man' in Blackfeet mythology. The creation myth of the Blackfeet is significant in the importance assigned to the buffalo, the tribe's principal source of food. After Na'pi made the earth, he made woman, then man, then the buffalo:

They were quite tame. He gave bows and arrows to the Indian and told them to shoot the buffalo. They did so and as the buffalo were tame, they killed a large number.

(John Macclean, 'Blackfoot Mythology', *The Journal of American Folk-Lore*, Vol. VI, July–September 1895)

4

IROQUOIS MYTHS AND LEGENDS

Iroquois gods and heroes

The myths of the Iroquois are of exceptional interest because of the portraits they present of several semi-historical heroes. The earliest substratum of the myths of this people deals with the adventures of their principal deity, Hi'nun, the Thunder-god, who, with his brother, the West Wind, finally overcame and exterminated the powerful race of Stone Giants. Coming to a later period, we find that a number of legends cluster round the names of the chiefs Atotarho and Hiawatha, who in all probability at one time really existed. These present a good instance of the rapidity with which myth gathers round a famous name. Atotarho, the mighty warrior, is now regarded as the wizard *par excellence* of the Iroquois, but probably this does not result from the fact that he was cunning and cruel, as some writers on the tribe appear to think, but from the circumstance that as a great warrior he was clothed in a garment of serpents, and these reptiles, besides being looked upon as powerful war-physic, also possessed a deep magical significance. The original Hiawatha (He who seeks the Wampum-belt) is pictured as the father of a long line of persons of the same name, who appear to have been important functionaries in the tribal government. To him was ascribed the honour of having established the great confederacy of the Iroquois, which so long rendered them formidable opponents to the tribes which surrounded them. Like many other heroes in myth – the Celtic Manahan, for example – Hiawatha possessed a magic canoe which would obey his slightest behest, and in which he finally quitted the terrestrial sphere for that shadowy region to which all heroes finally take their departure.

Hi'nun

Many interesting myths are related of the manner in which Hi'nun destroyed the monsters and giants which infested the early world. A hunter, caught in a heavy thunder-shower, took refuge in the woods. Crouching under the shelter of a great tree, he became aware of a mysterious voice which urged him to follow it. He was conscious of a sensation of slowly rising from the earth, and he soon found himself gazing downward from a point near the clouds, the height of many trees from the ground. He was surrounded by beings who had all the appearance of men, with one among them who seemed to be their chief. They asked him to cast his eyes toward the earth and tell them whether he could see a huge water-serpent. Unable to descry such a monster, the chief anointed his eyes with a sacred ointment, which gave him supernatural sight and permitted him to behold a dragon-like shape in the watery depths far below him. The chief commanded one of his warriors to dispatch the monster, but arrow after arrow failed to transfix it, whereupon the hunter was requested to display his skill as an archer. Drawing his bow, he took careful aim. The arrow whizzed down the depths and was speedily lost to sight, but a terrible commotion arose in the lake below, the body of the great serpent leaping from the blood-stained water with dreadful writhings and contortions. So appalling was the din that rose up to them that even the heavenly beings by whom the hunter was surrounded fell into a great trembling; but gradually the tempest of sound subsided, and the huge bulk of the mortally wounded serpent sank back into the lake, the surface of which became gradually more still, until finally all was peace once more. The chief thanked the hunter for the service he had rendered, and he was conducted back to earth. Thus was man first brought into contact with the beneficent Hi'nun, and thus did he learn the existence of a power which would protect him from forces unfriendly to humanity.

The Thunderers

Once in early Iroquois days three braves set out upon an expedition. After they had journeyed for some time a misfortune occurred, one of their number breaking his leg. The others fashioned a litter with the object of carrying him back to his home, as Indian custom exacted. Retracing their steps, they came to a range of high mountains, the steep slopes of which taxed their strength to the utmost. To rest themselves they placed the disabled man on the ground and withdrew to a little distance.

'Why should we be thus burdened with a wounded man?' said one to the other.

'You speak truly,' was the rejoinder. 'Why should we, indeed, since his hurt has come upon him by reason of his own carelessness?'

As they spoke their eyes met in a meaning glance, and one of them pointed to a deep hole or pit opening in the side of the mountain at a little distance from the place where they were sitting. Returning to the injured man, they raised him as if about to proceed on the journey, and when passing the brink of the pit suddenly hurled him into it with great force. Then without loss of time they set their faces homeward. When they arrived in camp they reported that their comrade had died of wounds received in a fight, but that he had not fallen into the enemy's hands, having received careful attention from them in his dying moments and honourable burial. The unfortunate man's aged mother was prostrate with grief at the sad news, but was somewhat relieved to think that her son had been kindly ministered to at the end.

When the brave who had been thrown into the pit regained his senses after the severe fall he had sustained he perceived a man of venerable aspect bending over him solicitously. When this person saw that the young man had regained consciousness he asked him what had been the intention of his comrades in so cruelly casting him into that abyss. The young man replied that his fellows had become tired of carrying him and had thus rid themselves of him. The old hermit – for so he seemed to be – made a hasty examination of the Indian's injuries, and announced that he would speedily cure him, on one condition. The other pledged his word to accept this, whatever it might be, whereupon the recluse told him that all he required was that he should hunt for him and bring home to him such game as he should slay. To this the brave gave a ready assent. The old man lost no time in performing his part of the bargain. He applied herbs to his injuries and assiduously tended his guest, who made a speedy and satisfactory recovery. The grateful warrior, once more enabled to follow the chase, brought home many trophies of his skill as a hunter to the cave on the mountain-side, and soon the pair had formed a strong attachment. One day, when in the forest, the warrior encountered an enormous bear, which he succeeded in slaying after a desperate struggle. As he was pondering how best he could remove it to the cave he became aware of a murmur of voices behind him, and glancing round he saw three men, or beings in the shape of men, clad in strange diaphanous garments, standing near. In reply to his question as to what brought them there, they told him that they were the Thunderers, or people of Hi'nun, whose mission it was to keep the earth in good order for the benefit of humanity, and to slay or destroy every agency inimical to mankind. They told him that the old man with whom he had been residing was by no means the sort of person he seemed to think, and that they had come to earth with the express intention of compassing his destruction. In this they requested his assistance, and promised him that if he would vouchsafe it he would speedily be transported back to his mother's lodge. Overjoyed at this proposal, the hunter did not scruple to return to the cave and tell the hermit that he had killed the bear, which he wished his help in bringing home. The old man seemed very uneasy, and begged him to examine the sky and tell him whether he perceived the least sign of clouds. The young brave reassured him and told him that not a cloud was to be seen, whereupon, emerging from his shelter, he made for the spot where the bear was lying. Hastily picking up the carcass, he requested his companion to place it all on his shoulders, which the young man did, expressing surprise at his great strength. He had proceeded with his burden for some distance when a terrific clap of thunder burst from the menacing black clouds which had speedily gathered overhead. In great terror the old man threw down his load and commenced to run with an agility which belied his years, but when a second peal broke forth he suddenly assumed the shape of a gigantic porcupine, which dashed through the undergrowth, discharging its quills like arrows as it ran. A veritable hail of thunderbolts now crashed down upon the creature's spiny back. As it reached the entrance to the cave one larger than the rest struck it with such tremendous force that it rolled dead into its den.

Then the Thunderers swooped down from the sky in triumph, mightily pleased at the death of their victim. The young hunter now requested them to discharge the promise they had made him to transport him back to his mother's lodge; so, having fastened cloud-wings on his shoulders, they speedily brought him thither, carrying him carefully through the air and depositing him just outside the hut. The widow was delighted to see her son, whom she had believed to be long dead, and the Thunderers were so pleased with the assistance he had lent them that they asked him to accompany them in their monster-destroying mission every spring. He assented, and on one of these expeditions flew earthward to drink from a certain pool. When he rejoined his companions they observed that the water with which his lips were moist had caused them to shine as if smeared with oil. At their request he indicated the pool from which he had drunk, and they informed him that in its depths there dwelt a monster for which they had searched for years. With that they hurled a great thunderbolt into the pool, which immediately dried up, revealing an immense grub of the species which destroys the standing crops. The monster was, indeed, the King of Grubs, and his death set back the conspiracies of his kind for many generations. The youth subsequently returned to earth, and having narrated to the members of his tribe the services which Hi'nun had performed on their behalf, they considered it fitting to institute a special worship of the deity, and, in fact, to make him supreme god of their nation. Even today many Iroquois allude to Hi'nun as their grandfather, and evince extraordinary veneration at the mention of his name.

Hiawatha

Much confusion exists with regard to the true status of the reputed Iroquois hero Hiawatha. We find him variously represented as a historical personage and a mythical demi-god, and as belonging to both the Iroquois and the Algonquins. In solid history and in the wildest myth he is a figure of equal importance. This confusion is largely due to the popularity of Longfellow's poem *Hiawatha*, which by its very excellence has given the greater prominence to the fallacies it contains. The fact is that Longfellow, following in the path of Schoolcraft, has really confused *two* personages in the character of Hiawatha, one the entirely mythical Manabozho, or Michabo – which name he at first intended to bestow on his poem – and the other the almost wholly historical

Hiawatha. Manabozho, according to tradition, was a demi-god of the Ojibways, and to him, and not to Hiawatha, must be credited the exploits described in the poem. There is no doubt that myths have grown up round the name of the Iroquois hero, for myth is the ivy that binds all historical ruins and makes them picturesque to the eye; but it has been proved that there is a solid structure of fact behind the legendary stories of Hiawatha, and even the period of his activity has been fixed with tolerable accuracy by modern American historians.

Hiawatha, or Hai-en-Wat-ha, was a chief of Iroquois stock, belonging either to the Onondaga or the Mohawk tribe. His most important feat was the union of the Five Nations of the Iroquois into a Grand League, an event which was of more than national significance, since it so largely affected the fortunes of European peoples when they afterward fought for American supremacy. As the Five Nations are known to have come together in the sixteenth century, it follows that Hiawatha must have lived and worked about that time. In later days the League was called the Six Nations, and still more recently the Seven Nations.

When the Iroquois, or 'Long House People', were found by the French and Dutch they occupied the western part of what is now New York State, and were at a much more advanced stage of culture than most of the Indian tribes. They tilled the ground, cultivating maize and tobacco, and were skilled in the arts of war and diplomacy. They were greatly strengthened by the Grand League, or 'Kayanerenh Kowa', which, as has been said, was founded by the chief Hiawatha, and were much the most important of the North American tribes.

If we look to tradition for an account of the origin of the Grand League, we learn that the union was effected by Hiawatha in the fourteenth century. The Hurons and Iroquois, we are told, were at one time one people, but later they separated, the Hurons going to the lake which is named after them, and the Iroquois to New York, where their five tribes were united under a General Council. But tradition is quite evidently wrong in assigning so early a date to this important event, for one of the two branches of the Iroquois family (that which comprises the Mohawks and the Oneidas) has left but few traces of an early occupation, and these, in the shape of some old town-sites, are judged to belong to the latter part of the sixteenth century.

The early connection between the Iroquois and the Hurons, and their subsequent separation, remains undisputed. The Iroquois family was divided into two branches, the Sinnekes (Onondagas, Cayugas, and Senecas) and the Caniengas (Mohawks and Oneidas), of which the subdivisions composed the Five Nations. The Sinnekes had established themselves in the western portion of New York, and the Caniengas at Hochelaga (Montreal) and elsewhere on the St Lawrence, where they lived amicably enough with their Algonquin neighbours. But in 1560 a quarrel arose between the Caniengas and the Algonquins, in which the latter called in the aid of the Hurons. This was the beginning of a long war, in which the Caniengas had the worst of it. Gradually the Caniengas were driven along the shores of Lake Champlain and Lake George till they reached the valley of the Mohawk River, where they established themselves in a country bordering on that of the Onondagas.

Now the Onondagas were a formidable tribe, fierce and warlike, and the Caniengas, being long accustomed to war, were not the most peaceable of nations, and ere long there was trouble between them, while both were at war with the Hurons. At the head of the Onondagas was the great chief Atotarho, whose sanguinary exploits and crafty stratagems had become the dread of the neighbouring peoples, and among his warriors was the generous Hiawatha. Hiawatha was filled with horror at the sight of the suffering caused by Atotarho's expeditions, and already his statesman's mind was forming projects of peace. He saw that in confederation lay the means not only of preserving peace among his people, but of withstanding alien foes as well. In two consecutive years he called an assembly to consider his plan, but on each occasion the grim presence of Atotarho made discussion impossible. Hiawatha in despair fled from the land of the Onondagas, journeyed eastward through the country of the Oneidas, and at last took up his residence among the Mohawks, into which tribe he was adopted. It has been said by some authorities, and the idea does not lack probability, that Hiawatha was originally a Mohawk, and that he spent some time among the Onondagas, afterward returning to his own people. At all events, the Mohawks proved more amenable to reason than the Onondagas had done. Among the chiefs of his adopted tribe Hiawatha found one – Dekanewidah – who fell in with his confederation plans, and agreed to work along with him. Messengers were dispatched to the Oneidas, who bade them return in a year, at the end of which period negotiations were renewed. The result was that the Oneida chiefs signed a treaty inaugurating the Kayanerenh Kowa. An embassy to the Onondagas was fruitless, as Atotarho persistently obstructed the new scheme; but later, when the Kayanerenh Kowa embraced the Cayugas, messages were once more sent to the powerful Onondagas, diplomatically suggesting that Atotarho should take the lead in the Grand Council. The grim warrior was mollified by this sop to his vanity, and condescended to accept the proposal. Not only that, but he soon became an enthusiastic worker in the cause of confederation, and secured the inclusion of the Senecas in the League.

The confederacy of the Five Nations was now complete, and the 'Silver Chain', as their Grand Council was called, met together on the shores of the Salt Lake. The number of chiefs chosen from each tribe bore some relation to its numerical status, the largest number, fourteen, being supplied by the Onondagas. The office of representative in the Council was to be an hereditary one, descending in the female line, as with the Picts of Scotland and other primitive peoples, and never from father to son.

So powerful did the League become that the name of 'Long House People' was held in the greatest awe. They annihilated their ancient enemies, the Hurons, and they attacked and subdued the Micmacs, Mohicans, Pawnees, Algonquins, Cherokees, and many other tribes. The effect of the League on British history is incalculable. When the Frenchman Champlain arrived in 1611 he interfered on behalf of the Hurons, an action whose far-reaching consequences he could not foresee, but from that period dated the hatred of the Iroquois for the French which ensured Britain's success in the long struggle between the European nations in America. Without the assistance of the native factor, who shall say how the struggle might have ended?

But the Iroquois were not altogether a bloodthirsty people. A strong bond of brotherhood existed between the Five Nations, among themselves they were kind and gentle, and in part at least Hiawatha's dream of peace was realized. It is not, of course, very easy to say how far Hiawatha intended the scheme of universal brotherhood with which he is credited. Whether he conceived a Grand League embracing all the nations of the earth or whether his full ambition was realized in the union of the Five Nations is a point which history does not make clear. But even in the more limited sense his work was a great one, and the lofty and noble character which Longfellow has given to his hero seems not unsuited to the actual Hiawatha, who realizes the ideal of the 'noble savage' more fully, perhaps, than anyone else in the annals of primitive peoples.

As in the case of King Arthur and Dietrich of Berne, many myths soon gathered round the popular and revered name of Hiawatha. Among barbarians three, or even two, generations usually suffice to render a great and outstanding figure mythical. But one prefers to think of this Iroquois statesman as a real man, a bright particular star in a dark sky of savagery and ignorance.

The Stone Giants

The Iroquois believed that in early days there existed a malignant race of giants whose bodies were fashioned out of stone. It is difficult to say how the idea of such beings arose, but it is possible that the generally distributed conception of a gigantic race springing from Mother Earth was in this instance fused with another belief that stones and rocks composed the earth's bony framework. We find an example of this belief in the beautiful old Greek myth of Deucalion and Pyrrha, which much resembles that of Noah. When after the great flood which submerged Hellas the survivors' ship grounded upon Mount Parnassus they inquired of the oracle of Themis in what manner the human race might be restored. They were bidden by the oracle to veil themselves and to throw the bones of their mother behind them. These they interpreted to mean the stones of the earth. Picking up loose pieces of stone, they cast them over their shoulders, and from those thrown by Deucalion there sprang men, while those cast by Pyrrha became women.

These Stone Giants of the Iroquois, dwelling in the far west, took counsel with one another and resolved to invade the Indian territory and exterminate the race of men. A party of Indians just starting on the war-path were apprised of the invasion, and were bidden by the gods to challenge the giants to combat. This they did, and the opposing bands faced each other at a spot near a great gulf. But as the monsters advanced upon their human enemies the god of the west wind, who was lying in wait for them, swooped down upon the Titans, so that they were hurled over the edge of the gulf, far down into the dark abyss below, where they perished miserably.

The Pigmies

In contradistinction to their belief in giants, the Iroquois imagined the existence of a race of pigmies, who had many of the attributes of the Teutonic gnomes. They were responsible for the beauty of terrestrial scenery, which they carved and sculptured in cliff, scar, and rock, and, like the thunder-gods, they protected the human race against the many monsters which infested the world in early times.

Witches and witchcraft

The Iroquois belief in witchcraft was very strong, and the following tale is supposed to account for the origin of witches and sorcery. A boy who was out hunting found a snake the colours of whose skin were so intensely beautiful that he resolved to capture it. He caught it and tended it carefully, feeding it on birds and small game, and housing it in a little bowl made of bark, which he filled with water. In the bottom of the bowl he placed down, small feathers, and wood fibre, and on going to feed the snake he discovered that these things had become living beings. From this he gathered that the reptile was endowed with supernatural powers, and he found that other articles placed in the water along with it soon showed signs of life. He procured more snakes and placed them in the bowl. Observing some men of the tribe rubbing ointment on their eyes to enable them to see more clearly, he used some of the water from the bowl in which the snakes were immersed upon his own, and lo! he found on climbing a tall tree that nothing was hidden from his sight, which pierced all intervening obstacles. He could see far into the earth, where lay hidden precious stones and rich minerals. His sight pierced the trunks of trees; he could see through mountains, and could discern objects lying deep down in the bed of a river.

He concluded that the greater the number of reptiles the snake-liquid contained the more potent would it become. Accordingly he captured several snakes, and suspended them over his bowl in such a manner that the essential oil they contained dropped into the water, with the result that the activity of the beings which had been so strangely bred in it was increased. In course of time he found that by merely placing one of his fingers in the liquid and pointing it at any person he could instantly bewitch him. He added some roots to the water in the bowl, some of which he then drank. By blowing this from his mouth a great light was produced, by rubbing his eyes with it he could see in the dark, and by other applications of it he could render himself invisible, or take the shape of a snake. If he dipped an arrow into the liquid and discharged it at any living being it would kill it although it might not strike it. Not content with discovering this magic fluid, the youth resolved to search for antidotes to it, and these he collected.

A 'medicine' legend

A similar legend is told by the Senecas to account for the origin of their 'medicine'. Nearly two hundred years ago – in the savage estimation this is a very great period of time – an Indian went into the woods on a hunting expedition. One night while asleep in his solitary camp he was awakened by a great noise of singing and drum-beating, such as is heard at festivals. Starting up, he made his way to the place whence the sounds came, and although he could not see anyone there he observed a heap of corn and a large squash vine with three squashes on it, and three ears of corn which lay apart from the rest. Feeling very uneasy, he once more pursued his hunting operations, and when night came again laid himself down to rest. But his sleep was destined to be broken yet a second time, and awaking he perceived a man bending over him, who said in menacing tones:

'Beware: what you saw was sacred. You deserve to die.'

A rustling among the branches denoted the presence of a number of people, who, after some hesitation, gathered round the hunter, and informed him that they would pardon his curiosity and would tell him their secret. 'The great medicine for wounds,' said the man who had first awakened him, 'is squash and corn. Come with me and I will teach you how to make and apply it.'

With these words he led the hunter to the spot at which he had surprised the 'medicine'-making operations on the previous night, where he beheld a great fire and a strange-looking laurel-bush, which seemed as if made of iron. Chanting a weird song, the people circled slowly round the bush to the accompaniment of a rattling of gourd-shells. On the hunter's asking them to explain this procedure, one of them heated a stick and thrust it right through his cheek. He immediately applied some of the 'medicine' to the wound, so that it healed instantly. Having thus demonstrated the power of the drug, they sang a tune that they called the 'medicine-song', which their pupil learned by heart.

The hunter then turned to depart, and all at once he saw that the beings who surrounded him were not human, as he had thought, but animals – foxes, bears, and beavers – who fled as he looked at them. Surprised and even terrified at the turn matters had taken, he made his way homeward with all speed, conning over the prescription which the strange beings had given him the while. They had told him to take one stalk of corn, to dry the cob and pound it very fine, then to take one squash, cut it up and pound it, and to mix the whole with water from a running stream, near its source. This prescription he used with very great success among his people, and it proved the origin of the great 'medicine' of the Senecas. Once a year at the season when the deer changes his coat they prepare it as the forest folk did, singing the weird song and dancing round it to the rhythmic accompaniment of the gourd-shell rattles, while they burn tobacco to the gods.

Great Head and the ten brothers
It was commonly believed among the Iroquois Indians that there existed a curious and malevolent being whom they called Great Head. This odd creature was merely an enormous head poised on slender legs. He made his dwelling on a rugged rock, and directly he saw any living person approach he would growl fiercely in true ogre fashion: 'I see thee, I see thee! Thou shalt die.'

Far away in a remote spot an orphaned family of ten boys

lived with their uncle. The older brothers went out every day to hunt, but the younger ones, not yet fitted for so rigorous a life, remained at home with their uncle, or at least did not venture much beyond the immediate vicinity of their lodge. One day the hunters did not return at their usual hour. As the evening passed without bringing any sign of the missing youths the little band at home became alarmed. At length the eldest of the boys left in the lodge volunteered to go in search of his brothers. His uncle consented, and he set off, but he did not return.

In the morning another brother said: 'I will go to seek my brothers.' Having obtained permission, he went, but he also did not come back. Another and another took upon himself the task of finding the lost hunters, but of the searchers as well as of those sought for there was no news forthcoming. At length only the youngest of the lads remained at home, and to his entreaties to be allowed to seek for his brothers the uncle turned a deaf ear, for he feared to lose the last of his young nephews.

One day when uncle and nephew were out in the forest the latter fancied he heard a deep groan, which seemed to proceed from the earth exactly under his feet. They stopped to listen. The sound was repeated – unmistakably a human groan. Hastily they began digging in the earth, and in a moment or two came upon a man covered with mould and apparently unconscious.

The pair carried the unfortunate one to their lodge, where they rubbed him with bear's oil till he recovered consciousness. When he was able to speak he could give no explanation of how he came to be buried alive. He had been out hunting, he said, when suddenly his mind became a blank, and he remembered nothing more till he found himself in the lodge with the old man and the boy. His hosts begged the stranger to stay with them, and they soon discovered that he was no ordinary mortal, but a powerful magician. At times he behaved very strangely. One night, while a great storm raged without, he tossed restlessly on his couch instead of going to sleep. At last he sought the old uncle.

'Do you hear that noise?' he said. 'That is my brother, Great Head, who is riding on the wind. Do you not hear him howling?'

The old man considered this astounding speech for a moment; then he asked: 'Would he come here if you sent for him?'

'No,' said the other, thoughtfully, 'but we might bring him here by magic. Should he come you must have food ready for him, in the shape of huge blocks of maple-wood, for that is what he lives on.'

The stranger departed in search of his brother Great Head, taking with him his bow, and on the way he came across a hickory-tree, whose roots provided him with arrows. About midday he drew near to the dwelling of his brother, Great Head. In order to see without being seen, he changed himself into a mole, and crept through the grass till he saw Great Head perched on a rock, frowning fiercely. 'I see thee!' he growled, with his wild eyes fixed on an owl. The man-mole drew his bow and shot an arrow at Great Head. The arrow became larger and larger as it flew toward the monster, but it returned to him who had fired it, and as it did so it regained its natural size. The man seized it and rushed back the way he had come. Very soon he heard Great Head in pursuit, puffing and snorting along on the wings of a hurricane. When the creature had almost overtaken him he turned and discharged another arrow. Again and again he repulsed his pursuer in this fashion, till he lured him to the lodge where his benefactors lived. When Great Head burst into the house the uncle and nephew began to hammer him vigorously with mallets. To their surprise the monster broke into laughter, for he had recognized his brother and was very pleased to see him. He ate the maple-blocks they brought him with a hearty appetite, whereupon they told him the story of the missing hunters.

'I know what has become of them,' said Great Head. 'They

have fallen into the hands of a witch. If this young man,' indicating the nephew, 'will accompany me, I will show him her dwelling, and the bones of his brothers.'

The youth, who loved adventure, and was besides very anxious to learn the fate of his brothers, at once consented to seek the home of the witch. So he and Great Head started off, and lost no time in getting to the place. They found the space in front of the lodge strewn with dry bones, and the witch sitting in the doorway singing. When she saw them she muttered the magic word which turned living people into dry bones, but on Great Head and his companion it had no effect whatever. Acting on a prearranged signal, Great Head and the youth attacked the witch and killed her. No sooner had she expired than her flesh turned into birds and beasts and fishes. What was left of her they burned to ashes.

Their next act was to select the bones of the nine brothers from among the heap, and this they found no easy task. But at last it was accomplished, and Great Head said to his companion: 'I am going home to my rock. When I pass overhead in a great storm I will bid these bones arise, and they will get up and return with you.'

The youth stood alone for a little while till he heard the sound of a fierce tempest. Out of the hurricane Great Head called to the brothers to arise. In a moment they were all on their feet, receiving the congratulations of their younger brother and each other, and filled with joy at their reunion.

The Seneca's revenge

A striking story is told of a Seneca youth who for many years and through a wearisome captivity nourished the hope of vengeance so dear to the Indian soul. A certain tribe of the Senecas had settled on the shores of Lake Erie, when they were surprised by their ancient enemies the Illinois, and in spite of a stout resistance many of them were slain, and a woman and a boy taken prisoner. When the victors halted for the night they built a great fire, and proceeded to celebrate their success by singing triumphant songs, in which they commanded the boy to join them. The lad pretended that he did not know their language, but said that he would sing their song in his own tongue, to which they assented; but instead of a paean in their praise he sang a song of vengeance, in which he vowed that if he were spared all of them would lose their scalps. A few days afterward the woman became so exhausted that she could walk no farther, so the Illinois slew her. But before she died she extracted a promise from the boy that he would avenge her, and would never cease to be a Seneca.

In a few days they arrived at the Illinois camp, where a council was held to consider the fate of the captive lad. Some were for instantly putting him to death, but their chief ruled that should he be able to live through their tortures he would be worthy of becoming an Illinois. They seized the wretched lad and held his bare feet to the glowing council-fire, then after piercing them they told him to run a race. He bounded forward, and ran so swiftly that he soon gained the Great House of the tribe, where he seated himself upon a wild-cat skin.

Another council was held, and the Illinois braves agreed that the lad possessed high courage and would make a great warrior; but others argued that he knew their war-path and might betray them, and it was finally decided that he should be burnt at the stake. As he was about to perish in this manner an aged warrior suggested that if he were able to withstand their last torture he should be permitted to live. Accordingly he held the unfortunate lad under water in a pool until only a spark of life remained in him, but he survived, and became an Illinois warrior.

Years passed, and the boy reached manhood and married a chief's daughter. His strength and endurance became proverbial, but the warriors of the tribe of his adoption would never permit him to take part in their warlike expeditions. At length a raid against the Senecas was mooted, and he begged so hard to be allowed to accompany the braves that at last they consented. Indeed, so great was their admiration of the skill with which he outlined a plan of campaign that they made him chief of the expedition. For many days the party marched toward the Seneca country; but when at last they neared it their scouts reported that there were no signs of the tribe, and that the Senecas must have quitted their territory. Their leader, however, proposed to go in search of the enemy himself, along with another warrior of the tribe, and this was agreed to.

When the pair had gone five or six miles the leader said to his companion that it would be better if they separated, as they would then be able to cover more ground. Passing on to where he knew he would find the Senecas, he warned them of their danger, and arranged that an ambush of his kinsfolk should lie in wait for the Illinois.

Returning to the Illinois camp, he reported that he had seen nothing, but that he well remembered the Seneca hiding-place. He asked to be given the bravest warriors, and assured the council that he would soon bring them the scalps of their foes. Suspecting nothing, they assented to his proposal, and he was followed by the flower of the Illinois tribe, all unaware that five hundred Senecas awaited them in the valley. The youth led his men right into the heart of the ambush; then, pretending to miss his footing, he fell. This was the signal for the Senecas to rise on every side. Yelling their war-cry, they rushed from their shelter and fell on the dismayed Illinois, who gave way on every side. The slaughter was immense. Vengeance nerved the arms of the Seneca braves, and of three hundred Illinois but two escaped. The leader of the expedition was borne in triumph to the Seneca village, where to listening hundreds he told the story of his capture and long-meditated revenge. He became a great chief among his people, and even to this day his name is uttered by them with honour and reverence.

The boy magician

In the heart of the wilderness there lived an old woman and her little grandson. The two found no lack of occupation from day to day, the woman busying herself with cooking and cleaning and the boy with shooting and hunting. The grandmother frequently spoke of the time when the child would grow up and go out into the world.

'Always go to the east,' she would say. 'Never go to the west, for there lies danger.'

But what the danger was she would not tell him, in spite of his importunate questioning. Other boys went west, he thought to himself, and why should not he? Nevertheless his grandmother made him promise that he would not go west.

Years passed by, and the child grew to be a man, though he still retained the curiosity and high spirits of his boyhood. His persistent inquiries drew from the old grandmother a reluctant explanation of her warning.

'In the west,' said she, 'there dwells a being who is anxious to do us harm. If he sees you it will mean death for both of us.'

This statement, instead of frightening the young Indian, only strengthened in him a secret resolution he had formed to go west on the first opportunity. Not that he wished to bring any misfortune on his poor old grandmother, any more than on himself, but he trusted to his strong arm and clear head to deliver them from their enemy. So with a laugh on his lips he set off to the west.

Toward evening he came to a lake, where he rested. He had not been there long when he heard a voice saying: 'Aha, my fine fellow, I see you!'

The youth looked all round him, and up into the sky above, but he saw no one.

'I am going to send a hurricane,' the mysterious voice continued, 'to break your grandmother's hut to pieces. How will you like that?'

'Oh, very well,' answered the young man gaily. 'We are always in need of firewood, and now we shall have plenty.'

'Go home and see,' the voice said mockingly. 'I daresay you will not like it so well.'

Nothing daunted, the young adventurer retraced his steps.

As he neared home a great wind sprang up, seeming to tear the very trees out by the roots.

'Make haste!' cried the grandmother from the doorway. 'We shall both be killed!'

When she had drawn him inside and shut the door she scolded him heartily for his disobedience, and bewailed the fate before them. The young man soothed her fears, saying: 'Don't cry, grandmother. We shall turn the lodge into a rock, and so we shall be saved.'

Having some skill in magic, he did as he had said, and the hurricane passed harmlessly over their heads. When it had ceased they emerged from their retreat, and found an abundance of firewood all round them.

The hailstorm

Next day the youth was on the point of setting off toward the west once more, but the urgent entreaties of his grandmother moved him to proceed eastward – for a time. Directly he was out of sight of the lodge he turned his face once more to the west. Arrived at the lake, he heard the voice once more, though its owner was still invisible.

'I am going to send a great hailstorm on your grandmother's hut,' it said. 'What do you think of that?'

'Oh,' was the response, 'I think I should like it. I have always wanted a bundle of spears.'

'Go home and see,' said the voice.

Away the youth went through the woods. The sky became darker and darker as he neared his home, and just as he was within a bowshot of the little hut a fierce hailstorm broke, and he thought he would be killed before he reached shelter.

'Alas!' cried the old woman when he was safely indoors, 'we shall be destroyed this time. How can we save ourselves?'

Again the young man exercised his magic powers, and transformed the frail hut into a hollow rock, upon which the shafts of the hailstorm spent themselves in vain. At last the sky cleared, the lodge resumed its former shape, and the young man saw a multitude of sharp, beautiful spear-heads on the ground.

'I will get poles,' said he, 'to fit to them for fishing.'

When he returned in a few minutes with the poles he found that the spears had vanished.

'Where are my beautiful spears?' he asked his grandmother.

'They were only ice-spears,' she replied. 'They have all melted away.'

The young Indian was greatly disappointed, and wondered how he could avenge himself on the being who had played him this malicious trick.

'Be warned in time,' said the aged grandmother, shaking her head at him. 'Take my advice and leave him alone.'

The charmed stone

But the youth's adventurous spirit impelled him to see the end of the matter, so he took a stone and tied it round his neck for a charm, and sought the lake once again. Carefully observing the direction from which the voice proceeded, he saw in the middle of the lake a huge head with a face on every side of it.

'Aha! uncle,' he exclaimed, 'I see you! How would you like it if the lake dried up?'

'Nonsense!' said the voice angrily, 'that will never happen.'

'Go home and see,' shouted the youth, mimicking the mocking tone the other had adopted on the previous occasions. As he spoke he swung his charmed stone round his head and threw it into the air. As it descended it grew larger and larger, and the moment it entered the lake the water began to boil.

The lad returned home and told his grandmother what he had done.

'It is of no use,' said she. 'Many have tried to slay him, but all have perished in the attempt.'

Next morning our hero went westward again, and found the lake quite dry, and the animals in it dead, with the exception of a large green frog, who was in reality the malicious being who had tormented the Indian and his grandmother. A quick blow with a stick put an end to the creature, and the triumphant youth bore the good news to his old grandmother, who from that time was left in peace and quietness.

The friendly skeleton

A little boy living in the woods with his old uncle was warned by him not to go eastward, but to play close to the lodge or walk toward the west. The child felt a natural curiosity to know what lay in the forbidden direction, and one day took advantage of his uncle's absence on a hunting expedition to wander away to the east. At length he came to a large lake, on the shores of which he stopped to rest. Here he was accosted by a man, who asked him his name and where he lived.

'Come,' said the stranger, when he had finished questioning the boy, 'let us see who can shoot an arrow the highest.'

This they did, and the boy's arrow went much higher than that of his companion.

The stranger then suggested a swimming match.

'Let us see,' he said, 'who can swim farthest under water without taking a breath.'

Again the boy beat his rival, who next proposed that they should sail out to an island in the middle of the lake, to see the beautiful birds that were to be found there. The child consented readily, and they embarked in a curious canoe, which was propelled by three swans harnessed to either side of it. Directly they had taken their seats the man began to sing, and the canoe moved off. In a very short time they had reached the island. Here the little Indian realized that his confidence in his new-found friend was misplaced. The stranger took all his clothes from him, put them in the canoe, and jumped in himself, saying:

'Come, swans, let us go home.'

The obedient swans set off at a good pace, and soon left the island far behind. The boy was very angry at having been so badly used, but when it grew dark his resentment changed to fear, and he sat down and cried with cold and misery. Suddenly he heard a husky voice close at hand, and, looking round, he saw a skeleton on the ground.

'I am very sorry for you,' said the skeleton in hoarse tones. 'I will do what I can to help you. But first you must do something for me. Go and dig by that tree, and you shall find a tobacco-pouch with some tobacco in it, a pipe, and a flint.'

The boy did as he was asked, and when he had filled the pipe he lit it and placed it in the mouth of the skeleton. He saw that the latter's body was full of mice, and that the smoke frightened them away.

'There is a man coming tonight with three dogs,' said the skeleton. 'He is coming to look for you. You must make tracks all over the island, so that they may not find you, and then hide in a hollow tree.'

Again the boy obeyed his gaunt instructor, and when he was safely hidden he saw a man come ashore with three dogs. All night they hunted him, but he had made so many tracks that the dogs were confused, and at last the man departed in anger. Next day the trembling boy emerged and went to the skeleton.

'Tonight,' said the latter, 'the man who brought you here is coming to drink your blood. You must dig a hole in the sand and hide. When he comes out of the canoe you must enter it. Say, "Come, swans, let us go home", and if the man calls you do not look back.'

The lost sister

Everything fell out as the skeleton had foretold. The boy hid in the sand, and directly he saw his tormentor step ashore he jumped into the canoe, saying hastily, 'Come, swans, let us go home.' Then he began to sing as he had heard the man do when they first embarked. In vain the man called him back; he refused to look round. The swans carried the canoe to a cave in a high rock, where the boy found his clothes, as well as a fire and food. When he had donned his garments and satisfied his hunger he lay down and slept. In the morning he returned to the island, where he found the tyrant quite dead. The skeleton now commanded him to sail eastward to seek for his sister, whom a fierce man had carried away. He set out eagerly on his new quest, and a three days' journey brought him to the place where his sister was. He lost no time in finding her.

'Come, my sister,' said he, 'let us flee away together.'

'Alas! I cannot,' answered the young woman. 'A wicked man keeps me here. It is time for him to return home, and he would be sure to catch us. But let me hide you now, and in the morning we shall go away.'

So she dug a pit and hid her brother, though not a moment too soon, for the footsteps of her husband were heard approaching the hut. The woman had cooked a child, and this she placed before the man.

'You have had visitors,' he said, seeing his dogs snuffing around uneasily.

'No,' was the reply, 'I have seen no one but you.'

'I shall wait till tomorrow,' said the man to himself. 'Then I shall kill and eat him.' He had already guessed that his wife had not spoken the truth. However, he said nothing more, but waited till morning, when, instead of going to a distant swamp to seek for food, as he pretended to do, he concealed himself at a short distance from the hut, and at length saw the brother and sister making for a canoe. They were hardly seated when they saw him running toward them. In his hand he bore a large hook, with which he caught the frail vessel; but the lad broke the hook with a stone, and the canoe darted out on to the lake. The man was at a loss for a moment, and could only shout incoherent threats after the pair. Then an idea occurred to him, and, lying down on the shore, he began to drink the water. This caused the canoe to rush back again, but once more the boy was equal to the occasion. Seizing the large stone with which he had broken the hook, he threw it at the man and slew him, the water at the same time rushing back into the lake. Thus the brother and sister escaped, and in three days they had arrived at the island, where they heartily thanked their benefactor, the skeleton. He, however, had still another task for the young Indian to perform.

'Take your sister home to your uncle's lodge,' said he; 'then return here yourself, and say to the many bones which you will find on the island, "Arise," and they shall come to life again.'

When the brother and sister reached their home they found that their old uncle had been grievously lamenting the loss of his nephew, and he was quite overjoyed at seeing them. On his recommendation they built a large lodge to accommodate the people they were to bring back with them. When it was completed, the youth revisited the island, bade the bones arise, and was delighted to see them obey his bidding and become men and women. He led them to the lodge he had built, where they all dwelt happily for a long time.

The pigmies

When the Cherokees were dwelling in the swamps of Florida the Iroquois made a practice of swooping down on them and raiding their camps. On one occasion the raiding party was absent from home for close on two years. On the eve of their return one of their number, a chieftain, fell ill, and the rest of the party were at a loss to know what to do with him. Obviously, if they carried him home with them he would considerably impede their progress. Besides, there was the possibility that he might not recover, and all their labour would be to no purpose. Thus they debated far into the night, and finally decided to abandon him to his fate and return by themselves. The sick man, unable to stir hand or foot, overheard their decision, but he bore it stoically, like an Indian warrior. Nevertheless, when he heard the last swish of their paddles as they crossed the river he could not help thinking of the friends and kindred he would probably never see again.

When the raiders reached home they were closely questioned as to the whereabouts of the missing chief, and the inquiries were all the more anxious because the sick man had been a great favourite among his people. The guilty warriors answered evasively. They did not know what had become of their comrade, they said. Possibly he had been lost or killed in Florida.

Meanwhile the sick man lay dying on the banks of the river. Suddenly he heard, quite close at hand, the gentle sound of a canoe. The vessel drew in close to the bank, and, full in view of the warrior, three pigmy men disembarked. They regarded the stranger with some surprise. At length one who seemed to be the leader advanced and spoke to him, bidding him await their return, and promising to look after him. They were going, he said, to a certain 'salt-lick', where many curious animals watered, in order to kill some for food.

The salt-lick

When the pigmies arrived at the place they found that no animals were as yet to be seen, but very soon a large buffalo bull came to drink. Immediately a buffalo cow arose from the lick, and when they had satisfied their thirst the two animals lay down on the bank. The pigmies concluded that the time was ripe for killing them, and, drawing their bows, they succeeded in dispatching the buffaloes. Returning to the sick man, they amply fulfilled their promise to take care of him, skilfully tending him until he had made a complete recovery. They then conveyed him to his friends, who now learned that the story told them by the raiders was false. Bitterly indignant at the deception and heartless cruelty of these men, they fell upon them and punished them according to their deserts.

Later the chief headed a band of people who were curious to see the lick, which they found surrounded by the bones of numberless large animals which had been killed by the pigmies.

This story is interesting as a record of what were perhaps the last vestiges of a pigmy folk who at one time inhabited the eastern portion of North America, before the coming of the Red Man.

The magical serpent

In the seventeenth century a strange legend concerning a huge serpent was found among the Hurons, who probably got it from the neighbouring Algonquins. This monster had on its head a horn which would pierce anything, even the hardest rock. Anyone possessing a piece of it was supposed to have very good fortune. The Hurons did not know where the creature was to be found, but said that the Algonquins were in the habit of selling them small pieces of the magic horn.

It is possible that the mercenary Shawnees had borrowed this myth from the Cherokees for their own purposes. At all events a similar legend existed among both tribes which told of a monster snake, the King of Rattlesnakes, who dwelt up among the mountain-passes, attended by a retinue of his kind. Instead of a crown, he wore on his head a beautiful jewel which possessed magic properties. Many a brave tried to obtain possession of this desirable gem, but all fell victims to the venomous reptiles. At length a more ingenious warrior clothed himself entirely in leather, and so rendered himself impervious to their attack. Making his way to the haunt of the serpents, he slew their monster chief. Then, triumphantly taking possession of the wonderful jewel, he bore it to his tribe, by whom it was regarded with profound veneration and jealously preserved.

The origin of medicine

An interesting Cherokee myth is that which recounts the origin of disease, and the consequent institution of curative medicine. In the old days, we are told, the members of the brute creation were gifted with speech and dwelt in amity with the human race, but mankind multiplied so quickly that the animals were crowded into the forests and desert places of the earth, so that the old friendship between them was soon forgotten. The breach was farther widened by the invention of lethal weapons, by the aid of which man commenced the wholesale slaughter of the beasts for the sake of their flesh and skins. The animals, at first surprised, soon grew angry, and resolved upon measures of retaliation. The bear tribe met in council, presided over by the Old White Bear, their chief. After several speakers had denounced mankind for their bloodthirsty tendencies, war was unanimously decided upon, but the lack of weapons was regarded as a serious drawback. However, it was suggested that man's instruments should be turned against himself, and as the bow and arrow were considered to be the principal human agency of destruction, it was resolved to fashion a specimen. A suitable piece of wood was procured, and one of the bears sacrificed himself to provide gut for a bowstring. When the weapon was completed it was discovered that the claws of the bears spoiled their shooting. One of the bears, however, cut his claws, and succeeded in hitting the mark, but the Old White Bear very wisely remarked that without claws they could not climb trees or bring down game, and that were they to cut them off they must all starve.

The deer also met in council, under their chief, the Little Deer, when it was decided that those hunters who slew one of their number without asking pardon in a suitable manner should be afflicted with rheumatism. They gave notice of this decision to the nearest settlement of Indians, and instructed them how to make propitiation when forced by necessity to kill one of the deer-folk. So when a deer is slain by the hunter the Little Deer runs to the spot, and, bending over the blood-stains, asks the spirit of the deer if it has heard the prayer of the hunter for pardon. If the reply be 'Yes', all is well, and the Little Deer departs; but if the answer be in the negative, he tracks the hunter to his cabin, and strikes him with rheumatism, so that he becomes a helpless cripple. Sometimes hunters who have not learned the proper formula for pardon attempt to turn aside the Little Deer from his pursuit by building a fire behind them in the trail.

The council of the fishes

The fishes and reptiles then held a joint council, and arranged to haunt those human beings who tormented them with hideous dreams of serpents twining round them and of eating fish which had become decayed. These snake and fish dreams seem to be of common occurrence among the Cherokees, and the services of the *shamans* to banish them are in constant demand.

Lastly, the birds and the insects, with the smaller animals, gathered together for a similar purpose, the grub-worm presiding over the meeting. Each in turn expressed an opinion, and the consensus was against mankind. They devised and named various diseases.

When the plants, which were friendly to man, heard what had been arranged by the animals, they determined to frustrate their evil designs. Each tree, shrub, and herb, down even to the grasses and mosses, agreed to furnish a remedy for some one of the diseases named. Thus did medicine come into being. When the *shaman* is in doubt as to what treatment to apply for the relief of a patient the spirit of the plant suggests a fitting remedy.

The wonderful kettle

A story is told among the Iroquois of two brothers who lived in the wilderness far from all human habitation. The elder brother went into the forest to hunt game, while the younger stayed at home and tended the hut, cooked the food, and gathered firewood.

One evening the tired hunter returned from the chase, and the younger brother took the game from him as usual and dressed it for supper. 'I will smoke awhile before I eat,' said the hunter, and he smoked in silence for a time. When he was tired of smoking he lay down and went to sleep.

'Strange,' said the boy; 'I should have thought he would want to eat first.'

When the hunter awoke he found that his brother had prepared the supper and was waiting for him.

'Go to bed,' said he; 'I wish to be alone.'

Wondering much, the boy did as he was bidden, but he could not help asking himself how his brother could possibly live if he did not eat. In the morning he observed that the hunter went away without tasting any food, and on many succeeding mornings and evenings the same thing happened.

'I must watch him at night,' said the boy to himself, 'for he must eat at night, since he eats at no other time.'

That same evening, when the lad was told as usual to go to bed, he lay down and pretended to be sound asleep, but all the time one of his eyes was open. In this cautious fashion he watched his brother, and saw him rise from his couch and pass through a trap-door in the floor, from which he shortly emerged bearing a rusty kettle, the bottom of which he scraped industriously. Filling it with water, he set it on the blazing fire. As he did so he struck it with a whip, saying at every blow: 'Grow larger, my kettle!'

The obedient kettle became of gigantic proportions, and after setting it aside to cool the man ate its contents with evident relish.

His watchful younger brother, well content with the result of his observation, turned over and went to sleep.

When the elder had set off next morning, the boy, filled with curiosity, opened the trap-door and discovered the kettle. 'I wonder what he eats,' he said, and there within the vessel was half a chestnut! He was rather surprised at this discovery, but he thought to himself how pleased his brother would be if on his return he found a meal to his taste awaiting him. When evening drew near he put the kettle on the fire, took a whip, and, hitting it repeatedly, exclaimed: 'Grow larger, my kettle!'

The kettle grew larger, but to the boy's alarm it kept on growing until it filled the room, and he was obliged to get on the roof and stir it through the chimney.

'What are you doing up there?' shouted the hunter, when he came within hail.

'I took your kettle to get your supper ready,' answered the boy.

'Alas!' cried the other, 'now I must die!'

He quickly reduced the kettle to its original proportions and put it in its place. But he still wore such a sad and serious air that his brother was filled with dismay, and prayed that he might be permitted to undo the mischief he had wrought. When the days went past and he found that his brother no longer went out to hunt or displayed any interest in life, but grew gradually thinner and more melancholy, his distress knew no bounds.

'Let me fetch you some chestnuts,' he begged earnestly. 'Tell me where they may be found.'

The white heron
'You must travel a full day's journey,' said the hunter in response to his entreaties. 'You will then reach a river which is most difficult to ford. On the opposite bank there stands a lodge, and near by a chestnut-tree. Even then your difficulties will only be begun. The tree is guarded by a white heron, which never loses sight of it for a moment. He is employed for that purpose by the six women who live in the lodge, and with their war-clubs they slay anyone who has the temerity to approach. I beg of you, do not think of going on such a hopeless errand.'

But the boy felt that were the chance of success even more slender he must make the attempt for the sake of his brother, whom his thoughtlessness had brought low.

He made a little canoe about three inches long, and set off on his journey, in the direction indicated by his brother. At the end of a day he came to the river, whose size had not been underestimated. Taking his little canoe from his pocket, he drew it out till it was of a suitable length, and launched it in the great stream. A few minutes sufficed to carry him to the opposite bank, and there he beheld the lodge and the chestnut-tree. On his way he had managed to procure some seeds of a sort greatly liked by herons, and these he scattered before the beautiful white bird strutting round the tree. While the heron was busily engaged in picking them up the young man seized his opportunity and gathered quantities of the chestnuts, which were lying thickly on the ground. Ere his task was finished, however, the heron perceived the intruder, and called a loud warning to the women in the lodge, who were not slow to respond. They rushed out with their fishing-lines in their hands, and gave chase to the thief. But fear, for his brother as well as for himself, lent the youth wings, and he was well out on the river in his canoe when the shrieking women reached the bank. The eldest threw her line and caught him, but with a sharp pull he broke it. Another line met with the same fate, and so on, until all the women had thrown their lines. They could do nothing further, and were obliged to watch the retreating canoe in impotent rage.

At length the youth, having come safely through the perils of the journey, arrived home with his precious burden of chestnuts. He found his brother still alive, but so weak that he could hardly speak. A meal of the chestnuts, however, helped to revive him, and he quickly recovered.

The stone giantess

In bygone times it was customary for a hunter's wife to accompany her husband when he sought the chase. A dutiful wife on these occasions would carry home the game killed by the hunter and dress and cook it for him.

There was once a chief among the Iroquois who was a very skilful hunter. In all his expeditions his wife was his companion and helper. On one excursion he found such large quantities of game that he built a wigwam at the place, and settled there for a time with his wife and child. One day he struck out on a new track, while his wife followed the path they had taken on the previous day, in order to gather the game killed then. As the woman turned her steps homeward after a hard day's work she heard the sound of another woman's voice inside the hut. Filled with surprise, she entered, but found to her consternation that her visitor was no other than a Stone Giantess. To add to her alarm, she saw that the creature had in her arms the chief's baby. While the mother stood in the doorway, wondering how she could rescue her child from the clutches of the giantess, the latter said in a gentle and soothing voice: 'Do not be afraid: come inside.'

The hunter's wife hesitated no longer, but boldly entered the wigwam. Once inside, her fear changed to pity, for the giantess was evidently much worn with trouble and fatigue. She told the hunter's wife, who was kindly and sympathetic, how she had travelled from the land of the Stone Giants, fleeing from her cruel husband, who had sought to kill her, and how she had finally taken shelter in the solitary wigwam. She besought the young woman to let her remain for a while, promising to assist her in her daily tasks. She also said she was very hungry, but warned her hostess that she must be exceedingly careful about the food she gave her. It must not be raw or at all underdone, for if once she tasted blood she might wish to kill the hunter and his wife and child.

So the wife prepared some food for her, taking care that it was thoroughly cooked, and the two sat down to dine together. The Stone Giantess knew that the woman was in the habit of carrying home the game, and she now declared that she would do it in her stead. Moreover, she said she already knew where it was to be found, and insisted on setting out for it at once. She very shortly returned, bearing in one hand a load of game which four men could scarcely have carried, and the woman recognized in her a very valuable assistant.

The time of the hunter's return drew near, and the Stone Giantess bade the wife go out and meet her husband and tell him of her visitor. The man was very well pleased to learn how the newcomer had helped his wife, and he gave her a hearty welcome. In the morning he went out hunting as usual. When he had disappeared from sight in the forest the giantess turned quickly to the woman and said:

'I have a secret to tell you. My cruel husband is after me, and in three days he will arrive here. On the third day your husband must remain at home and help me to slay him.'

When the third day came round the hunter remained at home, obedient to the instructions of his guest.

'Now,' said the giantess at last, 'I hear him coming. You must both help me to hold him. Strike him where I bid you, and we shall certainly kill him.'

The hunter and his wife were seized with terror when a great commotion outside announced the arrival of the Stone Giant, but the firmness and courage of the giantess reassured them, and with something like calmness they awaited the monster's approach. Directly he came in sight the giantess rushed forward, grappled with him and threw him to the ground.

'Strike him on the arms!' she cried to the others. 'Now on the nape of the neck!'

The trembling couple obeyed, and very shortly they had succeeded in killing the huge creature.

'I will go and bury him,' said the giantess. And that was the end of the Stone Giant.

The strange guest stayed on in the wigwam till the time came for the hunter and his family to go back to the settlement, when she announced her intention of returning to her own people.

'My husband is dead,' said she; 'I have no longer anything to fear.' Thus, having bade them farewell, she departed.

The healing waters

The Iroquois have a touching story of how a brave of their race once saved his wife and his people from extinction.

It was winter, the snow lay thickly on the ground, and there was sorrow in the encampment, for with the cold weather a dreadful plague had visited the people. There was not one but had lost some relative, and in some cases whole families had been swept away. Among those who had been most sorely bereaved was Nekumonta, a handsome young brave, whose parents, brothers, sisters, and children had died one by one before his eyes, the while he was powerless to help them. And now his wife, the beautiful Shanewis, was weak and ill. The dreaded disease had laid its awful finger on her brow, and she knew that she must shortly bid her husband farewell and take her departure for the place of the dead. Already she saw her dead friends beckoning to her and inviting her to join them, but it grieved her terribly to think that she must leave her young husband in sorrow and loneliness. His despair was piteous to behold when she broke the sad news to him, but after the first outburst of grief he bore up bravely, and determined to fight the plague with all his strength.

'I must find the healing herbs which the Great Manitou has planted,' said he. 'Wherever they may be, I must find them.'

So he made his wife comfortable on her couch, covering her with warm furs, and then, embracing her gently, he set out on his difficult mission.

All day he sought eagerly in the forest for the healing herbs, but everywhere the snow lay deep, and not so much as a blade of grass was visible. When night came he crept along the frozen ground, thinking that his sense of smell might aid him in his search. Thus for three days and nights he wandered through the forest, over hills and across rivers, in a vain attempt to discover the means of curing the malady of Shanewis.

When he met a little scurrying rabbit in the path he cried eagerly: 'Tell me, where shall I find the herbs which Manitou has planted?'

But the rabbit hurried away without reply, for he knew that the herbs had not yet risen above the ground, and he was very sorry for the brave.

Nekumonta came by and by to the den of a big bear, and of this animal also he asked the same question. But the bear could give him no reply, and he was obliged to resume his weary journey. He consulted all the beasts of the forest in turn, but from none could he get any help. How could they tell him, indeed, that his search was hopeless?

The pity of the trees

On the third night he was very weak and ill, for he had tasted no food since he had first set out, and he was numbed with cold and despair. He stumbled over a withered branch hidden under the snow, and so tired was he that he lay where he fell, and immediately went to sleep. All the birds and the beasts, all the multitude of creatures that inhabit the forest, came to watch over his slumbers. They remembered his kindness to them in former days, how he had never slain an animal unless he really needed it for food or clothing, how he had loved and protected the trees and the flowers. Their hearts were touched by his courageous fight for Shanewis, and they pitied his misfortunes. All that they could do to aid him they did. They cried to the Great Manitou to save his wife from the plague which held her, and the Great Spirit heard the manifold whispering and responded to their prayers.

While Nekumonta lay asleep there came to him the messenger of Manitou, and he dreamed. In his dream he saw his beautiful Shanewis, pale and thin, but as lovely as ever, and as he looked she smiled at him, and sang a strange, sweet song, like the murmuring of a distant waterfall. Then the scene changed, and it really was a waterfall he heard. In musical language it called him by name, saying: 'Seek us, O Nekumonta, and when you find us Shanewis shall live. We are the Healing Waters of the Great Manitou.'

Nekumonta awoke with the words of the song still ringing in his ears. Starting to his feet, he looked in every direction; but there was no water to be seen, though the murmuring sound of a waterfall was distinctly audible. He fancied he could even distinguish words in it.

The finding of the waters

'Release us!' it seemed to say. 'Set us free, and Shanewis shall be saved!'

Nekumonta searched in vain for the waters. Then it suddenly occurred to him that they must be underground,

directly under his feet. Seizing branches, stones, flints, he dug
feverishly into the earth. So arduous was the task that before
it was finished he was completely exhausted. But at last the
hidden spring was disclosed, and the waters were rippling
merrily down the vale, carrying life and happiness wherever
they went. The young man bathed his aching limbs in the
healing stream, and in a moment he was well and strong.

Raising his hands, he gave thanks to Manitou. With eager
fingers he made a jar of clay, and baked it in the fire, so that
he might carry life to Shanewis. As he pursued his way
homeward with his treasure his despair was changed to
rejoicing and he sped like the wind.

When he reached his village his companions ran to greet
him. Their faces were sad and hopeless, for the plague still
raged. However, Nekumonta directed them to the Healing
Waters and inspired them with new hope. Shanewis he found
on the verge of the Shadow-land, and scarcely able to murmur
a farewell to her husband. But Nekumonta did not listen to
her broken adieux. He forced some of the Healing Water
between her parched lips, and bathed her hands and her brow
till she fell into a gentle slumber. When she awoke the fever
had left her, she was serene and smiling, and Nekumonta's
heart was filled with a great happiness.

The tribe was forever rid of the dreaded plague, and the
people gave to Nekumonta the title of 'Chief of the Healing
Waters', so that all might know that it was he who had brought
them the gift of Manitou.

Sayadio in Spirit-land

A legend of the Wyandot tribe of the Iroquois relates how
Sayadio, a young Indian, mourned greatly for a beautiful sister
who had died young. So deeply did he grieve for her that at
length he resolved to seek her in the Land of Spirits. Long he
sought the maiden, and many adventures did he meet with.
Years passed in the search, which he was about to abandon as
wholly in vain, when he encountered an old man, who gave

him some good advice. This venerable person also bestowed upon him a magic calabash in which he might catch and retain the spirit of his sister should he succeed in finding her. He afterward discovered that this old man was the keeper of that part of the Spirit-land which he sought.

Delighted to have achieved so much, Sayadio pursued his way, and in due time reached the Land of Souls. But to his dismay he perceived that the spirits, instead of advancing to meet him as he had expected, fled from him in terror. Greatly dejected, he approached Tarenyawago, the spirit master of ceremonies, who took compassion upon him and informed him that the dead had gathered together for a great dance festival, just such as the Indians themselves celebrate at certain seasons of the year. Soon the dancing commenced, and Sayadio saw the spirits floating round in a mazy measure like wreaths of mist. Among them he perceived his sister, and sprang forward to embrace her, but she eluded his grasp and dissolved into air.

Much cast down, the youth once more appealed to the sympathetic master of ceremonies, who gave him a magic rattle of great power, by the sound of which he might bring her back. Again the spirit-music sounded for the dance, and the dead folk thronged into the circle. Once more Sayadio saw his sister, and observed that she was so wholly entranced with the music that she took no heed of his presence. Quick as thought the young Indian dipped up the ghost with his calabash as one nets a fish, and secured the cover, in spite of all the efforts of the captured soul to regain its liberty.

Retracing his steps earthward, he had no difficulty in making his way back to his native village, where he summoned his friends to come and behold his sister's resuscitation. The girl's corpse was brought from its resting-place to be reanimated with its spirit, and all was prepared for the ceremony, when a witless Indian maiden must needs peep into the calabash in her curiosity to see how a disembodied spirit looked. Instantly, as a bird rises when its cage bars are opened and flies forth to freedom, the spirit of Sayadio's sister flew from the calabash before the startled youth could dash forward and shut down the cover. For a while Sayadio could not realize his loss, but at length his straining eyes revealed to him that the spirit of his sister was not within sight. In a flash he saw the ruin of his hopes, and with a broken heart he sank senseless to the earth.

The Peace Queen

A brave of the Oneida tribe of the Iroquois hunted in the forest. The red buck flashed past him, but not swifter than his arrow, for as the deer leaped he loosed his shaft and it pierced the dappled hide.

The young man strode toward the carcass, knife in hand, but as he seized the horns the branches parted, and the angry face of an Onondaga warrior lowered between them.

'Leave the buck, Oneida,' he commanded fiercely. 'It is the spoil of my bow. I wounded the beast ere you saw it.'

The Oneida laughed. 'My brother may have shot at the buck,' he said, 'but what avails that if he did not slay it?

'The carcass is mine by right of forest law,' cried the other in a rage. 'Will you quit it or will you fight?'

The Oneida drew himself up and regarded the Onondaga scornfully.

'As my brother pleases,' he replied. Next moment the two were locked in a life-and-death struggle.

Tall was the Onondaga and strong as a great tree of the forest. The Oneida, lithe as a panther, fought with all the courage of youth. To and fro they swayed, till their breathing came thick and fast and the falling sweat blinded their eyes. At length they could struggle no longer, and by a mutual impulse they sprang apart.

The quarrel

'Ho! Onondaga,' cried the younger man, 'what profits it thus to strive for a buck? Is there no meat in the lodges of your people that they must fight for it like the mountain lion?'

'Peace, young man!' retorted the grave Onondaga. 'I had

not fought for the buck had not your evil tongue roused me. But I am older than you, and, I trust, wiser. Let us seek the lodge of the Peace Queen hard by, and she will award the buck to him who has the best right to it.'

'It is well,' said the Oneida, and side by side they sought the lodge of the Peace Queen.

Now the Five Nations in their wisdom had set apart a Seneca maiden dwelling alone in the forest as arbiter of quarrels between braves. This maiden the men of all tribes regarded as sacred and as apart from other women. Like the ancient Vestals, she could not become the bride of any man.

As the Peace Queen heard the wrathful clamour of the braves outside her lodge she stepped forth, little pleased that they should thus profane the vicinity of her dwelling.

'Peace!' she cried. 'If you have a grievance enter and state it. It is not fitting that braves should quarrel where the Peace Queen dwells.'

At her words the men stood abashed. They entered the lodge and told the story of their meeting and the circumstances of their quarrel.

When they had finished the Peace Queen smiled scornfully. 'So two such braves as you can quarrel about a buck?' she said. 'Go, Onondaga, as the elder, and take one half of the spoil, and bear it back to your wife and children.'

But the Onondaga stood his ground.

The offers

'O Queen,' he said, 'my wife is in the Land of Spirits, snatched from me by the Plague Demon. But my lodge does not lack food. I would wive again, and thine eyes have looked into my heart as the sun pierces the darkness of the forest. Will you come to my lodge and cook my venison?'

But the Peace Queen shook her head.

'You know that the Five Nations have placed Genetaska apart to be Peace Queen,' she replied firmly, 'and that her vows may not be broken. Go in peace.'

The Onondaga was silent.

Then spoke the Oneida. 'O Peace Queen,' he said, gazing steadfastly at Genetaska, whose eyes dropped before his glance, 'I know that you are set apart by the Five Nations. But it is in my mind to ask you to go with me to my lodge, for I love you. What says Genetaska?'

The Peace Queen blushed and answered: 'To you also I say, go in peace,' but her voice was a whisper which ended in a stifled sob.

The two warriors departed, good friends now that they possessed a common sorrow. But the Peace Maiden had forever lost her peace. For she could not forget the young Oneida brave, so tall, so strong, and so gentle.

Summer darkened into autumn, and autumn whitened into winter. Warriors innumerable came to the Peace Lodge for the settlement of disputes. Outwardly Genetaska was calm and untroubled, but though she gave solace to others her own breast could find none.

One day she sat by the lodge fire, which had burned down to a heap of cinders. She was thinking, dreaming of the young Oneida. Her thoughts went out to him as birds fly southward to seek the sun. Suddenly a crackling of twigs under a firm step roused her from her reverie. Quickly she glanced upward. Before her stood the youth of her dreams, pale and worn.

'Peace Queen,' he said sadly, 'you have brought darkness to the soul of the Oneida. No longer may he follow the hunt. The deer may sport in quiet for him. No longer may he bend the bow or throw the tomahawk in contest, or listen to the tale during the long nights round the camp-fire. You have his heart in your keeping. Say, will you not give him yours?'

Softly the Peace Queen murmured: 'I will.'

Hand in hand like two joyous children they sought his canoe, which bore them swiftly westward. No longer was Genetaska Peace Queen, for her vows were broken by the power of love.

The two were happy. But not so the men of the Five

Nations. They were wroth because the Peace Queen had broken her vows, and knew how foolish they had been to trust to the word of a young and beautiful woman. So with one voice they abolished the office of Peace Queen, and war and tumult returned once more to their own.

*   *   *

Contrary to Spence, there never was, in all likelihood, a person called 'Hiawatha'; it is not a personal name but a priestly title of the Onondaga tribe.

The social, political and religious life of sedentary agricultural Iroquois (maize of seventeen varieties being their main crop) in what is now New York state was more advanced than that of the hunting tribes. Indeed, the civilization of the Iroquois was the most advanced in North America with the exceptions of those in Southeast and Southwest. In politics they practised, as well as confederacy, a form of democracy, whereby clan mothers – much of Iroquois life was under maternal influence – selected fifty male *rotiyanehr* to represent the clans on the governing Grand Council. Great matters were referred back to the people in referenda, in which everyone had a vote.

This inclusivity was an important means by which the Iroquois maintained unity. So was the Iroquois' highly organized religion. Simply stated: A wandering band of 100 of nomads on the Plains could keep unity by blood and leadership, and had little need for complex religion. A people of 25,000, divided into five nations, required a considerable religion, full of mass ritual and ceremony to bind it together.

The complex theology of the Iroquois centred on a formless supreme power, 'The Great Spirit' or 'Ha-wen-ne-yu' who oversaw a world in constant flux and struggle between the dualities of light and dark, of good and evil. The creation myth of the Iroquois combines elements of the Earth Diver story with the image of a creator who descends from the heavens. Creation begins when a sky goddess named Atahensic plummets through a hole in the floor of heaven:

In the faraway days of this floating island there grew one stately tree that branched beyond the range of vision. Perpetually laden with fruit and blossoms, the air was fragrant with its perfume, and the people gathered to its shade where councils were held.

One day the Great Ruler said to his people: 'We will make a new place where another people may grow. Under our council tree is a great cloud sea which calls for our help. It is lonesome. It knows no rest and calls for light. We will talk to it. The roots of our council tree point to it and will show the way.'

Having commanded that the tree be uprooted, the Great Ruler peered into the depth where the roots had guided, and summoning Ata-en-sic, who was with child, bade her look down. Ata-en-sic saw nothing, but the Great Ruler knew that the sea voice was calling, and bidding her carry its life, wrapped around her a great ray of light and sent her down to the cloud sea.

Dazzled by the descending light enveloping Ata-en-sic, there was great consternation among the animals and birds inhabiting the cloud sea, and they counselled in alarm.

'If it falls it may destroy us,' they cried.

'Where can it rest?', asked the Duck.

'Only the oeh-da [earth] can hold it,' said the Beaver, 'the oeh-da which lies at the bottom of our waters, and I will bring it.' The Beaver went down but never returned. Then the Duck ventured, but soon its dead body floated to the surface.

Many of the divers had tried and failed when the Muskrat, knowing the way, volunteered to obtain it and soon returned bearing a small portion in his paw. 'But it is heavy,' said he, 'and will grow fast. Who will bear it?'

The Turtle was willing, and the oeh-da was placed on his hard shell.

Having received a resting place for the light, the water birds, guided by its glow, flew upward, and receiving the woman on their widespread wings, bore her down to the Turtle's back.

And Ha-nu-nah, the Turtle, became the Earth Bearer. When he stirs, the seas rise in great waves, and when restless and violent, earthquakes yawn and devour.

The oeh-da grew rapidly and had become an island when Ata-en-sic, hearing voices under her heart, one soft and soothing, the other loud and contentious, knew that her mission to people the island was nearing.

To her solitude two lives were coming, one peaceful and patient, the other restless and vicious. The latter, discovering light under her mother's arm, thrust himself through, to contentions and strife, the right born entered life for freedom and peace.

These were the Do-ya-da-no, the twin brothers, Spirits of Good and Evil. Foreknowing their powers, each claimed dominion and a struggle between them began, Hah-gwh-di-yu claiming the right to beautify the island, while Hah-gweh-da-et-gah determined to destroy. Each went his way, and where peace had reigned discord and strife prevailed.

> (From 'Myths and Legends of the New York State
> Iroquois', Harriet Maxwell Converse, New York State
> Museum, Bulletin 125, ed. Arthur C. Parker, 1908)

This was not evil exactly as the Christian tradition understood it, being more weighted to ill fortune than malevolence. Under the Great Spirit existed a gallery of lesser gods, the Invisible Agents or 'Ho-no-che-no-keh', who controlled natural events and human affairs, and to whom prayers and offerings were directed. In the Iroquois view ordinary humans could not communicate directly with the Great Spirit, but could do so indirectly by burning tobacco, which carried their prayers to spirits of the second rank. (Prior to European contact, the most common species of tobacco used was Nicotiana rustica; supplies were scarce and the plant was considered sacred.) Some of the most important spirits were Thunderer and 'The Three Sisters', the spirits of Maize, Beans, and Squash. Human sacrifice was rare, except for the torture and burning of captives in ceremonial fires; portions of slaughtered animals and the first of the crop were the more usual offerings. In dances the masked participants mimed and imitated the events they desired. Malign spirits could be driven out by the False Face Society or the Husk Society, with their hideous, impersonating masks. Used in the curing ceremonies of the False Face Societies, the masks were made of maple, white pine, poplar and basswood. False Face Masks were first carved in a living tree, then cut free and decorated. Evil could be warded off by the accumulation of orenda, the good, in-dwelling life force. It was believed that orenda survived after death, when not even otkon, the spirit of misfortune and decay, could harm it. However, the survival also depended on the judgement of the Great Spirit as to whether the recently deceased had led a virtuous life.

As with other farming tribes, the Iroquois had a different and fuller calendar of religious festivals to the nomadic hunters. The Iroquois held six regular festivals per year, based on the stages of crop growth; the first festival, which involved ritual cleansing (including vomiting), coincided with the rising of the sap in the local maple trees; there followed the festivals for planting corn, collecting the first strawberries, the appearance of the first corn ears, the harvest and the White Dog festival of the new year, in which a white dog was sent to the skies with a message of thanks to the Supreme Power above.

At the great festivals, the Keeper of the Wampum would recite tribal stories, using the beads of wampum (white or purple seashell) as mnemonics. Such priests were part time, male or female, there being no room in democratic Iroquois society for an all-powerful priesthood.

With a concept of a Supreme Being, a theology which understood the duality of good and evil, and a belief in the afterlife, Iroquois religion had enough obvious similarities to Christianity to gladden the heart of that faith's missionaries. Equally, the Seneca sachem (chief) Handsome Lake was able to seamlessly insert Quaker beliefs into his popular revamping of Iroquois religion in around 1800. Handsome Lake's amalgamation of Iroquois religion and Quakerism was published as the Code of Handsome Lake. It still has many adherents today.

5

SIOUX MYTHS AND LEGENDS

The Sioux or Dakota Indians
The Sioux or Dakota Indians dwell north of the Arkansas River on the right bank of the Mississippi, stretching over to Lake Michigan and up the valley of the Missouri. One of their principal tribes is the Iowa.

The Adventures of Ictinike
Many tales are told by the Iowa Indians regarding Ictinike, the son of the sun-god, who had offended his father, and was consequently expelled from the celestial regions. He possesses a very bad reputation among the Indians for deceit and trickery. They say that he taught them all the evil things they know, and they seem to regard him as a Father of Lies. The Omahas state that he gave them their war-customs, and for one reason or another they appear to look upon him as a species of war-god. A series of myths recount his adventures with several inhabitants of the wild. The first of these is as follows.

One day Ictinike encountered the Rabbit, and hailed him in

a friendly manner, calling him 'grandchild', and requesting him to do him a service. The Rabbit expressed his willingness to assist the god to the best of his ability, and inquired what he wished him to do.

'Oh, grandchild,' said the crafty one, pointing upward to where a bird circled in the blue vault above them, 'take your bow and arrow and bring down yonder bird.'

The Rabbit fitted an arrow to his bow, and the shaft transfixed the bird, which fell like a stone and lodged in the branches of a great tree.

'Now, grandchild,' said Ictinike, 'go into the tree and fetch me the game.'

This, however, the Rabbit at first refused to do, but at length he took off his clothes and climbed into the tree, where he stuck fast among the tortuous branches.

Ictinike, seeing that he could not make his way down, donned the unfortunate Rabbit's garments, and, highly amused at the animal's predicament, betook himself to the nearest village. There he encountered a chief who had two beautiful daughters, the elder of whom he married. The younger daughter, regarding this as an affront to her personal attractions, wandered off into the forest in a fit of the sulks. As she paced angrily up and down she heard someone calling to her from above, and, looking upward, she beheld the unfortunate Rabbit, whose fur was adhering to the natural gum which exuded from the bark of the tree. The girl cut down the tree and lit a fire near it, which melted the gum and freed the Rabbit. The Rabbit and the chief's daughter compared notes, and discovered that the being who had tricked the one and affronted the other was the same. Together they proceeded to the chief's lodge, where the girl was laughed at because of the strange companion she had brought back with her. Suddenly an eagle appeared in the air above them. Ictinike shot at and missed it, but the Rabbit loosed an arrow with great force and brought it to earth. Each morning a feather of the bird became another eagle, and each morning

Ictinike shot at and missed this newly created bird, which the Rabbit invariably succeeded in killing. This went on until Ictinike had quite worn out the Rabbit's clothing and was wearing a very old piece of tent skin; but the Rabbit returned to him the garments he had been forced to don when Ictinike had stolen his. Then the Rabbit commanded the Indians to beat the drums, and each time they were beaten Ictinike jumped so high that every bone in his body was shaken. At length, after a more than usually loud series of beats, he leapt to such a height that when he came down it was found that the fall had broken his neck. The Rabbit was avenged.

Ictinike and the buzzard

One day Ictinike, footsore and weary, encountered a buzzard, which he asked to oblige him by carrying him on its back part of the way. The crafty bird immediately consented, and, seating Ictinike between its wings, flew off with him.

They had not gone far when they passed above a hollow tree, and Ictinike began to shift uneasily in his seat as he observed the buzzard hovering over it. He requested the bird to fly onward, but for answer it cast him headlong into the tree-trunk, where he found himself a prisoner. For a long time he lay there in want and wretchedness, until at last a large hunting-party struck camp at the spot. Ictinike chanced to be wearing some racoon skins, and he thrust the tails of these through the cracks in the tree. Three women who were standing near imagined that a number of racoons had become imprisoned in the hollow trunk, and they made a large hole in it for the purpose of capturing them. Ictinike at once emerged, whereupon the women fled. Ictinike lay on the ground pretending to be dead, and as he was covered with the racoon-skins the birds of prey, the eagle, the rook, and the magpie, came to devour him. While they pecked at him the buzzard made his appearance for the purpose of joining in the feast, but Ictinike, rising quickly, tore the feathers from its scalp. That is why the buzzard has no feathers on its head.

Ictinike and the creators

In course of time Ictinike married and dwelt in a lodge of his own. One day he intimated to his wife that it was his intention to visit her grandfather the Beaver. On arriving at the Beaver's lodge he found that his grandfather-in-law and his family had been without food for a long time, and were slowly dying of starvation. Ashamed at having no food to place before their guest, one of the young beavers offered himself up to provide a meal for Ictinike, and was duly cooked and served to the visitor. Before Ictinike partook of the dish, however, he was earnestly requested by the Beaver not to break any of the bones of his son, but unwittingly he split one of the toe-bones. Having finished his repast, he lay down to rest, and the Beaver gathered the bones and put them in a skin. This he plunged into the river that flowed beside his lodge, and in a moment the young beaver emerged from the water alive.

'How do you feel, my son?' asked the Beaver.

'Alas! father,' replied the young beaver, 'one of my toes is broken.'

From that time every beaver has had one toe – that next to the little one – which looks as if it had been split by biting.

Ictinike shortly after took his leave of the Beavers, and pretended to forget his tobacco-pouch, which he left behind. The Beaver told one of his young ones to run after him with the pouch, but, being aware of Ictinike's treacherous character, he advised his offspring to throw it to the god when at some distance away. The young beaver accordingly took the pouch and hurried after Ictinike, and, obeying his father's instruction, was about to throw it to him from a considerable distance when Ictinike called to him: 'Come closer, come closer.'

The young beaver obeyed, and as Ictinike took the pouch from him he said: 'Tell your father that he must visit me.'

When the young beaver arrived home he acquainted his father with what had passed, and the Beaver showed signs of great annoyance.

'I knew he would say that,' he growled, 'and that is why I did not want you to go near him.'

But the Beaver could not refuse the invitation, and in due course returned the visit. Ictinike, wishing to pay him a compliment, was about to kill one of his own children wherewith to regale the Beaver, and was slapping it to make it cry in order that he might work himself into a passion sufficiently murderous to enable him to take its life, when the Beaver spoke to him sharply and told him that such a sacrifice was unnecessary. Going down to the stream hard by, the Beaver found a young beaver by the water, which was brought up to the lodge, killed and cooked, and duly eaten.

On another occasion Ictinike announced to his wife his intention of calling upon her grandfather the Musk-rat. At the Musk-rat's lodge he met with the same tale of starvation as at the home of the Beaver, but the Musk-rat told his wife to fetch some water, put it in the kettle, and hang the kettle over the fire. When the water was boiling the Musk-rat upset the kettle, which was found to be full of wild rice, upon which Ictinike feasted. As before, he left his tobacco-pouch with his host, and the Musk-rat sent one of his children after him with the article. An invitation for the Musk-rat to visit him resulted, and the call was duly paid. Ictinike, wishing to display his magical powers, requested his wife to hang a kettle of water over the fire, but, to his chagrin, when the water was boiled and the kettle upset instead of wild rice only water poured out. Thereupon the Musk-rat had the kettle refilled, and produced an abundance of rice, much to Ictinike's annoyance.

Ictinike then called upon his wife's grandfather the King-fisher, who, to provide him with food, dived into the river and brought up fish. Ictinike extended a similar invitation to him, and the visit was duly paid. Desiring to be even with his late host, the god dived into the river in search of fish. He soon found himself in difficulties, however, and if it had not been for the Kingfisher he would most assuredly have been drowned.

Lastly, Ictinike went to visit his wife's grandfather the Flying Squirrel. The Squirrel climbed to the top of his lodge and brought down a quantity of excellent black walnuts, which Ictinike ate. When he departed from the Squirrel's house he purposely left one of his gloves, which a small squirrel brought after him, and he sent an invitation by this messenger for the Squirrel to visit him in turn. Wishing to show his cleverness, Ictinike scrambled to the top of his lodge, but instead of finding any black walnuts there he fell and severely injured himself. Thus his presumption was punished for the fourth time.

The four beings alluded to in this story as the Beaver, Musk-rat, Kingfisher, and Flying Squirrel are four of the creative gods of the Sioux, whom Ictinike evidently could not equal so far as reproductive magic was concerned.

The story of Wabaskaha

An interesting story is that of Wabaskaha, an Omaha brave, the facts related in which occurred about a century ago. A party of Pawnees on the war-path raided the horses belonging to some Omahas dwelling beside Omaha Creek. Most of the animals were the property of Wabaskaha, who immediately followed on their trail. A few Omahas who had tried to rescue the horses had also been carried off, and on the arrival of the Pawnee party at the Republican River several of the Pawnees proposed to put their prisoners to death. Others, however, refused to participate in such an act, and strenuously opposed the suggestion. A wife of one of the Pawnee chiefs fed the captives, after which her husband gave them permission to depart.

After this incident quite a feeling of friendship sprang up between the two peoples, and the Pawnees were continually inviting the Omahas to feasts and other entertainments, but they refused to return the horses they had stolen. They told Wabaskaha that if he came for his horses in the autumn they would exchange them then for a certain amount of gunpowder, and that was the best arrangement he could come to with them. On his way homeward Wabaskaha mourned loudly for the horses, which constituted nearly the whole of his worldly possessions, and called upon Wakanda, his god, to assist and avenge him. In glowing language he recounted the circumstances of his loss to the people of his tribe, and so strong was their sense of the injustice done him that next day a general meeting was held in the village to consider his case. A pipe was filled, and Wabaskaha asked the men of his tribe to place it to their lips if they decided to take vengeance on the Pawnees. All did so, but the premeditated raid was postponed until the early autumn.

After a summer of hunting the braves sought the war-path. They had hardly started when a number of Dakotas arrived at their village, bringing some tobacco. The Dakotas announced their intention of joining the Omaha war-party, the trail of which they took up accordingly. In a few days the Omahas arrived at the Pawnee village, which they attacked at daylight. After a vigorous defence the Pawnees were almost exterminated, and all their horses captured. The Dakotas who had elected to assist the Omaha war-party were, however, slain to a man. Such was the vengeance of Wabaskaha.

This story is interesting as an account of a veritable Indian raid, taken from the lips of Joseph La Flèche, a Dakota Indian.

The men-serpents
Twenty warriors who had been on the war-path were returning homeward worn-out and hungry, and as they went they scattered in search of game to sustain them on their way,

Suddenly one of the braves, placing his ear to the ground, declared that he could hear a herd of buffaloes approaching.

The band was greatly cheered by this news, and the plans made by the chief to intercept the animals were quickly carried into effect.

Nearer and nearer came the supposed herd. The chief lay very still, ready to shoot when it came within range. Suddenly he saw, to his horror, that what approached them was a huge snake with a rattle as large as a man's head. Though almost paralysed with surprise and terror, he managed to shoot the monster and kill it. He called up his men, who were not a little afraid of the gigantic creature, even though it was dead, and for a long time they debated what they should do with the carcass. At length hunger conquered their scruples and made them decide to cook and eat it. To their surprise, they found the meat as savoury as that of a buffalo, which it much resembled. All partook of the fare, with the exception of one boy, who persisted in refusing it, though they pressed him to eat.

When the warriors had finished their meal they lay down beside the camp-fire and fell asleep. Later in the night the chief awoke and was horrified to find that his companions had turned to snakes, and that he himself was already half snake, half man. Hastily he gathered his transformed warriors, and they saw that the boy who had not eaten of the reptile had retained his own form. The lad, fearing that the serpents might attack him, began to weep, but the snake-warriors treated him very kindly, giving him their charms and all they possessed.

At their request he put them into a large robe and carried them to the summit of a high hill, where he set them down under the trees.

'You must return to our lodges,' they told him, 'and in the summer we will visit our kindred. See that our wives and children come out to greet us.'

The boy carried the news to his village, and there was much weeping and lamentation when the friends of the warriors heard of their fate. But in the summer the snakes came and sat in a group outside the village, and all the people crowded round them, loudly venting their grief. The horses which had belonged to the snakes were brought out to them, as well as their moccasins, leggings, whips, and saddles.

'Do not be afraid of them,' said the boy to the assembled people. 'Do not flee from them, lest something happen to you also.' So they let the snakes creep over them, and no harm befell.

In the winter the snakes vanished altogether, and with them their horses and other possessions, and the people never saw them more.

The three tests

There dwelt in a certain village a woman of remarkable grace and attractiveness. The fame of her beauty drew suitors from far and near, eager to display their prowess and win the love of this imperious creature – for, besides being beautiful, she was extremely hard to please, and set such tests for her lovers as none had ever been able to satisfy.

A certain young man who lived at a considerable distance had heard of her great charms, and made up his mind to woo and win her. The difficulty of the task did not daunt him, and, full of hope, he set out on his mission.

As he travelled he came to a very high hill, and on the summit he saw a man rising and sitting down at short intervals. When the prospective suitor drew nearer he observed that the man was fastening large stones to his ankles. The youth approached him, saying: 'Why do you tie these great stones to your ankles?'

'Oh,' replied the other, 'I wish to chase buffaloes, and yet whenever I do so I go beyond them, so I am tying stones to my ankles that I may not run so fast.'

'My friend,' said the suitor, 'you can run some other time. In the meantime I am without a companion: come with me.'

The Swift One agreed, and they walked on their way together. Ere they had gone very far they saw two large lakes. By the side of one of them sat a man, who frequently bowed his head to the water and drank. Surprised that his thirst was not quenched, they said to him: 'Why do you sit there drinking of the lake?'

'I can never get enough water. When I have finished this lake I shall start on the other.'

'My friend,' said the suitor, 'do not trouble to drink it just now. Come and join us.'

The Thirsty One complied, and the three comrades journeyed on. When they had gone a little farther they noticed a man walking along with his face lifted to the sky. Curious to know why he acted thus, they addressed him.

'Why do you walk with your eyes turned skyward?' said they.

'I have shot an arrow,' he said, 'and I am waiting for it to reappear.'

'Never mind your arrow,' said the suitor. 'Come with us.'

'I will come,' said the Skilful Archer.

As the four companions journeyed through a forest they beheld a strange sight. A man was lying with his ear to the ground, and if he lifted his head for a moment he bowed it again, listening intently. The four approached him, saying: 'Friend, for what do you listen so earnestly?'

'I am listening,' said he, 'to the plants growing. This forest is full of plants, and I am listening to their breathing.'

'You can listen when the occasion arises,' they told him. 'Come and join us.'

He agreed, and so they travelled to the village where dwelt the beautiful maiden.

When they had reached their destination they were quickly surrounded by the villagers, who displayed no small curiosity as to who their visitors were and what object they had in coming so far. When they heard that one of the strangers desired to marry the village beauty they shook their heads over him. Did he not know the difficulties in the way? Finding that he would not be turned from his purpose, they led him to a huge rock which overshadowed the village, and described the first test he would be required to meet.

'If you wish to win the maiden,' they said, 'you must first of all push away that great stone. It is keeping the sunlight from us.'

'Alas!' said the youth, 'it is impossible.'

'Not so,' said his companion of the swift foot; 'nothing could be more easy.'

Saying this, he leaned his shoulder against the rock, and with a mighty crash it fell from its place. From the breaking up of it came the rocks and stones that are scattered over all the world.

The second test was of a different nature. The people brought the strangers a large quantity of food and water, and bade them eat and drink. Being very hungry, they succeeded in disposing of the food, but the suitor sorrowfully regarded the great kettles of water.

'Alas!' said he, 'who can drink up that?'

'I can,' said the Thirsty One, and in a twinkling he had drunk it all.

The people were amazed at the prowess of the visitors. However, they said, 'There is still another test,' and they brought out a woman who was a very swift runner, so swift that no one had ever outstripped her in a race.

The race

'You must run a race with this woman,' said they. 'If you win you shall have the hand of the maiden you have come to seek.'

Naturally the suitor chose the Swift One for this test. When the runners were started the people hailed them as fairly matched, for they raced together till they were out of sight.

When they reached the turning-point the woman said: 'Come, let us rest for a little.'

The man agreed, but no sooner had he sat down than he fell asleep. The woman seized her opportunity. Making sure that her rival was sleeping soundly, she set off for the village, running as hard as she could.

Meanwhile the four comrades were anxiously awaiting the return of the competitors, and great was their disappointment when the woman came in sight, while there was yet no sign of their champion.

The man who could hear the plants growing bent his ear to the ground.

'He is asleep,' said he; 'I can hear him snoring.'

The Skilful Archer came forward, and as he bit the point off an arrow he said: 'I will soon wake him.'

He shot an arrow from the bowstring with such a wonderful aim that it wounded the sleeper's nose, and roused him from his slumbers. The runner started to his feet and looked round for the woman. She was gone. Knowing that he had been tricked, the Swift One put all his energy into an effort to overtake her. She was within a few yards of the winning-post when he passed her. It was a narrow margin, but nevertheless the Swift One had gained the race for his comrade.

The youth was then married to the damsel, whom he found to be all that her admirers had claimed, and more.

The snake-ogre

One day a young brave, feeling at variance with the world in general, and wishing to rid himself of the mood, left the lodges of his people and journeyed into the forest. By and by he came to an open space, in the centre of which was a high hill. Thinking he would climb to the top and reconnoitre, he directed his footsteps thither, and as he went he observed a man coming in the opposite direction and making for the same spot. The two met on the summit, and stood for a few moments silently regarding each other. The stranger was the first to speak, gravely inviting the young brave to accompany him to his lodge and sup with him. The other accepted the invitation, and they proceeded in the direction the stranger indicated.

On approaching the lodge the youth saw with some surprise that there was a large heap of bones in front of the door. Within sat a very old woman tending a pot. When the young man learned that the feast was to be a cannibal one, however, he declined to partake of it. The woman thereupon boiled some corn for him, and while doing so told him that his host was nothing more nor less than a snake-man, a sort of ogre who killed and ate human beings. Because the brave was young and very handsome the old woman took pity on him, bemoaning the fate that would surely befall him unless he could escape from the wiles of the snake-man.

'Listen,' said she: 'I will tell you what to do. Here are some moccasins. When the morning comes put them on your feet, take one step, and you will find yourself on that headland you see in the distance. Give this paper to the man you will meet there, and he will direct you further. But remember that however far you may go, in the evening the Snake will overtake you. When you have finished with the moccasins take them off, place them on the ground facing this way, and they will return.'

'Is that all?' said the youth.

'No,' she replied. 'Before you go you must kill me and put a robe over my bones.'

The magic moccasins

The young brave forthwith proceeded to carry these instructions into effect. First of all he killed the old woman, and disposed of her remains in accordance with her bidding. In the morning he put on the magic moccasins which she had provided for him, and with one great step he reached the distant headland. Here he met an old man, who received the paper from him, and then, giving him another pair of moccasins, directed him to a far-off point where he was to deliver another piece of paper to a man who would await him there. Turning the first moccasins homeward, the young brave put the second pair to use, and took another gigantic step. Arrived at the second stage of his journey from the Snake's lodge, he found it a repetition of the first. He was directed to another distant spot, and from that to yet another. But when he delivered his message for the fourth time he was treated somewhat differently.

'Down there in the hollow,' said the recipient of the paper, 'there is a stream. Go toward it, and walk straight on, but do not look at the water.'

The youth did as he was bidden, and shortly found himself on the opposite bank of the stream.

He journeyed up the creek, and as evening fell he came upon a place where the river widened to a lake. Skirting its shores, he suddenly found himself face to face with the Snake. Only then did he remember the words of the old woman, who had warned him that in the evening the Snake would overtake him. So he turned himself into a little fish with red fins, lazily moving in the lake.

The Snake's quest

The Snake, high on the bank, saw the little creature, and cried: 'Little Fish! have you seen the person I am looking for? If a bird had flown over the lake you must have seen it, the water is so still, and surely you have seen the man I am seeking?'

'Not so,' replied the Little Fish, 'I have seen no one. But if he passes this way I will tell you.'

So the Snake continued down-stream, and as he went there was a little grey toad right in his path.

'Little Toad,' said he, 'have you seen him for whom I am seeking? Even if only a shadow were here you must have seen it.'

'Yes,' said the Little Toad, 'I have seen him, but I cannot tell you which way he has gone.'

The Snake doubled and came back on his trail. Seeing a very large fish in shallow water, he said: 'Have you seen the man I am looking for?'

'That is he with whom you have just been talking,' said the Fish, and the Snake turned homeward. Meeting a musk-rat he stopped.

'Have you seen the person I am looking for?' he said. Then, having his suspicions aroused, he added craftily: 'I think that you are he.'

But the Musk-rat began a bitter complaint.

'Just now,' said he, 'the person you seek passed over my lodge and broke it.'

So the Snake passed on, and encountered a red-breasted turtle.

He repeated his query, and the Turtle told him that the object of his search was to be met with farther on.

'But beware,' he added, 'for if you do not recognize him he will kill you.'

Following the stream, the Snake came upon a large green frog floating in shallow water.

'I have been seeking a person since morning,' he said. 'I think that you are he.'

The Frog allayed his suspicions, saying: 'You will meet him farther down the stream.'

The Snake next found a large turtle floating among the green scum on a lake. Getting on the Turtle's back, he said: 'You must be the person I seek,' and his head rose higher and higher as he prepared to strike.

'I am not,' replied the Turtle. 'The next person you meet will be he. But beware, for if you do not recognize him he will kill you.'

When he had gone a little farther down the Snake attempted to cross the stream. In the middle was an eddy. Crafty as he was, the Snake failed to recognize his enemy, and the eddy drew him down into the water and drowned him. So the youth succeeded in slaying the Snake who had sought throughout the day to kill him.

The story of the salmon

A certain chief who had a very beautiful daughter was unwilling to part with her, but knowing that the time must come when she would marry he arranged a contest for her suitors, in which the feat was to break a pair of elk's antlers hung in the centre of the lodge.

'Whoever shall break these antlers,' the old chief declared, 'shall have the hand of my daughter.'

The quadrupeds came first – the Snail, Squirrel, Otter, Beaver, Wolf, Bear, and Panther; but all their strength and skill

would not suffice to break the antlers. Next came the Birds,
but their efforts also were unavailing. The only creature left
who had not attempted the feat was a feeble thing covered
with sores, whom the mischievous Blue Jay derisively
summoned to perform the task. After repeated taunts from the
tricky bird, the creature rose, shook itself, and became whole
and clean and very good to look upon, and the assembled
company saw that it was the Salmon. He grasped the elk's
antlers and easily broke them in five pieces. Then, claiming his
prize, the chief's daughter, he led her away.

Before they had gone very far the people said: 'Let us go
and take the chief's daughter back,' and they set off in pursuit
of the pair along the sea-shore.

When Salmon saw what was happening he created a bay
between himself and his pursuers. The people at length
reached the point of the bay on which Salmon stood, but he
made another bay, and when they looked they could see him
on the far-off point of that one. So the chase went on, till
Salmon grew tired of exercising his magic powers.

Coyote and Badger, who were in advance of the others,
decided to shoot at Salmon. The arrow hit him in the neck and
killed him instantly. When the rest of the band came up they
gave the chief's daughter to the Wolves, and she became the
wife of one of them.

In due time the people returned to their village, and the
Crow, who was Salmon's aunt, learnt of his death. She
hastened away to the spot where he had been killed, to seek
for his remains, but all she could find was one salmon's egg,
which she hid in a hole in the river-bank. Next day she found
that the egg was much larger, on the third day it was a small
trout, and so it grew till it became a full-grown salmon, and at
length a handsome youth.

Salmon's magic bath
Leading young Salmon to a mountain pool, his grand-aunt
said: 'Bathe there, that you may see spirits.'

One day Salmon said: 'I am tired of seeing spirits. Let me go away.'

The old Crow thereupon told him of his father's death at the hands of Badger and Coyote.

'They have taken your father's bow,' she said.

The Salmon shot an arrow toward the forest, and the forest went on fire. He shot an arrow toward the prairie, and it also caught fire.

'Truly,' muttered the old Crow, 'you have seen spirits.'

Having made up his mind to get his father's bow, Salmon journeyed to the lodge where Coyote and Badger dwelt. He found the door shut, and the creatures with their faces blackened, pretending to lament the death of old Salmon. However, he was not deceived by their tricks, but boldly entered and demanded his father's bow. Four times they gave him other bows, which broke when he drew them. The fifth time it was really his father's bow he received. Taking Coyote and Badger outside, he knocked them together and killed them.

The wolf lodge

As he travelled across the prairie he stumbled on the habitation of the Wolves, and on entering the lodge he encountered his father's wife, who bade him hide before the monsters returned. By means of strategy he got the better of them, shot them all, and sailed away in a little boat with the woman. Here he fell into a deep sleep, and slept so long that at last his companion ventured to wake him. Very angry at being roused, he turned her into a pigeon and cast her out of the boat, while he himself, as a salmon, swam to the shore.

Near the edge of the water was a lodge, where dwelt five beautiful sisters. Salmon sat on the shore at a little distance, and took the form of an aged man covered with sores. When the eldest sister came down to speak to him he bade her carry him on her back to the lodge, but so loathsome a creature was he that she beat a hasty retreat. The second sister did likewise, and the third, and the fourth. But the youngest sister proceeded to carry him to the lodge, where he became again a young and handsome brave. He married all the sisters, but the youngest was his head-wife and his favourite.

The drowned child

On the banks of a river there dwelt a worthy couple with their only son, a little child whom they loved dearly. One day the boy wandered away from the lodge and fell into the water, and no one was near enough to rescue him. Great was the distress of the parents when the news reached them, and all his kindred were loud in their lamentations, for the child had been a favourite with everybody. The father especially showed signs of the deepest grief, and refused to enter his lodge till he should recover the boy. All night he lay outside on the bare ground, his cheek pillowed on his hand. Suddenly he heard a faint sound, far under the earth. He listened intently: it was the crying of his lost child! Hastily he gathered all his relatives round him, told them what he had heard, and besought them piteously to dig into the earth and bring back his son. This task they hesitated to undertake, but they willingly collected horses and goods in abundance, to be given to anyone who would venture.

Two men came forward who claimed to possess supernatural powers, and to them was entrusted the work of finding the child. The grateful father gave them a pipe filled with tobacco, and promised them all his possessions if their mission should succeed. The two gifted men painted their bodies, one making himself quite black, the other yellow. Going to the neighbouring river, they plunged into its depths, and so arrived at the abode of the Water-god. This being and his wife, having no children of their own, had adopted the Indian's little son who was supposed to have been drowned, and the two men, seeing him alive and well, were pleased to think that their task was as good as accomplished.

'The father has sent for his son,' they said. 'He has

commanded us to bring him back. We dare not return without him.'

'You are too late,' responded the Water-god. 'Had you come before he had eaten of my food he might safely have returned with you. But he wished to eat, and he has eaten, and now, alas! he would die if he were taken out of the water.'[1]

Sorrowfully the men rose to the surface and carried the tidings to the father.

'Alas!' they said, 'he has eaten in the palace of the Water-god. He will die if we bring him home.'

Nevertheless the father persisted in his desire to see the child.

'I must see him,' he said, and the two men prepared for a second journey, saying: 'If you get him back, the Water-god will require a white dog in payment.'

The Indian promised to supply the dog. The two men painted themselves again, the one black, the other yellow. Once more they dived through the limpid water to the palace of the god.

'The father must have his child,' they said. 'This time we dare not return without him.'

So the deity gave up the little boy, who was placed in his father's arms, dead. At the sight the grief of his kindred burst out afresh. However, they did not omit to cast a white dog into the river, nor to pay the men lavishly, as they had promised.

Later the parents lost a daughter in the same manner, but as she had eaten nothing of the food offered her under the water she was brought back alive, on payment by her relatives of a tribute to the Water-god of four white-haired dogs.

The Snake-wife

A certain chief advised his son to travel. Idling, he pointed out, was not the way to qualify for chieftainship.

---

[1] See p. 65, 'The Soul's Journey'.

'When I was your age,' said he, 'I did not sit still. There was hard work to be done. And now look at me: I have become a great chief.'

'I will go hunting, father,' said the youth. So his father furnished him with good clothing, and had a horse saddled for him.

The young man went off on his expedition, and by and by fell in with some elk. Shooting at the largest beast, he wounded it but slightly, and as it dashed away he spurred his horse after it. In this manner they covered a considerable distance, till at length the hunter, worn out with thirst and fatigue, reined in his steed and dismounted. He wandered about in search of water till he was well-nigh spent, but after a time he came upon a spring, and immediately improvised a song of thanksgiving to the deity, Wakanda, who had permitted him to find it. His rejoicing was somewhat premature, however, for when he approached the spring a snake started up from it. The youth was badly scared, and retreated to a safe distance without drinking. It seemed as though he must die of thirst after all. Venturing to look back after a time, he saw that the snake had disappeared, and very cautiously he returned. Again the snake darted from the water, and the thirsty hunter was forced to flee. A third return to the spring had no happier results, but when his thirst drove him to a fourth attempt the youth found, instead of a snake, a very beautiful woman. She offered him a drink in a small cup, which she replenished as often as he emptied it. So struck was he by her grace and beauty that he promptly fell in love with her. When it was time for him to return home she gave him a ring, saying: 'When you sit down to eat, place this ring on a seat and say, "Come, let us eat," and I will come to you.'

Having bidden her farewell, the young man turned his steps homeward, and when he was once more among his kindred he asked that food might be placed before him. 'Make haste,' said he, 'for I am very hungry.'

Quickly they obeyed him, and set down a variety of dishes.

When he was alone the youth drew the ring from his finger and laid it on a seat. 'Come,' he said, 'let us eat.'

Immediately the Snake-woman appeared and joined him at his meal. When she had eaten she vanished as mysteriously as she had come, and the disconsolate husband (for the youth had married her) went out of the lodge to seek her. Thinking she might be among the women of the village, he said to his father: 'Let the women dance before me.'

An old man was deputed to gather the women together, but not one of them so much as resembled the Snake-woman.

Again the youth sat down to eat, and repeated the formula which his wife had described to him. She ate with him as before, and vanished when the meal was over.

'Father,' said the young man, 'let the very young women dance before me.'

But the Snake-woman was not found among them either.

Another fleeting visit from his wife induced the chief's son to make yet another attempt to find her in the community.

'Let the young girls dance,' he said. Still the mysterious Snake-woman was not found.

One day a girl overheard voices in the youth's lodge, and, peering in, saw a beautiful woman sharing his meal. She told the news to the chief, and it soon became known that the chief's son was married to a beautiful stranger.

The youth, however, wished to marry a woman of his own tribe; but the maiden's father, having heard that the young man was already married, told his daughter that she was only being made fun of.

So the girl had nothing more to do with her wooer, who turned for consolation to his ring. He caused food to be brought, and placed the ring on a seat.

The ring unavailing
'Come,' he said, 'let us eat.'

There was no response; the Snake-woman would not appear.

The youth was greatly disappointed, and made up his mind to go in search of his wife.

'I am going a-hunting,' said he, and again his father gave him good clothes and saddled a horse for him.

When he reached the spot where the Snake-woman had first met him, he found her trail leading up to the spring, and beyond it on the other side. Still following the trail, he saw before him a very dilapidated lodge, at the door of which sat an old man in rags. The youth felt very sorry for the tattered old fellow, and gave him his fine clothes, in exchange for which he received the other's rags.

'You think you are doing me a good turn,' said the old man, 'but it is I who am going to do you one. The woman you seek has gone over the Great Water. When you get to the other shore talk with the people you shall meet there, and if they do not obey you send them away.'

In addition to the tattered garments, the old man gave him a hat, a sword, and a lame old horse.

At the edge of the Great Water the youth prepared to cross, while his companion seated himself on the shore, closed his eyes, and recited a spell. In a moment the young man found himself on the opposite shore. Here he found a lodge inhabited by two aged Thunder-men, who were apparently given to eating human beings. The young stranger made the discovery that his hat rendered him invisible, and he was able to move unseen among the creatures. Taking off his hat for a moment, he took the pipe from the lips of a Thunder-man and pressed it against the latter's hand.

'Oh,' cried the Thunder-man, 'I am burnt!'

But the youth had clapped on his hat and disappeared.

'It is not well,' said the Thunder-man gravely. 'A stranger has been here and we have let him escape. When our brother returns he will not believe us if we tell him the man has vanished.'

Shortly after this another Thunder-man entered with the body of a man he had killed. When the brothers told him their story he was quite sceptical.

'If I had been here,' said he, 'I would not have let him escape.'

As he spoke the youth snatched his pipe from him and pressed it against the back of his hand.

'Oh,' said the Thunder-man, 'I am burnt!'

'It was not I,' said one brother.

'It was not I,' said the other.

'It was I,' said the youth, pulling off his hat and appearing among them. 'What were you talking about among yourselves? Here I am. Do as you said.'

But the Thunder-men were afraid.

'We were not speaking,' they said, and the youth put on his hat and vanished.

'What will our brother say,' cried the three in dismay, 'when he hears that a man has been here and we have not killed him? Our brother will surely hate us.'

In a few minutes another Thunder-man came into the lodge, carrying the body of a child. He was very angry when he heard that they had let a man escape.

The youth repeated his trick on the newcomer – appeared for a moment, then vanished again. The fifth and last of the brothers was also deceived in the same manner.

Seeing that the monsters were now thoroughly frightened, the young man took off his magic hat and talked with them.

The finding of the Snake-wife

'You do wrong,' said he, 'to eat men like this. You should eat buffaloes, not men. I am going away. When I come back I will visit you, and if you are eating buffaloes you shall remain, but if you are eating men I shall send you away.'

The Thunder-men promised they would eat only buffaloes in future, and the young man went on his way to seek for the Snake-woman. When at last he came to the village where she dwelt he found she had married a man of another tribe, and in a great rage he swung the sword the magician had given him and slew her, and her husband, and the whole village, after which he returned the way he had come. When he reached the lodge of the Thunder-men he saw that they had not kept their promise to eat only buffaloes.

'I am going to send you above,' he said. 'Hitherto you have destroyed men, but when I have sent you away you shall give them cooling rain to keep them alive.'

So he sent them above, where they became the thunder-clouds.

Proceeding on his journey, he again crossed the Great Water with a single stride, and related to the old wizard all that had happened.

'I have sent the Thunder-men above, because they would not stop eating men. Have I done well?'

'Very well.'

'I have killed the whole village where the Snake-woman was, because she had taken another husband. Have I done well?'

'Very well. It was for that I gave you the sword.' The youth returned to his father, and married a very beautiful woman of his own village.

A subterranean adventure

There lived in a populous village a chief who had two sons and one daughter, all of them unmarried. Both the sons were in the habit of joining the hunters when they went to shoot buffaloes, and on one such occasion a large animal became separated from the herd. One of the chief's sons followed it, and when the pursuit had taken him some distance from the rest of the party the buffalo suddenly disappeared into a large pit. Before they could check themselves man and horse had plunged in after him. When the hunters returned the chief was greatly disturbed to learn that his son was missing. He sent the criers in all directions, and spared no pains to get news of the youth.

'If any person knows the whereabouts of the chief's son,' shouted the criers, 'let him come and tell.'

This they repeated again and again, till at length a young man came forward who had witnessed the accident.

'I was standing on a hill,' he said, 'and I saw the hunters, and I saw the son of the chief. And when he was on level ground he disappeared, and I saw him no more.'

He led the men of the tribe to the spot, and they scattered to look for signs of the youth. They found his trail; they followed it to the pit, and there it stopped.

They pitched their tents round the chasm, and the chief begged his people to descend into it to search for his son.

'If any man among you is brave and stout-hearted,' he said, 'let him enter.'

There was no response.

'If anyone will go I will make him rich.'

Still no one ventured to speak.

'If anyone will go I will give him my daughter in marriage.'

There was a stir among the braves and a youth came forward.

'I will go,' he said simply.

Ropes of hide were made by willing hands, and secured to a skin shaped to form a sort of bucket.

After arranging signals with the party at the mouth of the pit, the adventurous searcher allowed himself to be lowered. Once fairly launched in the Cimmerian depths his eyes became accustomed to the darkness, and he saw first the buffalo, then the horse, then the young brave, quite dead. He put the body of the chief's son into the skin bucket, and gave the signal for it to be drawn up to the surface. But so great was the excitement that when his comrades had drawn up the dead man they forgot about the living one still in the pit, and hurried away.

Lost underground

By and by the hero got tired of shouting, and wandered off into the darkness.

He had not gone very far when he met an old woman.

Respectfully addressing her, he told her his story and begged her to aid his return to his own country.

'Indeed I cannot help you,' she said, 'but if you will go to the house of the wise man who lives round the corner you may get what you want.'

Having followed the direction she had indicated with a withered finger, the youth shortly arrived at a lodge. Hungry and weary, he knocked somewhat impatiently. Receiving no answer, he knocked again, still more loudly. This time there was a movement inside the lodge, and a woman came to the door. She led him inside, where her husband sat dejectedly, not even rising to greet the visitor. Sadly the woman told him that they were mourning the death of their only son. At a word from his wife the husband looked at the youth. Eagerly he rose and embraced him.

'You are like our lost child,' said he. 'Come and we will make you our son.'

The young brave then told him his story.

'We shall treat you as our child,' said the Wise Man. 'Whatever you shall ask we will give you, even should you desire to leave us and to return to your own people.'

Though he was touched by the kindness of the good folk, there was yet nothing the youth desired so much as to return to his kindred.

'Give me,' said he, 'a white horse and a white mule.'

The return to Earth

The old man bade him go to where the horses were hobbled, and there he found what he had asked for. He also received from his host a magic piece of iron, which would enable him to obtain whatever he desired. The rocks even melted away at a touch of this talisman. Thus equipped, the adventurer rode off.

Shortly afterward he emerged in his own country, where the first persons he met were the chief and his wife, to whom he disclosed his identity, as he was by this time very much changed. They were sceptical at first, but soon they came to recognize him, and gave him a very cordial reception.

He married the chief's daughter, and was made head chieftain by his father-in-law. The people built a lodge for him in the centre of the encampment, and brought him many valuable presents of clothing and horses. On his marriage-day the criers were sent out to tell the people that on the following day no one must leave the village or do any work.

On the morrow all the men of the tribe went out to hunt buffaloes, and the young chieftain accompanied them. By means of his magic piece of iron he charmed many buffaloes, and slew more than did the others.

Now it so happened that the chief's remaining son was very jealous of his brother-in-law. He thought his father should have given him the chieftainship, and the honours accorded by the people to his young relative were exceedingly galling to him. So he made up his mind to kill the youth and destroy his beautiful white horse. But the sagacious beast told its master that someone was plotting against his life, and, duly warned, he watched in the stable every night.

On the occasion of a second great buffalo hunt the wicked schemer found his opportunity. By waving his robe he scared the buffaloes and caused them to close in on the youth and trample him to death. But when the herd had scattered and moved away there was no trace of the young brave or of his milk-white steed. They had returned to the Underworld.

White Feather the giant-killer

There once dwelt in the heart of a great forest an old man and his grandchild. So far as he could remember, the boy had never seen any human being but his grandfather, and though he frequently questioned the latter on the subject of his relatives he could elicit no information from him. The truth was that they had perished at the hands of six great giants. The nation to which the boy belonged had wagered their children against those of the giants that they would beat the latter in a race.

Unfortunately the giants won, the children of the rash Indians were forfeited, and all were slain with the exception of little Chácopee, whose grandfather had taken charge of him. The child learned to hunt and fish, and seemed quite contented and happy.

One day the boy wandered away to the edge of a prairie, where he found traces of an encampment. Returning, he told his grandfather of the ashes and tent-poles he had seen, and asked for an explanation. Had his grandfather set them there? The old man responded brusquely that there were no ashes or tent-poles: he had merely imagined them. The boy was sorely puzzled, but he let the matter drop, and next day he followed a different path. Quite suddenly he heard a voice addressing him as 'Wearer of the White Feather'. Now there had been a tradition in his tribe that a mighty man would arise among them wearing a white feather and performing prodigies of valour. But of this Chácopee as yet knew nothing; so he could only look about him in a startled way. Close by him stood a man, which fact was in itself sufficiently astonishing to the boy, who had never seen anyone but his grandfather; but to his further bewilderment he perceived that the man was made of wood from the breast downward, only the head being of flesh.

'You do not wear the white feather yet,' the curious stranger resumed, 'but you will by and by. Go home and sleep. You will dream of a pipe, a sack, and a large white feather. When you wake you will see these things by your side. Put the feather on your head and you will become a very great warrior. If you want proof, smoke the pipe and you will see the smoke turn into pigeons.'

He then proceeded to tell him who his parents were, and of the manner in which they had perished, and bade him avenge their death on the giants. To aid him in the accomplishment of this feat he gave him a magic vine which would be invisible to the giants, and with which he must trip them up when they ran a race with him.

Chácopee returned home, and everything happened as the Man of Wood had predicted. The old grandfather was greatly surprised to see a flock of pigeons issuing from the lodge, from which Chácopee also shortly emerged, wearing on his head a white feather. Remembering the prophecy, the old man wept to think that he might lose his grandchild.

In search of the giants

Next morning Chácopee set off in search of the giants, whom he found in a very large lodge in the centre of the forest. The giants had learned of his approach from the 'little spirits who carry the news'. Among themselves they mocked and scoffed at him, but outwardly they greeted him with much civility, which, however, in nowise deceived him as to their true feelings. Without loss of time they arranged a race between Chácopee and the youngest giant, the winner of which was to cut off the head of the other. Chácopee won, with the help of his magic vine, and killed his opponent. Next morning he appeared again, and decapitated another of his foes. This happened on five mornings. On the sixth he set out as usual, but was met by the Man of Wood, who informed him that on his way to the giants' lodge he would encounter the most beautiful woman in the world.

Chácopee's downfall

'Pay no attention to her,' he said earnestly. 'She is there for your destruction. When you see her turn yourself into an elk, and you will be safe from her wiles.'

Chácopee proceeded on his way, and sure enough before long he met the most beautiful woman in the world. Mindful of the advice he had received, he turned himself into an elk, but, instead of passing by, the woman, who was really the sixth giant, came up to him and reproached him with tears for taking the form of an elk when she had travelled so far to become his wife. Chácopee was so touched by her grief and beauty that he resumed his own shape and endeavoured to console her with gentle words and caresses. At last he fell asleep with his head in her lap. The beautiful woman once more became the cruel giant, and, seizing his axe, the monster broke Chácopee's back; then, turning him into a dog, he bade him rise and follow him. The white feather he stuck in his own head, fancying that magic powers accompanied the wearing of it.

In the path of the travellers there lay a certain village in which dwelt two young girls, the daughters of a chief. Having heard the prophecy concerning the wearer of the white feather, each made up her mind that she would marry him when he should appear. Therefore, when they saw a man approaching with a white feather in his hair the elder ran to meet him, invited him into her lodge, and soon after married him. The younger, who was gentle and timid, took the dog into her home and treated him with great kindness.

One day while the giant was out hunting he saw the dog casting a stone into the water. Immediately the stone became a beaver, which the dog caught and killed. The giant strove to emulate this feat, and was successful, but when he went home and ordered his wife to go outside and fetch the beaver only a stone lay by the door. Next day he saw the dog plucking a withered branch and throwing it on the ground, where it became a deer, which the dog slew. The Giant performed this magic feat also, but when his wife went to the door of the lodge to fetch the deer she saw only a piece of rotten wood. Nevertheless the giant had some success in the chase, and his wife repaired to the home of her father to tell him what a skilful hunter her husband was. She also spoke of the dog that lived with her sister, and his skill in the chase.

The transformation
The old chief suspected magic, and sent a deputation of youths and maidens to invite his younger daughter and her dog to visit him. To the surprise of the deputation, no dog was there, but an exceedingly handsome warrior. But alas! Chácopee

could not speak. The party set off for the home of the old chief, where they were warmly welcomed.

It was arranged to hold a general meeting, so that the wearer of the white feather might show his prowess and magical powers. First of all they took the giant's pipe (which had belonged to Chácopee), and the warriors smoked it one after the other. When it came to Chácopee's turn he signified that the giant should precede him. The giant smoked, but to the disappointment of the assembly nothing unusual happened. Then Chácopee took the pipe, and as the smoke ascended it became a flock of pigeons. At the same moment he recovered his speech, and recounted his strange adventures to the astounded listeners. Their indignation against the giant was unbounded, and the chief ordered that he should be given the form of a dog and stoned to death by the people.

Chácopee gave a further proof of his right to wear the white feather. Calling for a buffalo-hide, he cut it into little pieces and strewed it on the prairie. Next day he summoned the braves of the tribe to a buffalo-hunt, and at no great distance they found a magnificent herd. The pieces of hide had become buffaloes. The people greeted this exhibition of magic art with loud acclamations, and Chácopee's reputation was firmly established with the tribe.

Chácopee begged the chief's permission to take his wife on a visit to his grandfather, which was readily granted, and the old man's gratitude and delight more than repaid them for the perils of their journey.

How the Rabbit caught the Sun
Once upon a time the Rabbit dwelt in a lodge with no one but his grandmother to keep him company. Every morning he went hunting very early, but no matter how early he was he always noticed that someone with a very long foot had been before him and had left a trail. The Rabbit resolved to discover the identity of the hunter who forestalled him, so one fine morning he rose even earlier than usual, in the hope of

encountering the stranger. But all to no purpose, for the mysterious one had gone, leaving behind him, as was his wont, the trail of the long foot.

This irritated the Rabbit profoundly, and he returned to the lodge to consult with his grandmother.

'Grandmother,' he grumbled, 'although I rise early every morning and set my traps in the hope of snaring game, someone is always before me and frightens the game away. I shall make a snare and catch him.'

'Why should you do so?' replied his grandmother. 'In what way has he harmed you?'

'It is sufficient that I hate him,' replied the querulous Rabbit, and departed. He secreted himself among the bushes and waited for nightfall. He had provided himself with a stout bowstring, which he arranged as a trap in the place where the footprints were usually to be found. Then he went home, but returned very early to examine his snare.

When he arrived at the spot he discovered that he had caught the intruder, who was, indeed, no less a personage than the Sun. He ran home at the top of his speed to acquaint his grandmother with the news. He did not know what he had caught, so his grandmother bade him seek the forest once more and find out. On returning he saw that the Sun was in a violent passion.

'How dare you snare me!' he cried angrily. 'Come hither and untie me at once!'

The Rabbit advanced cautiously, and circled round him in abject terror. At last he ducked his head and, running in, cut the bowstring which secured the Sun with his knife. The Sun immediately soared upward, and was quickly lost to sight. And the reason why the hair between the Rabbit's shoulders is yellow is that he was scorched there by the great heat which came from the Sun-god when he loosed him.

How the Rabbit slew the devouring hill

In the long ago there existed a hill of ogre-like propensities which drew people into its mouth and devoured them. The

Rabbit's grandmother warned him not to approach it upon any account.

But the Rabbit was rash, and the very fact that he had been warned against the vicinity made him all the more anxious to visit it. So he went to the hill, and cried mockingly: 'Pahe-Wathahuni, draw me into your mouth! Come, devour me!'

But Pahe-Wathahuni knew the Rabbit, so he took no notice of him.

Shortly afterward a hunting-party came that way, and Pahe-Wathahuni opened his mouth, so that they took it to be a great cavern, and entered. The Rabbit, waiting his chance, pressed in behind them. But when he reached Pahe-Wathahuni's stomach the monster felt that something disagreed with him, and he vomited the Rabbit up.

Later in the day another hunting-party appeared, and Pahe-Wathahuni again opened his capacious gullet. The hunters entered unwittingly, and were devoured. And once more the Rabbit entered, disguised as a man by magic art. This time the cannibal hill did not eject him. Imprisoned in the monster's entrails, he saw in the distance the whitened bones of folk who had been devoured, the still undigested bodies of others, and some who were yet alive.

Mocking Pahe-Wathahuni, the Rabbit said: 'Why do you not eat? You should have eaten that very fat heart.' And, seizing his knife, he made as if to devour it. At this Pahe-Wathahuni set up a dismal howling; but the Rabbit merely mocked him, and slit the heart in twain. At this the hill split asunder, and all the folk who had been imprisoned within it went out again, stretched their arms to the blue sky, and hailed the Rabbit as their deliverer; for it was Pahe-Wathahuni's heart that had been sundered.

The people gathered together and said: 'Let us make the Rabbit chief.' But he mocked them and told them to be gone, that all he desired was the heap of fat the hill had concealed within its entrails, which would serve him and his old grandmother for food for many a day. With that the Rabbit went homeward, carrying the fat on his back, and he and his grandmother rejoiced exceedingly and were never in want again.

*   *   *

The Sioux were one of the largest tribes in North America, with an aboriginal population of 30,000 and divided into three main sub-groups, the Eastern (Santee), Central (Yankton) and Western (Teton) Sioux. The tribe called itself Dakota in the Santee dialect, Nakota in the Yankton dialect, and Lakota in the Teton dialect. 'Sioux' derives from the Chippewa word *nadowessioux*, meaning 'enemy' or 'snake'. Truly, the Sioux were the opponents of many, after they descended onto the Plains from the wooded headwaters of the Mississippi in the sixteenth century, under pressure from the Ojibwa (themselves on a chain of displacement caused by the advance of European settlement) and under enticing lure of the horses now wandering free and for the taking on the ocean of grass. The Sioux were both hunters and farmers, with the exception of the western bands which became fully committed to a nomadic, horse-riding, buffalo-hunting lifestyle. The Sioux, it is thought, lost their 'digging sticks' and were horsed in the 1720s.

The religion of the Sioux, like other nomads of the Plains, centred on an omniscient Sky God, Watan Tanka, who watched and directed the animals of the earth, not least the buffalo on which the livelihood of the prairie tribes depended. Watan Tanka was also, as discussed previously, an all pervasive force. Between the Sky God and Earth there was a realm in which planets and stars, thunder and eagles, rainbows and lightning lived, all of them spirits that could come down to earth in human form. These spirits lived a mirror existence to the Sioux, travelling with their skin-tents (teepees) across the sky. Since the sky spirits could, among other things bring drought or alter the migration of the buffalo, the Sioux sought to propitiate them by offerings of pain, including in the famous Sun Dance.

The Sun Dance was the most important religious ceremony of the Sioux and other Plains Indians of North America, and for the nomads, an occasion when the bands congregated to reaffirm their religious beliefs about the universe and their part in it through ritual and ceremony. Traditionally, a Sun Dance was held by each tribe once a year in late spring when the buffalo themselves gathered after the Plains winter. The festival usually lasted for eight days, and culminated in the building of a symbolic lodge to represent man's home, at the centre of which was a pole denoting the distance between earth and heaven. Distinguished warriors who vowed their lives to the Sun danced around this pole, to which they were attached by ropes that were skewered through their breasts. The artist and explorer George Catlin witnessed a Sioux Sun Dance in c. 1843:

An inch or more of the flesh on each shoulder, or each breast was taken up between the thumb and finger by the man who held the knife in his right hand; and the knife, which had been ground sharp on both edges, and then hacked and notched with the blade of another, to make it produce as much pain as possible, was forced through the flesh below the fingers, and being withdrawn, was followed with a splint or skewer, from the other, who held a bunch of such in his left hand, and was ready to force them through the wound. There were then two cords lowered down from the top of the lodge, which were fastened to these splints or skewers, and they instantly began to haul him up; he was thus raised until his body was suspended from the ground where he rested, until the knife and a splint were passed through the flesh or integuments in a similar manner on each arm below the shoulder, below the elbow, on the thighs, and below the knees.

In some instances they remained in a reclining position on the ground until this painful operation was finished, which was performed, in all instances, exactly on the same parts of the body and limbs; and which, in its progress, occupied some five or six minutes.

Each one was then instantly raised with the cords, until the weight of his body was suspended by them, and then, while the blood was streaming down their limbs, the bystanders hung upon the splints each man's appropriate shield, bow and quiver, &c; and in many instances, the skull of a buffalo with the horns on it, was attached to each lower arm and each lower leg, for the purpose, probably, of preventing by their great weight, the struggling, which might otherwise have taken place to their disadvantage whilst they were hung up.

Fixing their eyes on the sun, the warriors followed its path across the sky all day, slowly circling the pole. If any Sun Dancers succeeded on staying on their feet until sunset they became medicine-men.

The Sun Dance ceremony (Wiwanyag Wachipi) was only one of the seven sacred rites brought the Sioux by the mythical White Buffalo Calf Woman, the others being: the Sweat Lodge Ceremony (Inipi); the Keeping of the Soul Ceremony (Wanagi Yuhapi), the Making of Relatives Ceremony (Hunkapi), Preparing a Girl for Womanhood (Ishnata Awicalowan), the Throwing the Ball ceremony (Tapa Wanka Yap), and the Vision Quest (Hanblecheyapi). She also brought the *canupa*, the sacred red pipe, and taught the Sioux the pipe ceremony to send their prayers to Wakan Tanka.

In this sextet of rites the Vision Quest stands alongside the Sun Dance ceremony for its importance. Although used primarily by healers and shamans, the Vision Quest was not exclusively reserved for them. The purpose of a vision quest was for the participant to receive guidance from the spirit world, by experiencing a dream containing guidance from their particular animal spirit, ancestors, or cultural figures from Sioux mythology. As with all other aspects of Sioux, the Vision Quest was highly formalized, requiring the seeker to venture to an isolated spot, and fast and pray until the vision came.

Until the middle of the nineteenth century, the Sioux had little contact with the white man; however, when the Europeans did penetrate the plains by the railroad, buffalo hunters, and pioneer settlers, the Sioux early determined on resistance. The Sioux Wars, which ended at Wounded Knee Creek in 1890 after twenty eight years of fighting, were the bloodiest of the Indian Wars west of the Mississippi. They witnessed too, the greatest defeat inflicted on the US Army by the Native Peoples.

In June 1876 Sitting Bull, already a medicine-man, subjected himself to a Sun Dance. During the ritual the Huncpapa leader saw a vision of a great number of white soldiers falling from the sky upside down. And so predicted a great victory by his people over the blue coats.

On 25–26 June of that year, the victory duly came when the Lakota, allied with Arapaho and Northern Cheyenne, defeated the US 7th Cavalry under George Armstrong Custer at Little Big Horn – or to the Indians, Greasy Grass. Custer and his entire command of 264 men were killed.

But it was a pyrrhic victory for the Native People. An enraged American nation demanded vengeance. All reservations on the northern plains were placed under military control, while Congress passed a law compelling the free Sioux to hand over their Black Hills, plus the Powder River and Big Horn ranges and move onto reservations. The Black Hills were a sacred site; in some Sioux creation myths, it was on the Black Hill that the only human survivor of the great flood, a girl, was taken by the rescuing eagle Wanblee. Her twin children by Wanblee became the Sioux nation.

Throughout the remainder of 1876 the Indians still at large on the plains were harassed by the US Army's most redoubtable Indian-fighting officers, Crook, Mackenzie and Miles. Over the next twelve months small bands of Sioux and Cheyenne limped into US forts and agencies, until only the Huncpapa Sioux bands of Sitting Bull and Gall were left roaming free. To evade the US Army they slipped over the border to Canada. While they hoped to find sanctuary, they found only starvation and disease. Crossing back into the USA, they too surrendered. At midday on 19 July 1881, starving and dressed in rags, Sitting Bull rode into Fort Burford in Dakota. With him were just 143 followers.

It was another medicine man who prompted the last spasm of violence between the Sioux and the Army. Just before dawn on New Year's Day 1889 a Paiute shaman, Wovoka, dreamed that he visited the Great Spirit in heaven, who told him that a time was coming when dead tribesmen would be resurrected and the buffalo restored to the plains, and the Great Spirit return. If the Indians were virtuous and performed the proper ritual dance – the Ghost Dance – they could hasten the coming of the new order. This was not the first outbreak of the Ghost Dance; it had originated in California/ Nevada c. 1870, following a vision by the Paiute prophet Wodziwob, but led by Wovoka (the son of Wodziwob's assistant) it found mass Indian appeal – especially amongst the disillusioned Sioux, who adapted the Ghost Dance to their Sun Dance. They also added two dangerous twists to Wovoka's essentially peaceful message, adding the belief that the dances would bring about a landslide that would destroy the white men, while the 'Ghost Shirts' worn by the dancers would repel bullets. By mid-autumn 1890 the Sioux were in something akin to religious frenzy, with thousands of them participating in Ghost Dances, shuffling round in great circles until, exhausted, they reached a delirium where they saw the dead come to life. The movement culminated in the massacre of the Sioux by alarmed US soldiers at Wounded Knee on 29 December 1890.

6

MYTHS AND LEGENDS OF THE PAWNEES

The Pawnees, or Caddoan Indians
The Caddoan stock, the principal representatives of which are the Pawnees, are now settled in Oklahoma and North Dakota. From the earliest period they seem to have been cultivators of the soil, as well as hunters, and skilled in the arts of weaving and pottery-making. They possessed an elaborate form of religious ceremonial. The following myths well exemplify how strongly the Pawnee was gifted with the religious sense.

The sacred bundle
A certain young man was very vain of his personal appearance, and always wore the finest clothes and richest adornments he could procure. Among other possessions he had a down feather of an eagle, which he wore on his head when he went to war, and which possessed magical properties. He was unmarried, and cared nothing for women, though doubtless there was more than one maiden of the village who would not

have disdained the hand of the young hunter, for he was as brave and good-natured as he was handsome.

One day while he was out hunting with his companions – the Indians hunted on foot in those days – he got separated from the others, and followed some buffaloes for a considerable distance. The animals managed to escape, with the exception of a young cow, which had become stranded in a mud-hole. The youth fitted an arrow to his bow, and was about to fire, when he saw that the buffalo had vanished and only a young and pretty woman was in sight. The hunter was rather perplexed, for he could not understand where the animal had gone to, nor where the woman had come from. However, he talked to the maiden, and found her so agreeable that he proposed to marry her and return with her to his tribe. She consented to marry him, but only on condition that they remained where they were. To this he agreed, and gave her as a wedding gift a string of blue and white beads he wore round his neck.

One evening when he returned home after a day's hunting he found that his camp was gone, and all round about were the marks of many hoofs. No trace of his wife's body could he discover, and at last, mourning her bitterly, he returned to his tribe.

Years elapsed, and one summer morning as he was playing the stick game with his friends a little boy came toward him, wearing round his neck a string of blue and white beads.

'Father,' he said, 'mother wants you.'

The hunter was annoyed at the interruption.

'I am not your father,' he replied. 'Go away.'

The boy went away, and the man's companions laughed at him when they heard him addressed as 'father', for they knew he was a woman-hater and unmarried.

However, the boy returned in a little while. He was sent away again by the angry hunter, but one of the players now suggested that he should accompany the child and see what he wanted. All the time the hunter had been wondering where he had seen the beads before. As he reflected he saw a buffalo cow and calf running across the prairie, and suddenly he remembered.

Taking his bow and arrows, he followed the buffaloes, whom he now recognized as his wife and child. A long and wearisome journey they had. The woman was angry with her husband, and dried up every creek they came to, so that he feared he would die of thirst, but the strategy of his son obtained food and drink for him until they arrived at the home of the buffaloes. The big bulls, the leaders of the herd, were very angry, and threatened to kill him. First, however, they gave him a test, telling him that if he accomplished it he should live. Six cows, all exactly alike, were placed in a row, and he was told that if he could point out his wife his life would be spared. His son helped him secretly, and he succeeded. The old bulls were surprised, and much annoyed, for they had not expected him to distinguish his wife from the other cows. They gave him another test. He was requested to pick out his son from among several calves. Again the young buffalo helped him to perform the feat. Not yet satisfied, they decreed that he must run a race. If he should win they would let him go. They chose their fastest runners, but on the day set for the race a thin coating of ice covered the ground, and the buffaloes could not run at all, while the young Indian ran swiftly and steadily, and won with ease.

The magic feather

The chief bulls were still angry, however, and determined that they would kill him, even though he had passed their tests. So they made him sit on the ground, all the strongest and fiercest bulls round him. Together they rushed at him, and in a little while his feather was seen floating in the air. The chief bulls called on the others to stop, for they were sure that he must be trampled to pieces by this time. But when they drew back there sat the Indian in the centre of the circle, with his feather in his hair.

It was, in fact, his magic feather to which he owed his escape, and a second rush which the buffaloes made had as little effect on him. Seeing that he was possessed of magical powers, the buffaloes made the best of matters and welcomed him into their camp, on condition that he would bring them gifts from his tribe. This he agreed to do.

When the Indian returned with his wife and son to the village people they found that there was no food to be had; but the buffalo-wife produced some meat from under her robe, and they ate of it. Afterward they went back to the herd with gifts, which pleased the buffaloes greatly. The chief bulls, knowing that the people were in want of food, offered to return with the hunter. His son, who also wished to return, arranged to accompany the herd in the form of a buffalo, while his parents went ahead in human shape. The father warned the people that they must not kill his son when they went to hunt buffaloes, for, he said, the yellow calf would always return leading more buffaloes.

By and by the child came to his father saying that he would no more visit the camp in the form of a boy, as he was about to lead the herd eastward. Ere he went he told his father that when the hunters sought the chase they should kill the yellow calf and sacrifice it to Atius Tiráwa, tan its hide, and wrap in the skin an ear of corn and other sacred things. Every year they should look out for another yellow calf, sacrifice it, and keep a piece of its fat to add to the bundle. Then when food was scarce and famine threatened the tribe the chiefs should gather in council and pay a friendly visit to the young buffalo, and he would tell Tiráwa of their need, so that another yellow calf might be sent to lead the herd to the people.

When he had said this the boy left the camp. All was done as he had ordered. Food became plentiful, and the father became a chief, greatly respected by his people. His buffalo-wife, however, he almost forgot, and one night she vanished. So distressed was the chief, and so remorseful for his neglect of her, that he never recovered, but withered away and died.

But the sacred bundle was long preserved in the tribe as a magic charm to bring the buffalo.

Their sacred bundles were most precious to the Indians, and were guarded religiously. In times of famine they were opened by the priests with much ceremony. The above story is given to explain the origin of that belonging to the Pawnee tribe.

The Bear-man

There was once a boy of the Pawnee tribe who imitated the ways of a bear; and, indeed, he much resembled that animal. When he played with the other boys of his village he would pretend to be a bear, and even when he grew up he would often tell his companions laughingly that he could turn himself into a bear whenever he liked.

His resemblance to the animal came about in this manner. Before the boy was born his father had gone on the war-path, and at some distance from his home had come upon a tiny bear-cub. The little creature looked at him so wistfully and was so small and helpless that he could not pass by without taking notice of it. So he stooped and picked it up in his arms, tied some Indian tobacco round its neck, and said: 'I know that the Great Spirit, Tiráwa, will care for you, but I cannot go on my way without putting these things round your neck to show that I feel kindly toward you. I hope that the animals will take care of my son when he is born, and help him to grow up a great and wise man.' With that he went on his way.

On his return he told his wife of his encounter with the Little Bear, told her how he had taken it in his arms and looked at it and talked to it. Now there is an Indian superstition that a woman, before a child is born, must not look fixedly at or think much about any animal, or the infant will resemble it. So when the warrior's boy was born he was found to have the ways of a bear, and to become more and more like that animal the older he grew. The boy, quite aware of the resemblance, often went away by himself into the forest, where he used to pray to the Bear.

The Bear-man slain

On one occasion, when he was quite grown up, he accompanied a war party of the Pawnees as their chief. They travelled a considerable distance, but ere they arrived at any village they fell into a trap prepared for them by their enemies, the Sioux. Taken completely off their guard, the Pawnees, to the number of about forty, were slain to a man. The part of the country in which this incident took place was rocky and cedar-clad and harboured many bears, and the bodies of the dead Pawnees lay in a ravine in the path of these animals. When they came to the body of the Bear-man a she-bear instantly recognized it as that of their benefactor, who had sacrificed smokes to them, made songs about them, and done them many a good turn during his lifetime. She called to her companion and begged him to do something to bring the Bear-man to life again. The other protested that he could do nothing. 'Nevertheless,' he added, 'I will try. If the sun were shining I might succeed, but when it is dark and cloudy I am powerless.'

The resuscitation of the Bear-man

The sun was shining but fitfully that day, however. Long intervals of gloom succeeded each gleam of sunlight. But the two bears set about collecting the remains of the Bear-man, who was indeed sadly mutilated, and, lying down on his body, they worked over him with their magic medicine till he showed signs of returning life. At length he fully regained consciousness, and, finding himself in the presence of two bears, was at a loss to know what had happened to him. But the animals related how they had brought him to life, and the sight of his dead comrades lying around him recalled what had gone before. Gratefully acknowledging the service the bears had done him, he accompanied them to their den. He was still very weak, and frequently fainted, but ere long he recovered his strength and was as well as ever, only he had no hair on his head, for the Sioux had scalped him. During his sojourn with the bears he was taught all the things that they knew – which was a great deal, for all Indians know that the bear is one of the wisest of animals. However, his host begged him not to regard the wonderful things he did as the outcome of his own strength, but to give thanks to Tiráwa, who had made the bears and had given them their wisdom and greatness. Finally he told the Bear-man to return to his people, where he would become a very great man, great in war and in wealth. But at the same time he must not forget the bears, nor cease to imitate them, for on that would depend much of his success.

'I shall look after you,' he concluded. 'If I die, you shall die; if I grow old, you shall grow old along with me. This tree' – pointing to a cedar – 'shall be a protector to you. It never becomes old; it is always fresh and beautiful, the gift of Tiráwa. And if a thunderstorm should come while you are at home throw some cedar-wood on the fire and you will be safe.'

Giving him a bear-skin cap to hide his hairless scalp, the Bear then bade him depart.

Arrived at his home, the young man was greeted with amazement, for it was thought that he had perished with the rest of the war party. But when he convinced his parents that it was indeed their son who visited them, they received him joyfully. When he had embraced his friends and had been congratulated by them on his return, he told them of the bears, who were waiting outside the village. Taking presents of Indian tobacco, sweet-smelling clay, buffalo-meat, and beads, he returned to them, and again talked with the he-bear. The latter hugged him, saying: 'As my fur has touched you, you will be great; as my hands have touched your hands, you will be fearless; and as my mouth touches your mouth, you will be wise.' With that the bears departed.

True to his words, the animal made the Bear-man the greatest warrior of his tribe. He was the originator of the Bear Dance, which the Pawnees still practise. He lived to an advanced age, greatly honoured by his people.

*   *   *

'Pawnee' is likely derived from the Caddoan *pariki*, meaning 'horn', referring to the distinctive manner in which Pawnee males wore the scalplock, coiled over the forehead in a queue bound with hide and stiffened with grease. Essentially, the Pawnee were a confederation of Hokan-Caddoan speakers, who migrated north-eastwards until they settled on the Platte River, Nebraska. In prehistoric times the chief tribes were the Skidi, the Pitahauerat, the Chaui, and the Kitkachaki. They practised both hunting and farming, cultivating pumpkins, beans and maize, the last being regarded as a sacred gift, and honoured as 'mother'.

The complex religion of the Pawnee was based on following the rules and rhythms of the gods of the big sky over their Plains heartland. They were the most assiduous astronomers of the Plains.

In Pawnee mythology Tiráwa was the Great Spirit and creator, who positioned the star-gods in the sky. When Bright Star (the Evening Star) and Great Star (the Morning Star, probably Venus, but possibly Mars) mated, woman was created. Then Sakuru (the Sun) copulated with Pah (the Moon), and man was born. A number of lesser, earthly gods, usually identified with animals, acted as the aids of human and intermediaries with the higher gods. Worship of the heavenly gods centred on sacred objects donated by them, called by Europeans sacred or medicine bundles. More accurately, the bundles were portable shrines, which formed the centre of a ceremony. (One of the most famous of the Plains bundles was the 'Sacred Canoe' of the Mandan tribe, which was made of ancient willow boards believed to have come from a raft on which first humans survived the flood.) Each village possessed one of these bundles, which was in the care of a hereditary keeper, but its relevant ceremonies were in the charge of a priesthood open to all eligible aspirants.

For the Pawnee almost every aspect of existence was dominated by celestial observation, divination and worship, so much so that each lodge had four poles to represent the four stars that held up the heavens. From the movement of the stars the Pawnee priests sitting in an earth lodge that served as an observatory (it had an especially enlarged smoke-hole and a large eastwards facing door) determined when to sow seeds in the spring and when to harvest the crop in the autumn. But for the crops to grow, for the buffalo to appear on the grassland required the pleasing of the gods in ceremony. A series of ceremonies related to the coming of life and its increase began with the first thunder in spring and closed with the harvest of 'Mother Corn' in the autumn. For the Skidi Pawnee the apex of the ceremonial cycle was the Morning Star ceremony in which a young girl was ritually sacrificed. The echo of the creation story, in which the male Morning Star overcomes the female Evening Star to produce life on earth, is obvious.

The ceremony was held in April. Until recently white scholars believed that the ceremony was irregular; however new research suggests that the ceremony was an annual event. It began with warriors of the Skidi Pawnee capturing a young girl, usually around the age of fourteen, from a neighbouring tribe. Brought to the Skidi's village, the girl was ritually prepared for slaughter, a process that could take months. The actual ceremony is well described by the ethnologist Ralph Linton in his report 'The Sacrifice to the Morning Star by the Skidi Pawnee', Leaflet No. 6, Field Museum of Natural History, Chicago, 1922:

> The priest built two little fires of sweet grass, one to the east, and the other to the west of the fireplace. The girl was taken to the eastern fire, undressed, and her body bathed in the smoke. Her guardian then painted her whole body red and dressed her in a black skirt and robe which were kept in the sacred bundle between sacrifices. The man who had captured the girl then went to the altar, and was dressed by the priest in another costume, also kept in the bundle. He was given black leggings and moccasins, his face and hair were painted red, and a fan-shaped head-dress of twelve eagle feathers was attached to his hair in such a way that it stood out straight over the back of his head at right angles to his body. This was the costume in which the Morning Star usually appeared in visions, and with its assumption the captor seems to have become a personification of that deity.
>
> After these ceremonies had been performed, the captor left the

lodge and passed through the village, entering every lodge and warning those who were to take part in the ceremony to come to the chief's lodge. Each family gave him a little red and black paint and certain other objects which were needed in the ceremony. When he had completed the circuit, he returned to the chief's lodge, and errand men were sent out to invite the chiefs and priests of all the villages to come to the ceremony. The Pawnee village was a social as well as a geographical unit. Several villages might live together. Each of the priests and chiefs had his prescribed place in the circle, while the space behind them was packed with spectators. So great was the eagerness of the people to see the ceremony that many of them tore holes in the roof and walls of the lodge, leaving it a complete wreck.

When all the invited guests had taken their places, the chief priest told the priests of the Four Direction bundles to go into the woods and bring back four thick poles about twelve feet long. The priest of the northeast was to bring an elm; he of the northwest, a box elder; he of the southwest, a cotton wood; and he of the southeast, a willow. When they had returned, the four poles were laid on the fireplace with their ends together so that they formed a cross whose arms pointed to the four directions. The poles had to be long enough to last for the entire four days of the ceremony, and as they burned, they were pushed in toward the centre, the cross being always maintained.

The ceremonies which followed are not fully known, but they consisted of many songs and dances, with feasting, and continued for three days and nights. During this time, and for the three days after the slaying of the sacrifice, the ordinary rules of conduct were set aside, and the priests announced to the people that if any man approached any woman during this period, she was to go with him willingly, that the tribe might increase.

Toward morning of each night, the representative of the northeast village danced around the fireplace, and taking the pole brought by the priest of that direction, pointed its glowing end toward the girl's body. This was repeated by the representative of the other directions in turn, but the girl's body was never touched with the brand. Indeed, the girl was treated with the greatest respect and consideration throughout the ceremony. She was told that the entire performance was given in her honour, and everything was done to lull her suspicions and keep her in a pleasant frame of mind.

On the afternoon of the fourth day, the chief priest selected four men from the Four Band village to secure the materials for the scaffold. Under the direction of the leader of the war party which had captured the girl, they went to the nearest thick timber and searched until they found a hackberry tree near the centre of the grove. At this tree they made an offering of smoke to the gods, and then went northeast from it to find an elm, northwest to find a box elder, southwest to find a cotton wood, and southeast to find a willow. These were to serve for the lower cross-bars of the scaffold. They then went east until they found an elm and a cotton wood large enough to be used as uprights. Finally, they went west and cut a willow to serve as the top cross-bar.

When the men had departed to search for the timber, the priests sang a song describing their actions. At its conclusion the chief priest sent the two chiefs of the Morning Star village, accompanied by a warrior, to select the site of the scaffold. This had to be some place near the village which had, to the east of it, a depression or ravine large enough to conceal several men. When the chiefs had made their choice, the warrior accompanying them gave his war-cry. An errand man had been stationed outside the lodge to listen for this, and as soon as he heard and reported it, the priest of the Skull bundle ran to the place, bearing the sacred bow and two arrows. The two chiefs had stationed themselves at the points where the uprights of the scaffold were to stand, and the priest shot an arrow into the ground in front of each of them, thus marking the place where the hole was to be dug. Between these arrows four priests then dug away the soil to a depth of about a foot, making a rectangular pit approximately the size of the wrapper of a sacred bundle when fully unfolded. The floor of the excavation was then covered with white, downy feathers. This pit was called knsaru, and represented the garden which the Evening Star kept in the west, or, according to another account, the reproductive organs of the Evening Star. The white feathers with which it was lined symbolized the milk of women and animals and the juice of young corn. After the pit had been completed, the holes for the uprights of the scaffold were dug by two young girls.

While the digging was going on, the party sent after the timbers had returned. The two uprights of the scaffold were first erected, then each cross-bar was tied on by a warrior from the village of the direction which it represented. Before tying it, the warrior would recount some deed. One would say, 'I made a sacrifice of meat and carried it to the priest on my back. After the ceremony was performed, the priest whispered to me, "You, young man, have brought meat here by means of the pack string. You will have an opportunity before the summer is over to lasso a pony in the enemy's country. The gods now know you. Do not fear to go on the war path I went." We found a village, and others became afraid and ran. I went east by myself and found the enemy's horses. I went among them and found one with an eagle-wing fan tied to its tail. I captured it and rode home. Since then I have made many sacrifices.' The top cross-bar was tied by two men each of whom had made a sacrifice, but these did not recount any adventures in war.

It is probable that the scaffold was also painted at this time, although the ceremonies connected with the painting are not remembered. The two uprights were painted red and black, the former symbolizing day, and the latter, night. The lowest cross-bar was black, and symbolized the northeast; and its animal guardian, the bear. The second was red, symbolizing: the southeast and the wolf. The third was yellow, symbolizing the northwest and the mountain lion; and the fourth white, symbolizing the southwest and the wildcat. The top cross-bar represented the west, and was painted blue or black and white, symbolizing clouds and rain.

By the time the scaffold was completed, it was about sunset, and the people dispersed. All spectators were sent out of the lodge, and the door was closed. The chief priest then drew upon the floor of the lodge four circles, one for each of the world quarters, and outlined them with white downy feathers. Each of these circles represented a region penetrated by the Morning Star in his search for the Evening Star and also the magic animal which he had overcome there. The white feathers symbolized the foam about their mouths when they attacked him. When the circles had been made, the spectators were readmitted, and the priests sang a song descriptive of the journey of the Morning Star, while the chief priest danced around the lodge with a war club, destroying the circles one by one. When the song was finished, he straightened up and said, 'Chiefs, priests, warriors, old men, I have destroyed the regions once controlled by the mysterious woman who wanted darkness forever. These animals were under her control, when the Morning Star travelled in darkness looking for her. She placed an obstacle in the southeast, which was controlled by the wolf. The Morning Star destroyed this obstacle, but preserved the mysterious animal. He continued his journey, travelled to the southwest, and again met an obstacle which he destroyed, but preserved the animal, a wildcat. He continued his journey, and when he came to the northwest, he again met an obstacle. He destroyed it, but preserved the animal, a mountain lion. He went on to the northeast, and again destroyed an obstacle, but preserved its guardian, the bear. In the centre of the earth in darkness he found the woman, conquered her, touched her with his war club, and turned her into the earth. The Morning Star then called the mysterious animals to him and said, 'You beings are now under my control. Stand in the places where I found you, and watch over the people who shall be placed upon the earth and guard them. All powers you have you shall keep. You shall exist as long as the earth lasts. You are now placed as upright posts so that you will always hold up the heavens. Priests, chiefs, warriors, old men, I have this night followed the journey of the Morning Star. We will not forget these beings which he placed in the four directions, for he promised that they should partake of all offerings which the people made to the heavens. Let us begin singing the songs given to us by Mother White Star in the west (the Evening Star).'

When the chief priest had finished his speech, all began to sing the prescribed songs, resting and smoking informally after each. Like most ceremonial songs, these were long, with many repetitions, and were often obscure in meaning. As each song was finished, a tally stick, taken from a bunch kept in the sacred bundle, was laid down. The idea underlying this part of the ritual seems to have been that the girl at first belonged to the people and to the world of human affairs, but that, as each song was sung, she became more removed from them until, when the last tally was laid down, she had been won from the people, like a prize in a game, and belonged to the gods.

The singing usually lasted until about two hours before dawn. A priest then climbed on the roof of the lodge and announced to the people that the girl was about to be prepared for the sacrifice, and that it was time for everyone to set out for the scaffold. The chief priest undressed the girl, went through the motions of washing her and combing her hair, and painted the right half of her body red and the left half black. Her skirt was then replaced, black moccasins were put on her feet, and a black robe fastened around her shoulders.

Lastly a head-dress of twelve black-tipped eagle feathers, arranged like a fan, was fastened on her head.

When the girl had been dressed, all resumed their seats and sang another song at the conclusion of which she was told to rise; and two men, chosen to lead her to the scaffold, came forward and placed thongs around her wrists. All then passed out of the lodge, with the girl in the lead and the priests following behind chanting.

The rate at which the procession moved toward the scaffold depended largely upon the disposition of the girl. Everything was done to conceal the truth from her, and force was not used unless absolutely necessary. If she mounted the scaffold of her own free will, it was considered an especially auspicious omen. The procession was timed to reach the scaffold a few minutes before the Morning Star rose, so that the men who tied her to it could complete their work and leave her alone when the star appeared.

While the girl was being tied to the scaffold, the men chosen for the last rites had assembled in the ravine to the east of it, where they were concealed from her view. A small fire was kindled there, and they prepared their paraphernalia. At the moment the Morning Star appeared, two men came forward bearing firebrands. They were dressed as priests, and had owl skins hung from their necks, showing that they represented the messengers of the Morning Star.

They took their places on either side of the girl, and with their brands touched her lightly in the groin and armpit. They then returned to the ravine, and a third man ran out, carrying the bow from the Skull bundle and a sacred arrow made for the sacrifice. As he came, he gave his war cry, and the people called to him and encouraged him as though he was attacking an enemy. Coming close to the girl, he sent his arrow through her heart, and ran back to the ravine. This part was usually taken by the man who had captured her. A fourth man then came forward with the club from the Morning Star bundle and struck the girl on the head.

A fire had been kindled to the southeast of the scaffold, and as soon as the girl was dead, her guardian came forward with a flint knife, and her captor with the dried heart and tongue of a buffalo. The guardian mounted the scaffold and cut open the body, while the captor held the meat below and caught the blood. The guardian thrust his hand into the thoracic cavity and painted his face with the blood. Sometimes he is said to have removed her liver and given it to the members of the Bear Medicine Society, who cut it into small pieces and ate it to acquire magical powers. The blood-soaked meat was burned on the fire near the scaffold as an offering to all the gods.

When these rites had been performed, the men among the spectators gave their war cries and crowded forward to shoot arrows into the body. It was thought desirable that as many arrows should be shot as there were males in the tribe, and boys too young to draw a bow were helped by their fathers or mothers. When each man had shot his arrow, the spectators dispersed and returned to the villages where feasting and dancing continued for three days.

The priests, the guardian, and those intimately connected with the ceremony remained at the scaffold. When the crowd had gone, the guardian removed the arrows from the body one by one and handed them to an assistant who divided them into four bundles and laid these bundles northeast, northwest, southeast, and southwest of the fireplace. The body was then taken down and carried a short distance to the east of the scaffold, where it was laid face down. The sacred arrow was drawn from its heart and laid upon it. All then returned to the village, and the place was avoided for some time.

It was believed that the soul of the girl left her body at the moment she was struck with the club and went straight to Tiráwa, who sent it to the Morning Star. The Morning Star clothed it with flint from his fireplace in the dawn and placed it among the stars in the heavens. Her body was thought to be not like ordinary bodies. Even after her death it possessed life. Things would be born from it, and the earth would be fertilized by it.

The Morning Star ceremony was a religious duty, rather than voyeuristic, sadistic entertainment. Even so, it sickened many Pawnee and in 1818, Petalesharo, and his father Chief Latelesharo, rescued the Comanche victim and banished live sacrifices thereafter. They were not entirely successful. Human sacrifice at Morning Star ceremonies continued intermittently until 1838.

7

MYTHS AND LEGENDS OF THE NORTH AND NORTH-WEST INDIANS

Haida demi-gods

There is a curious Haida story told of the origin of certain supernatural people, who are supposed to speak through the *shamans*, or medicine-men, and of how they got their names.

Ten brothers went out to hunt with their dogs. While they were climbing a steep rocky mountain a thick mist enveloped them, and they were compelled to remain on the heights. By and by they made a fire, and the youngest, who was full of mischief, cast his bow in it. When the bow was burnt the hunters were astonished to see it on the level ground below. The mischievous brother thereupon announced his intention of following his weapon, and by the same means. Though the others tried hard to dissuade him, he threw himself on the blazing fire, and was quickly consumed. His brothers then beheld him on the plain vigorously exhorting them to follow his example. One by one they did so, some boldly, some timorously, but all found themselves at last on the level ground.

As the brothers travelled on they heard a wren chirping, and they saw that one of their number had a blue hole in his heart. Farther on they found a hawk's feather, which they tied in the hair of the youngest. They came at length to a deserted village on the shores of an inlet, and took possession of one of the huts. For food they ate some mussels, and having satisfied their hunger they set out to explore the settlement. Nothing rewarded their search but an old canoe, moss-grown and covered with nettles. When they had removed the weeds and scraped off the moss they repaired it, and the mischievous one who had led them into the fire made a bark bailer for it, on which he carved the representation of a bird. Another, who had in his hair a bunch of feathers, took a pole and jumped into the canoe. The rest followed, and the canoe slid away from the shore. Soon they came in sight of a village where a *shaman* was performing.

Attracted by the noise and the glow of the fire, the warrior at the bow stepped ashore and advanced to see what was going on. 'Now,' he heard the *shaman* say; 'the chief Supernatural-being-who-keeps-the-bow-off is coming ashore.' The Indian was ashamed to hear himself thus mistakenly, as he thought, referred to as a supernatural being, and returned to the canoe. The next one advanced to the village. 'Chief Hawk-hole is coming ashore,' said the *shaman*. The Indian saw the blue hole at his heart, and he also was ashamed, and returned to his brothers. The third was named Supernatural-being-on-whom-the-daylight-rests, the fourth Supernatural-being-on-the-water-on-whom-is-sunshine, the fifth Supernatural-puffin-on-the-water, the sixth Hawk-with-one-feather-sticking-out-of-the-water, the seventh Wearing-clouds-around-his-neck, the eighth Supernatural-being-with-the-big-eyes, the ninth Supernatural-being-lying-on-his-back-in-the-canoe, and the eldest, and last, Supernatural-being-half-of-whose-words-are-raven. Each as he heard his name pronounced returned to the canoe. When they had all heard the *shaman*, and were assembled once more, the eldest brother said, 'We have indeed become supernatural people,' which was quite true, for by burning themselves in the fire they had reached the Land of Souls.[1]

The supernatural sister

The ten brothers floated round the coast till they reached another village. Here they took on board a woman whose arms had been accidentally burned by her husband, who mistook them for the arms of someone embracing his wife. The woman was severely burned and was in great distress. The supernatural brothers made a crack in the bottom of the canoe and told the woman to place her hands in it. Her wounds were immediately healed. They called her their sister, and seated her in the canoe to bail out the water. When they came to the Djū, the stream near which dwelt Fine-weather-woman,[2] the latter came and talked to them, repeating the names which the *shaman* had given them, and calling their sister Supernatural-woman-who-does-the-bailing.

'Paddle to the island you see in the distance,' she added. 'The wizard who lives there is he who paints those who are to become supernatural beings. Go to him and he will paint you. Dance four nights in your canoe and you will be finished.'

They did as she bade them, and the wizard dressed them in a manner becoming to their position as supernatural beings. He gave them dancing hats, dancing skirts, and puffin-beak rattles, and drew a cloud over the outside of their canoe.

The birth of Sîñ

The Haida of British Columbia and the Queen Charlotte Islands possess a striking myth relating to the incarnation of the Sky-god, their principal deity. The daughter of a certain chief went one day to dig in the beach. After she had worked

---

[1] This myth would appear to explain the fancied resemblance between smoke and the shadowy or vaporous substance of which spirits or ghosts are supposed to be composed.

[2] See page 256.

some time she dug up a cockle-shell. She was about to throw it to one side when she thought she heard a sound coming from it like that of a child crying. Examining the shell, she found a small baby inside. She carried it home and wrapped it in a warm covering, and tended it so carefully that it grew rapidly and soon began to walk.

She was sitting beside the child one day when he made a movement with his hand as if imitating the drawing of a bowstring, so to please him she took a copper bracelet from her arm and hammered it into the shape of a bow, which she strung and gave him along with two arrows. He was delighted with the tiny weapon, and immediately set out to hunt small game with it. Every day he returned to his foster-mother with some trophy of his skill. One day it was a goose, another a woodpecker, and another a blue jay.

One morning he awoke to find himself and his mother in a fine new house, with gorgeous door-posts splendidly carved and illuminated in rich reds, blues, and greens. The carpenter who had raised this fine building married his mother, and was very kind to him. He took the boy down to the sea-shore, and caused him to sit with his face looking toward the expanse of the Pacific. And so long as the lad looked across the boundless blue there was fair weather.

His father used to go fishing, and one day Sîñ – for such was the boy's name – expressed a wish to accompany him. They obtained devil-fish for bait, and proceeded to the fishing-ground, where the lad instructed his father to pronounce certain magical formula, the result of which was that their fishing-line was violently agitated and their canoe pulled round an adjacent island three times. When the disturbance stopped at last they pulled in the line and dragged out a monster covered with piles of halibut.

One day Sîñ went out wearing a wren-skin. His mother beheld him rise in stature until he soared above her and brooded like a bank of shining clouds over the ocean. Then he descended and donned the skin of a blue jay. Again he rose over the sea, and shone resplendently. Once more he soared upward, wearing the skin of a woodpecker, and the waves reflected a colour as of fire.

Then he said: 'Mother, I shall see you no more. I am going away from you. When the sky looks like my face painted by my father there will be no wind. Then the fishing will be good.'

His mother bade him farewell, sadly, yet with the proud knowledge that she had nurtured a divinity. But her sorrow increased when her husband intimated that it was time for him to depart as well. Her supernatural son and husband, however, left her a portion of their power. For when she sits by the inlet and loosens her robe the wind scurries down between the banks and the waves are ruffled with tempest; and the more she loosens the garment the greater is the storm. They call her in the Indian tongue Fine-weather-woman. But she dwells mostly in the winds, and when the cold morning airs draw up from the sea landward she makes an offering of feathers to her glorious son. The feathers are flakes of snow, and they serve to remind him that the world is weary for a glimpse of his golden face.

Master-carpenter and South-east

A Haida myth relates how Master-carpenter, a supernatural being, went to war with South-east (the south-east wind) at Sqa-i, the town lying farthest south on the Queen Charlotte Islands. The south-east wind is particularly rude and boisterous on that coast, and it was with the intention of punishing him for his violence that Master-carpenter challenged him. First of all, however, he set about building a canoe for himself. The first one he made split, and he was obliged to throw it away. The second also split, notwithstanding the fact that he had made it stouter than the other. Another and another he built, making each one stronger than the last, but every attempt ended in failure, and at last, exceedingly vexed at his unskilfulness, he was on the point of giving the task up. He would have done so, indeed, but for the intervention of Greatest Fool. Hitherto Master-carpenter had been trying to form two canoes from one log by means of wedges. Greatest Fool stood watching him for a time, amused at his clumsiness, and finally showed him that he ought to use bent wedges. And though he was perhaps the last person from whom Master-carpenter might expect to learn anything, the unsuccessful builder of canoes adopted the suggestion, with the happiest results. When at length he was satisfied that he had made a good canoe he let it down into the water, and sailed off in search of South-east.

By and by he floated right down to his enemy's abode, and when he judged himself to be above it he rose in the canoe and flung out a challenge. There was no reply. Again he called, and this time a rapid current began to float past him, bearing on its surface a quantity of seaweed. The shrewd Master-carpenter fancied he saw the matted hair of his enemy floating among the seaweed. He seized hold of it, and after it came South-east. The latter in a great passion began to call on his nephews to help him. The first to be summoned was Red-storm-cloud. Immediately a deep red suffused the sky. Then the stormy tints died away, and the wind rose with a harsh murmur. When this wind had reached its full strength another was summoned, Taker-off-of-the-tree-tops. The blast increased to a hurricane, and the tree-tops were blown off and carried away and fell thickly about the canoe, where Master-carpenter was making use of his magic arts to protect himself. Again another wind was called up, Pebble-rattler, who set the stones and sand flying about as he shrieked in answer to the summons. Maker-of-the-thick-sea-mist came next, the spirit of the fog which strikes terror into the hearts of those at sea, and he was followed by a numerous band of other nephews, each more to be dreaded than the last. Finally Tidal-wave came and covered Master-carpenter with water, so that he was obliged to give in. Relinquishing his hold on South-east, he managed to struggle to the shore. It was said by some that

South-east died, but the *shamans*, who ought to know, say that he returned to his own place.

South-east's mother was named Tomorrow, and the Indians say that if they utter that word they will have bad weather, for South-east does not like to hear his mother's name used by anyone else.

The Beaver and the Porcupine

This is the tale of a feud between the beavers and the porcupines. Beaver had laid in a plentiful store of food, but Porcupine had failed to do so, and one day when the former was out hunting the latter went to his lodge and stole his provision. When Beaver returned he found that his food was gone, and he questioned Porcupine about the matter.

'Did you steal my food?' he asked.

'No,' answered Porcupine. 'One cannot steal food from supernatural beings, and you and I both possess supernatural powers.'

Of course this was mere bluff on the part of Porcupine, and it in nowise deceived his companion.

'You stole my food!' said Beaver angrily, and he tried to seize Porcupine with his teeth. But the sharp spines of the latter disconcerted him, though he was not easily repulsed. For a time he fought furiously, but at length he was forced to retreat, with his face covered with quills from his spiny adversary. His friends and relatives greeted him sympathetically. His father summoned all the Beaver People, told them of the injuries his son had received, and bade them avenge the honour of their clan. The people at once repaired to the abode of Porcupine, who, from the fancied security of his lodge, heaped insults and abuse on them. The indignant Beaver People pulled his house down about his ears, seized him, and carried him, in spite of his threats and protests, to a desolate island, where they left him to starve.

It seemed to Porcupine that he had not long to live. Nothing grew on the island save two trees, neither of which was edible, and there was no other food within reach. He called loudly to his friends to come to his assistance, but there was no answer. In vain he summoned all the animals who were related to him. His cries never reached them.

When he had quite given up hope he fancied he heard something whisper to him: 'Call upon Cold-weather, call upon North-wind.' At first he did not understand, but thought his imagination must be playing tricks with him. Again the voice whispered to him: 'Sing North songs, and you will be saved.' Wondering much, but with hope rising in his breast, Porcupine did as he was bidden, and raised his voice in the North songs. 'Let the cold weather come,' he sang, 'let the water be smooth.'

The finding of Porcupine

After a time the weather became very cold, a strong wind blew from the north, and the water became smooth with a layer of ice. When it was sufficiently frozen to bear the weight of the Porcupine People they crossed over to the island in search of their brother. They were greatly rejoiced to see him, but found him so weak that he could hardly walk, and he had to be carried to his father's lodge.

When they wanted to know why Beaver had treated him so cruelly he replied that it was because he had eaten Beaver's food. The Porcupine People, thinking this a small excuse, were greatly incensed against the beavers, and immediately declared war on them. But the latter were generally victorious, and the war by and by came to an inglorious end for the porcupines. The spiny tribe still, however, imagined that they had a grievance against Beaver, and plotted to take his life. They carried him to the top of a tall tree, thinking that as the beavers could not climb he would be in the same plight as their brother had been on the island. But by the simple expedient of eating the tree downward from the top Beaver was enabled to return to his home.

The devil-fish's daughter

A Haida Indian was sailing in his canoe with his two children
and his wife at low tide. They had been paddling for some
time, when they came to a place where some devil-fish stones
lay, and they could discern the devil-fish's tracks and see
where its food was lying piled up. The man, who was a
shaman, landed upon the rocks with the intention of finding
and killing the devil-fish, but while he was searching for it the
monster suddenly emerged from its hole and dragged him
through the aperture into its den. His wife and children,
believing him to be dead, paddled away.

The monster which had seized the man was a female
devil-fish, and she dragged him far below into the precincts of
the town where dwelt her father, the devil-fish chief, and there
he married the devil-fish which had captured him. Many years
passed, and at length the man became homesick and greatly
desired to see his wife and family once more. He begged the
chief to let him go, and after some demur his request was
granted.

The *shaman* departed in one canoe, and his wife, the
devil-fish's daughter, in another. The canoes were magical, and
sped along of themselves. Soon they reached his father's town
by the aid of the enchanted craft. He had brought much
wealth with him from the devil-fish kingdom, and with this
he traded and became a great chief. Then his children found
him and came to him. They were grown up, and to celebrate
his home-coming he held a great feast. Five great feasts he
held, one after another, and at each of them his children and
his human wife were present.

But the devil-fish wife began to pine for the sea-life. One
day while her husband and she sat in his father's house he
began to melt. At the same time the devil-fish wife disappeared betwixt the planks of the flooring. Her husband then
assumed the devil-fish form, and a second soft, slimy body
followed the first through the planks. The devil-fish wife and
her husband had returned to her father's realm.

This myth, of course, approximates to those of the seal-wives who escape from their mortal husbands, and the swan- and other bird-brides who, pining for their natural environment, take wing one fine day and leave their earth-mates.

Chinook tales

The Chinooks formerly dwelt on Columbia River, from the Dalles to its mouth, and on the Lower Willamette. With the exception of a few individuals, they are now extinct, but their myths have been successfully collected and preserved. They were the natives of the north-west coast, cunning in bargaining, yet dwelling on a communal plan. Their chief physical characteristic was a high and narrow forehead artificially flattened. Concerning this people Professor Daniel Wilson says:

'The Chinooks are among the most remarkable of the flat-headed Indians, and carry the process of cranial distortion to the greatest excess. They are in some respects a superior race, making slaves of other tribes, and evincing considerable skill in such arts as are required in their wild forest and coast life. Their chief war-implements are bows and arrows, the former made from the yew-tree, and the latter feathered and pointed with bone. Their canoes are hollowed out of the trunk of the cedar-tree, which attains to a great size in that region, and are frequently ornamented with much taste and skill. In such a canoe the dead Chinook chief is deposited, surrounded with all the requisites for war, or the favourite occupations of life: presenting a correspondence in his sepulchral rites to the ancient pagan viking, who, as appears alike from the contents of the Scandinavian *Skibssaetninger* and from the narratives of the sagas, was interred or consumed in his war-galley, and the form of that favourite scene of ocean triumphs perpetuated in the earthwork that covered his ashes.'

The story of Blue Jay and Ioi

The Chinooks tell many stories of Blue Jay, the tricky, mischievous totem-bird, and among these tales there are three which are concerned with his sister Ioi. Blue Jay, whose disposition resembled that of the bird he symbolized, delighted in tormenting Ioi by deliberately misinterpreting her commands, and by repeating at every opportunity his favourite phrase, 'Ioi is always telling lies'.

In the first of the trilogy Ioi requested her brother to take a wife from among the dead, to help her with her work in house and field. To this Blue Jay readily assented, and he took for his spouse a chieftain's daughter who had been recently buried. But Ioi's request that his wife should be an old one he disregarded.

'Take her to the Land of the Supernatural People,' said Ioi, when she had seen her brother's bride, 'and they will restore her to life.'

Blue Jay set out on his errand, and after a day's journey arrived with his wife at a town inhabited by the Supernatural Folk.

'How long has she been dead?' they asked him, when he stated his purpose in visiting them.

'A day,' he replied.

The Supernatural People shook their heads.

'We cannot help you,' said they. 'You must travel to the town where people are restored who have been dead for a day.'

Blue Jay obediently resumed his journey, and at the end of another day he reached the town to which he had been directed, and told its inhabitants why he had come.

'How long has she been dead?' they asked.

'Two days,' said he.

'Then we can do nothing,' replied the Supernatural Folk, 'for we can only restore people who have been dead one day. However, you can go to the town where those are brought to life who have been dead two days.'

Another day's journey brought Blue Jay and his wife to the third town. Again he found himself a day late, and was directed to a fourth town, and from that one to yet another. At the fifth town, however, the Supernatural People took pity on him, and recovered his wife from death. Blue Jay they made a chieftain among them, and conferred many honours upon him.

After a time he got tired of living in state among the Supernatural People, and returned home.

When he was once more among his kindred his young brother-in-law, the chief's son, learned that his sister was alive and married to Blue Jay.

Hastily the boy carried the news to his father, the old chief, who sent a message to Blue Jay demanding his hair in payment for his wife. The messenger received no reply, and the angry chief gathered his people round him and led them to Blue Jay's lodge. On their approach Blue Jay turned himself into a bird and flew away, while his wife swooned. All the efforts of her kindred could not bring the woman round, and they called on her husband to return. It was in vain, however: Blue Jay would not come back, and his wife journeyed finally to the Land of Souls.

The marriage of Ioi

The second portion of the trilogy relates how the Ghost-people, setting out one night from the Shadow-land to buy a wife, took Ioi, the sister of Blue Jay, who disappeared before morning. After a year had elapsed her brother decided to go in search of her. But though he inquired the way to the Ghost-country from all manner of birds and beasts, he got a satisfactory answer from none of them, and would never have arrived at his destination at all had he not been carried thither at last by supernatural means.

In the Ghost-country he found his sister, surrounded by heaps of bones, which she introduced to him as his relatives by marriage. At certain times these relics would attain a semblance of humanity, but instantly became bones again at the sound of a loud voice.

A fishing expedition in Shadow-land

At his sister's request Blue Jay went fishing with his young brother-in-law. Finding that when he spoke in a loud tone he caused the boy to become a heap of bones in the canoe, Blue Jay took a malicious pleasure in reducing him to that condition. It was just the sort of trick he loved to play.

The fish they caught were nothing more than leaves and branches, and Blue Jay, in disgust, threw them back into the water. But, to his chagrin, when he returned his sister told him that they were really fish, and that he ought not to have flung them away. However, he consoled himself with the reflection, 'Ioi is always telling lies.'

Besides teasing Ioi, he played many pranks on the inoffensive Ghosts. Sometimes he would put the skull of a child on the shoulders of a man, and vice versa, and take a mischievous delight in the ludicrous result when they came 'alive'.

On one occasion, when the prairies were on fire, Ioi bade her brother extinguish the flames. For this purpose she gave him five buckets of water, warning him that he must not pour it on the burning prairies until he came to the fourth of them. Blue Jay disobeyed her, as he was wont to do, and with dire results, for when he reached the fifth prairie he found he had no water to pour on it. While endeavouring to beat out the flames he was so seriously burned that he died, and returned to the Ghosts as one of themselves, but without losing his mischievous propensities.

Blue Jay and Ioi go visiting

The third tale of the trilogy tells how Blue Jay and Ioi went to visit their friends. The Magpie was the first to receive the visitors, and by means of magic he provided food for them. Putting a salmon egg into a kettle of boiling water, he placed the kettle on the fire, and immediately it was full of salmon eggs, so that when they had eaten enough Blue Jay and Ioi were able to carry a number away.

On the following day the Magpie called for the kettle they had borrowed. Blue Jay tried to entertain his visitor in the same magical fashion as the latter had entertained him. But his attempt was so ludicrous that the Magpie could not help laughing at him.

The pair's next visit was to the Duck, who obtained food for them by making her children dive for trout. Again there was twice as much as they could eat, and Blue Jay and Ioi carried away the remainder on a mat. During the return visit of the Duck Blue Jay tried to emulate this feat also, using Ioi's children instead of the ducklings. His attempt was again unsuccessful.

The two visited in turn the Black Bear, the Beaver, and the Seal, all of whom similarly supplied refreshment for them in a magical manner. But Blue Jay's attempts at imitating these creatures were futile.

A visit to the Shadows concluded the round, and the adventurers returned home.

The heaven-sought bride

A brother and sister left destitute by the death of their father, a chief of the Chinooks, were forced to go hunting sea-otters every day to obtain a livelihood. As they hunted the mists came down, and with them the Supernatural People, one of whom became enamoured of the girl. The ghostly husband sent his wife gifts of stranded timber and whale-meat, so that when her son was born she might want for nothing. The mischievous Blue Jay, hearing of the abundance of meat in the young chief's house, apprised his own chief of the circumstance and brought all the village to share it. The Supernatural People, annoyed that their bounty should be thus misused, abducted the young chief's sister, along with her child.

The woman's aunt, the Crow, gathered many potentilla and other roots, placed them in her canoe, and put out to sea. She came to the country of the Supernatural Folk, and when they saw her approaching they all ran down to the beach to greet her. They greedily snatched at the roots she had brought with her and devoured them, eating the most succulent and throwing away those that were not so much to their taste. The Crow soon found her niece, who laughed at her for bringing such fare to such a land.

'Do you think they are men that you bring them potentilla roots?' she cried. 'They only eat certain of the roots you have fetched hither because they have magical properties. The next time you come bring the sort of roots they seized upon – and you can also bring a basket of potentilla roots for me.'

The whale-catcher
She then called upon a dog which was gambolling close at hand.

'Take this dog,' she said to the Crow. 'It belongs to your grand-nephew. When you come near the shore say, "Catch a whale, dog," and see what happens.'

The Crow bade farewell to her niece, and, re-entering her canoe, steered for the world of mortals again. The dog lay quietly in the stern. When about half-way across the Crow recollected her niece's advice.

'Catch a whale, good dog,' she cried encouragingly.

The dog arose, and at that moment a whale crossed the path of the canoe. The dog sank his teeth in the great fish, and the frail bark rocked violently.

'Hold him fast, good fellow!' cried the Crow excitedly. 'Hold him fast!' But the canoe tossed so dangerously and shipped so much water that in a great fright she bade the dog let go. He did so, and lay down in the stern again.

The Crow arrived at the world of men once more, and after landing turned round to call her wonderful dog ashore. But no trace of him was visible. He had disappeared.

Once more the Crow gathered many roots and plants, taking especial care to collect a good supply of the sort the Supernatural People were fond of, and gathering only a small basket of potentilla. For the second time she crossed over to the land of the Divine Beings, who, on espying her succulent cargo, devoured it at once. She carried the potentilla roots to her niece, and when in her house noticed the dog she had received and lost. Her niece informed her that she should not have ordered the animal to seize the whale in mid-ocean, but should have waited until she was nearer the land. The Crow departed once more, taking the dog with her.

When they approached the land of men the Crow called to the animal to catch a whale, but it stirred not. Then the Crow poured some water over him, and he started up and killed a large whale, the carcass of which drifted on to the beach, when the people came down and cut it up for food.

The Chinooks visit the Supernaturals

Some time after this the young chief expressed a desire to go to see his sister, so his people manned a large canoe and set forth. The chief of the Supernatural People, observing their approach, warned his subjects that the mortals might do something to their disadvantage, and by means of magic he covered the sea with ice. The air became exceedingly cold, so cold, indeed, that Blue Jay, who had accompanied the young chief, leapt into the water. At this one of the Supernatural People on shore laughed and cried out: 'Ha, ha! Blue Jay has drowned himself!' At this taunt the young chief in the canoe arose, and, taking the ice which covered the surface of the sea, cast it away. At sight of such power the Supernatural Folk became much alarmed.

The chief and his followers now came to land, and, walking up the beach, found it deserted. Not a single Supernatural Person was to be seen. Espying the chief's house, however, the Chinooks approached it. It was guarded by sea-lions, one at each side of the door. The chief cautiously warned his people against attempting an entrance. But the irrepressible Blue Jay tried to leap past the sea-lions, and got severely bitten for his pains. Howling dismally, he rushed seaward. The young chief, annoyed that the Divine Beings should have cause for laughter against any of his people, now darted forward, seized the monsters one in each hand, and hurled them far away.

At this second feat the Supernatural Folk set up a hubbub of rage and dismay, which was turned to loud laughter when Blue Jay claimed the deed as his, loudly chanting his own praises. The Chinooks, taking heart, entered the lodge. But the Supernatural Folk vanished, leaving only the chief's sister behind.

The Chinooks had had nothing to eat since leaving their own country, and Blue Jay, who, like most worthless folk, was always hungry, complained loudly that he was famished. His brother Robin sullenly ordered him to be silent. Suddenly a Supernatural Being with a long beak emerged from under the bed, and, splitting wood with his beak, kindled a large fire.

'Robin,' said Blue Jay, 'that is the spirit of our great-grandfather's slave.'

Soon the house was full of smoke, and a voice was heard calling out for the Smoke-eater. An individual with an enormous belly made his appearance, and swallowed all the smoke, so that the house became light. A small dish was brought, containing only one piece of meat. But the mysterious voice called for the Whale-meat-cutter, who appeared, and sliced the fragment so with his beak that the plate was full to overflowing. Then he blew upon it, and it became a large canoe full of meat, which the Chinooks finished, much to the amazement of the Supernatural People.

The four tests
After a while a messenger from the Divine People approached and asked to be told whether the Indians would accept a challenge to a diving contest, the defeated to lose their lives. This was agreed to, and Blue Jay was selected to dive for the Chinooks. He had taken the precaution of placing some bushes in his canoe, which he threw into the water before diving with his opponent, a woman. When his breath gave out he came to the surface, concealing his head under the floating

bushes. Then he sank into the water again, and cried to his opponent: 'Where are you?' 'Here I am,' she replied. Four times did Blue Jay cunningly come up for breath, hidden beneath the bushes, and on diving for the last time he found the woman against whom he was pitted lying at the bottom of the sea, almost unconscious. He took his club, which he had concealed beneath his blanket, and struck her on the nape of the neck. Then he rose and claimed the victory.

The Supernatural People, much chagrined, suggested a climbing contest, to which Blue Jay readily agreed, but he was warned that if he was beaten he would be dashed to pieces. He placed upright a piece of ice which was so high that it reached the clouds. The Supernaturals matched a chipmunk against him. When the competitors had reached a certain height Blue Jay grew tired, so he used his wings and flew upward. The chipmunk kept her eyes closed and did not notice the deception. Blue Jay hit her on the neck with his club, so that she fell, and Blue Jay was adjudged the winner.

A shooting match was next proposed by the exasperated Supernaturals, in which the persons engaged were to shoot at one another. This the Chinooks won by taking a beaver as their champion and tying a millstone in front of him. A sweating match was also won by the Chinooks taking ice with them into the superheated caves where the contest took place.

As a last effort to shame the Chinooks the Divine People suggested that the two chiefs should engage in a whale-catching contest. This was agreed to, and the Supernatural chief's wife, after warning them, placed Blue Jay and Robin under her armpits to keep them quiet. As they descended to the beach, she said to her brother: 'Four whales will pass you, but do not harpoon any until the fifth appears.'

Robin did as he was bid, but the woman had a hard time in keeping the curious Blue Jay hidden. The four whales passed, but the young chief took no heed. Then the fifth slid by. He thrust his harpoon deep into its blubber, and cast it ashore. The Supernatural chief was unsuccessful in his attempts, and so the Chinooks won again. On the result being known Blue Jay could no longer be restrained, and, falling from under the woman's arm, he was drowned.

On setting out for home the chief was advised to tie Robin's blanket to a magical rope with which his sister provided him. When the Chinooks were in the middle of the ocean the Supernatural People raised a great storm to encompass their destruction. But the charm the chief's sister had given them proved efficacious, and they reached their own land in safety.

Blue Jay's death may be regarded as merely figurative, for he appears in many subsequent Chinook tales.

This myth is undoubtedly one of the class which relates to the 'harrying of Hades'. See the remarks at the conclusion of the myth of 'The Thunderer's son-in-law'.

The Thunderer's son-in-law

There were five brothers who lived together. Four of them were accustomed to spend their days in hunting elk, while the fifth, who was the youngest, was always compelled to remain at the camp. They lived amicably enough, save that the youngest grumbled at never being able to go to the hunting. One day as the youth sat brooding over his grievance the silence was suddenly broken by a hideous din which appeared to come from the region of the doorway. He was at a loss to understand the cause of it, and anxiously wished for the return of his brothers. Suddenly there appeared before him a man of gigantic size, strangely apparelled. He demanded food, and the frightened boy, remembering that they were well provided, hastily arose to satisfy the stranger's desires. He brought out an ample supply of meat and tallow, but was astonished to find that the strange being lustily called for more. The youth, thoroughly terrified, hastened to gratify the monster's craving, and the giant ate steadily on, hour after hour, until the brothers returned at the end of the day to discover the glutton devouring the fruits of their hunting. The monster appeared not to heed the brothers, but, anxious to satisfy his enormous appetite, he still ate. A fresh supply of meat had been secured, and this the brothers placed before him. He continued to gorge himself throughout the night and well into the next day. At last the meat was at an end, and the brothers became alarmed. What next would the insatiable creature demand? They approached him and told him that only skins remained, but he replied: 'What shall I eat, grandchildren, now that there are only skins and you?' They did not appear to understand him until they had questioned him several times. On realizing that the glutton meant to devour them, they determined to escape, so, boiling the skins, which they set before him, they fled through a hole in the hut. Outside they placed a dog, and told him to send the giant in the direction opposite to that which they had taken. Night fell, and the monster slept, while the dog kept a weary vigil over the exit by which his masters had escaped. Day dawned as the giant crept through the gap. He asked the dog: 'Which way went your masters?' The animal replied by setting his head in the direction opposite to the true one. The giant observed the sign, and went on the road the dog indicated. After proceeding for some distance he found that the young men could not have gone that way, so he returned to the hut, to find the dog still there. Again he questioned the animal, who merely repeated his previous movement. The monster once more set out, but, unable to discover the fugitives, he again returned. Three times he repeated these fruitless journeys. At last he succeeded in getting on to the right path, and shortly came within sight of the brothers.

The Thunderer

Immediately they saw their pursuer they endeavoured to outrun him, but without avail. The giant gained ground, and soon overtook the eldest, whom he slew. He then made for the others, and slew three more. The youngest only was left. The lad hurried on until he came to a river, on the bank of which was a man fishing, whose name was the Thunderer.

This person he implored to convey him to the opposite side. After much hesitation the Thunderer agreed, and, rowing him over the stream, he commanded the fugitive to go to his hut, and returned to his nets. By this time the monster had gained the river, and on seeing the fisherman he asked to be ferried over also. The Thunderer at first refused, but was eventually persuaded by the offer of a piece of twine. Afraid that the boat might capsize, the Thunderer stretched himself across the river, and commanded the giant to walk over his body. The monster, unaware of treachery, readily responded, but no sooner had he reached the Thunderer's legs than the latter set them apart, thus precipitating him into the water. His hat also fell in after him. The Thunderer now gained his feet, and watched the giant drifting helplessly down the stream. He did not wish to save the monster, for he believed him to be an evil spirit. 'Okulam [Noise of Surge] will be your name,' he said. 'Only when the storm is raging will you be heard. When the weather is very bad your hat will also be heard.' As he concluded this prophecy the giant disappeared from sight. The Thunderer then gathered his nets together and went to his hut. The youth whom he had saved married his daughter, and continued to remain with him. One day the youth desired to watch his father-in-law fishing for whales. His wife warned him against doing so. He paid no heed to her warning, however, but went to the sea, where he saw the Thunderer struggling with a whale. His father-in-law flew into a great rage, and a furious storm arose. The Thunderer looked toward the land, and immediately the storm increased in fury, with thunder and lightning, so he threw down his dip-net and departed for home, followed by his son-in-law.

Storm-raising
On reaching the house the young man gathered some pieces of coal and climbed a mountain. There he blackened his face, and a high wind arose which carried everything before it. His father-in-law's house was blown away, and the Thunderer,

seeing that it was hopeless to attempt to save anything from the wreck, commanded his daughter to seek for her husband. She hurried up the mountain-side, where she found him, and told him he was the cause of all the destruction, but concluded: 'Father says you may look at him tomorrow when he catches whales.' He followed his wife back to the valley and washed his face. Immediately he had done so the storm abated. Going up to his father-in-law, he said: 'Tomorrow I shall go down to the beach, and you shall see me catching whales.' Then the Thunderer and he rebuilt their hut. On the following morning they went down to the sea-shore together. The young man cast his net into the sea. After a little while a whale entered the net. The youth quickly pulled the net toward him, reached for the whale, and flung it at the feet of his father-in-law. Thunderer was amazed, and called to him: 'Ho, ho, my son-in-law, you are just as I was when I was a young man.'

The beast comrades

Soon after this the Thunderer's daughter gave birth to two sons. The Thunderer sent the young man into the woods to capture two wolves with which he used to play when a boy. The son-in-law soon returned with the animals, and threw them at the feet of the Thunderer. But they severely mauled the old man, who, seeing that they had forgotten him, cried piteously to his son-in-law to carry them back to the forest. Shortly after this he again despatched his son-in-law in search of two bears with which he had also been friendly. The young man obeyed. But the bears treated the old man as the wolves had done, so he likewise returned them to their native haunts. For the third time the son-in-law went into the forest, for two grizzly bears, and when he saw them he called: 'I come to carry you away.' The bears instantly came toward him and suffered themselves to be carried before the Thunderer. But they also had forgotten their former playmate, and immediately set upon him, so that the young man was compelled to return with them to the forest. Thunderer had scarcely recovered from this last attack when he sent his son-in-law into the same forest after two panthers, which in his younger days had also been his companions. Without the slightest hesitation the young man arose and went into the wood, where he met the panthers. He called to them in the same gentle manner: 'I come to take you away.' The animals seemed to understand, and followed him. But Thunderer was dismayed when he saw how wild they had grown. They would not allow him to tame them, and after suffering their attack he sent them back to the forest. This ended the Thunderer's exciting pastime.

The tests

The Thunderer then sent his son-in-law to split a log of wood. When this had been done he put the young man's strength to the test by placing him within the hollow trunk and closing the wood around him. But the young man succeeded in freeing himself, and set off for the hut carrying the log with him. On reaching his home he dropped the wood before the door, and caused the earth to quake. The Thunderer jumped up in alarm and ran to the door rejoicing in the might of his son-in-law. 'Oh, my son-in-law,' he cried, 'you are just as I was when I was young!' The two continued to live together and the young man's sons grew into manhood. One day the Thunderer approached his son-in-law and said: 'Go to the Supernatural Folk and bring me their hoops.'

The Spirit-land

The son-in-law obeyed. He travelled for a long distance, and eventually reached the land of the spirits. They stood in a circle, and he saw that they played with a large hoop. He then remembered that he must secure the hoop. But he was afraid to approach them, as the light of the place dazzled him. He waited until darkness had set in, and, leaving his hiding-place, dashed through the circle and secured the hoop. The Supernatural People pursued him with torches. Just as this was taking place his wife remembered him. She called to her children: 'Now whip your grandfather.' This they did, while the old man wept. This chastisement brought rain upon the Supernatural People and extinguished their torches. They dared not pursue the young man farther, so they returned to their country. The adventurer was now left in peace to continue his homeward journey. He handed over the hoop to Thunderer, who now sent him to capture the targets of the Spirit Folk. The son-in-law gladly undertook the journey, and again entered the bright region of Spirit-land. He found the Supernaturals shooting at the targets, and when night had fallen he picked them up and ran away. The spirits lit their torches and followed him. His wife once more was reminded of her absent husband, and commanded her sons to repeat the punishment upon their grandfather. The rain recommenced and the torches of the pursuers were destroyed. The young man returned in peace to his dwelling and placed the targets before his father-in-law. He had not been long home before a restless spirit took possession of him. He longed for further adventure, and at last decided to set out in quest of it. Arraying himself in his fine necklaces of teeth and strapping around his waist two quivers of arrows, he bade farewell to his wife and sons. He journeyed until he reached a large village, which consisted of five rows of houses. These he carefully inspected. The last house was very small, but he entered it. He was met by two old women, who were known as the Mice. Immediately they saw him they muttered to each other: 'Oh, now Blue Jay will make another chief unhappy.' On the young man's arrival in the village Blue Jay became conscious of a stranger in the midst of the people. He straightaway betook himself to the house of the Mice. He then returned to his chief, saying that a strange chief wished to hold a shooting match. Blue Jay's chief seemed quite willing to enter into the contest with the stranger, so he sent Blue Jay back to the house to inform the young chief of his willingness. Blue Jay led the stranger down to the beach where the targets stood. Soon the old chief arrived and the shooting match began. But the adventurer's skill could not compare with the old chief's, who finally defeated him. Blue Jay now saw his opportunity. He sprang upon the stranger, tore out his hair, cut off his head, and severed the limbs from his body. He carried the pieces to the house and hung up the head. At night-fall the Mice fed the head and managed to keep it alive. This process of feeding went on for many months, the old women never tiring of their task. A full year had passed, and the unfortunate adventurer's sons began to fear for his safety. They decided to search for him. Arming themselves, they made their way to the large village in which their father was imprisoned. They entered the house of the Mice, and there saw the two old women, who asked: 'Oh, chiefs, where did you come from?'

'We search for our father,' they replied. But the old women warned them of Blue Jay's treachery, and advised them to depart. The young men would not heed the advice, and succeeded in drawing from the women the story of their father's fate. When they heard that Blue Jay had used their father so badly they were very angry. Blue Jay, meanwhile, had become aware of the arrival of two strangers, and he went to the small house to smell them out. There he espied the youths, and immediately returned to inform his chief of their presence in the village. The chief then sent him back to invite the strangers to a shooting match, but they ignored the invitation. Three times Blue Jay made the journey, and at last the youths looked upon him, whereupon his hair immediately took fire. He ran back to his chief and said: 'Oh, these strangers are more powerful than we are. They looked at me and my hair caught fire.' The chief was amazed, and went down to the beach to await the arrival of the strangers. When the young men saw the targets they would not shoot, and declared that they were bad. They immediately drew them out of the ground and replaced them by their own, the brilliance of which dazzled the sight of their opponent. The chief was defeated. He lost his life and the people were subdued. The youths then cast Blue Jay into the river, saying as they did so: 'Green Sturgeon shall be your name. Henceforth you shall not make chiefs miserable. You shall sing "Watsetsetsetse", and it shall be a bad omen.' This performance over, they restored their father from his death-slumber, and spoke kindly to the Mice, saying: 'Oh, you pitiful ones, you shall eat everything that is good. You shall eat berries.' Then, after establishing order in this strange land, they returned to their home, accompanied by their father.

This curious story is an example of what is known in mythology as the 'harrying of Hades'. The land of the supernatural or subterranean beings always exercises a profound fascination over the minds of barbarians, and such tales are invented by their story-tellers for the purpose of minimizing the terrors which await them when they them-selves must enter the strange country by death. The incident of the glutton would seem to show that two tales have been amalgamated, a not uncommon circumstance in primitive story-telling. In these stories the evil or supernatural power is invariably defeated, and it is touching to observe the child-like attempts of the savage to quench the dread of death, common to all mankind, by creating amusement at the ludicrous appearance of the dreadful beings whom he fears. The sons of the Thunderer are, of course, hero-gods whose effulgence confounds the powers of darkness, and to some extent they resemble the Hun-Apu and Xbalanque of the Central American *Popol Vuh*, who travel to the dark kingdom of Xibalba to rescue their father and uncle, and succeed in over-throwing its hideous denizens.[3]

The myth of Stikŭa

As an example of a myth as taken from the lips of the Indian by the collector we append to this series of Chinook tales the story of Stikŭa in all its pristine ingenuousness. Such a tale well

---

[3] See the author's *Myths of Mexico and Peru* p. 220.

exemplifies the difference of outlook between the aboriginal and the civilized mind, and exhibits the many difficulties with which collectors of such myths have to contend.

Many people were living at Nakotat. Now their chief died. He had [left] a son who was almost grown up. It was winter and the people were hungry. They had only mussels and roots to eat. Once upon a time a hunter said: 'Make yourselves ready.' All the men made themselves ready, and went seaward in two canoes. Then the hunter speared a sea-lion. It jumped and drifted on the water [dead]. They hauled it ashore. Blue Jay said 'Let us boil it here.' They made a fire and singed it. They cut it and boiled it. Blue Jay said: 'Let us eat it here, let us eat all of it.' Then the people ate. Raven tried to hide a piece of meat in his mat, and carried it to the canoe. [But] Blue Jay had already seen it; he ran [after him] took it and threw it into the fire. He burned it. Then they went home. They gathered large and small mussels. In the evening they came home. Then Blue Jay shouted: 'Stikŭa, fetch your mussels.' Stikŭa was the name of Blue Jay's wife. Then noise of many feet [was heard], and Stikŭa and the other women came running down to the beach. They went to fetch mussels. The women came to the beach and carried the mussels to the house. Raven took care of the chief's son. The boy said: 'Tomorrow I shall accompany you.' Blue Jay said to him: 'What do you want to do? The waves will carry you away, you will drift away; even I almost drifted away.'

The next morning they made themselves ready. They went into the canoe, and the boy came down to the beach. He wanted to accompany them, and held on to the canoe. 'Go to the house, go to the house,' said Blue Jay. The boy went up, but he was very sad. Then Blue Jay said: 'Let us leave him.' The people began to paddle. Then they arrived at the sea-lion island. The hunter went ashore and speared a sea-lion. It jumped and drifted on the water [dead]. They hauled it ashore and pulled it up from the water. Blue Jay said: 'Let us eat it here; let us eat all of it, else our chief's son would always want to come here.' They singed it, carved it, and boiled it there. When it was done they ate it all. Raven tried to hide a piece in his hair, but Blue Jay took it out immediately and burned it. In the evening they gathered large and small mussels, and then they went home. When they approached the beach Blue Jay shouted: 'Stikŭa, fetch your mussels!' Then noise of many feet [was heard]. Stikŭa and her children and all the other women came running down to the beach and carried the mussels up to the house. Blue Jay had told all those people: 'Don't tell our chief's son, else he will want to accompany us.' In the evening the boy said: 'Tomorrow I shall accompany you.' But Blue Jay said: 'What do you want to do? The waves will carry you away.' But the boy replied: 'I must go.'

In the morning they made themselves ready for the third time. The boy went down to the beach and took hold of the canoe. But Blue Jay pushed him aside and said: 'What do you want here? Go to the house.' The boy cried and went up to the house. [When he turned back] Blue Jay said: 'Now paddle away. We will leave him.' The people began to paddle, and soon they reached the sea-lion island. The hunter went ashore and speared one large sea-lion. It jumped and drifted on the water [dead]. They hauled it toward the shore, landed, pulled it up and singed it. They finished singeing it. Then they carved it and boiled it, and when it was done they began to eat. Blue Jay said: 'Let us eat it all. Nobody must speak about it, else our chief's son will always want to accompany us.' A little [meat] was still left when they had eaten enough. Raven tried to take a piece with him. He tied it to his leg and said his leg was broken. Blue Jay burned all that was left over. Then he said to Raven: 'Let me see your leg.' He jumped at it, untied it, and found the piece of meat at Raven's leg. He took it and burned it. In the evening they gathered large and small mussels. Then they went home. When they were near home Blue Jay shouted: 'Stikŭa, fetch your mussels!' Then noise of many feet [was heard], and Stikŭa [her children and the other women] came down to the beach and carried the mussels up to the house. The [women and children] and the chief's son ate the mussels all night. Then that boy said: 'Tomorrow I shall accompany you.' Blue Jay said: 'What do you want to do? You will drift away. If I had not taken hold of the canoe I should have drifted away twice.'

On the next morning they made themselves ready for the fourth time. The boy rose and made himself ready also. The people hauled their canoes into the water and went aboard. The boy tried to board a canoe also, but Blue Jay took hold of him and threw him into the water. He stood in the water up to his waist. He held the canoe, but Blue Jay struck his hands. There he stood. He cried, and cried, and went up to the house. The people went; they paddled, and soon they reached the sea-lion island. The hunter went ashore and speared a sea-lion. It jumped and drifted on the water [dead]. Again they towed it to the island, and pulled it ashore. They singed it. When they had finished singeing it they carved it and boiled it. When it was done Blue Jay said: 'Let us eat it here.' They ate half of it and were satiated. They slept because they had eaten too much. Blue Jay awoke first, and burned all that was left. In the evening they gathered large and small mussels and went home. When they were near the shore he shouted: 'Stikŭa, fetch your mussels!' Noise of many feet [was heard] and Stikŭa [her children and the other women] came running down to the beach and carried up the mussels. The boy said: 'Tomorrow I shall accompany you.' But Blue Jay said: 'What do you want to do? We might capsize and you would be drowned.'

Early on the following morning the people made themselves ready. The boy arose and made himself ready also. Blue Jay and the people hauled their canoes down to the water. The boy tried to board, but Blue Jay threw him into the water. He tried to hold the canoe. The water reached up to his armpits. Blue Jay struck his hands [until he let go]. Then the boy cried and cried. Blue Jay and the other people went away.

After some time the boy went up from the beach. He took

his arrows and walked round a point of land. There he met a young eagle and shot it. He skinned it and tried to put the skin on. It was too small; it reached scarcely to his knees. Then he took it off, and went on. After a while he met another eagle. He shot it and it fell down. It was a white-headed eagle. He skinned it and tried the skin on, but it was too small; it reached a little below his knees. He took it off, left it, and went on. Soon he met a bald-headed eagle. He shot it twice and it fell down. He skinned it and put the skin on. It was nearly large enough for him, and he tried to fly. He could fly downward only. He did not rise. He turned back, and now he could fly. Now he went round the point seaward from Nakotat. When he had nearly gone round he smelled smoke of burning fat. When he came round the point he saw the people of his town. He alighted on top of a tree and looked down. [He saw that] they had boiled a sea-lion and that they ate it. When they had nearly finished eating he flew up. He thought: 'Oh, I wish Blue Jay would see me.' Then Blue Jay looked up [and saw] the bird flying about. 'Ah, a bird came to get food from us.' Five times the eagle circled over the fire; then it descended. Blue Jay took a piece of blubber and said: 'I will give you this to eat.' The bird came down, grasped the piece of meat, and flew away. 'Ha!' said Blue Jay, 'that bird has feet like a man.' When the people had eaten enough they slept. Raven again hid a piece of meat. Toward evening they awoke and ate again; then Blue Jay burned the rest of their food. In the evening they gathered large and small mussels and went home. When the boy came home he lay down at once. They approached the village, and Blue Jay shouted: 'Fetch your mussels, Stikŭa!' Noise of many feet [was heard] and Stikŭa [and the other women] ran down to the beach and carried up the mussels. They tried to rouse the boy, but he did not arise.

The next morning the people made themselves ready and launched their canoe. The chief's son stayed in bed and did not attempt to accompany them. After sunrise he rose and called the women and children and said: 'Wash yourselves; be quick.'

The women obeyed and washed themselves. He continued: 'Comb your hair.' Then he put down a plank, took a piece of meat out [from under his blanket, showed it to the women, and said]: 'Every day your husbands eat this.' He put two pieces side by side on the plank, cut them to pieces, and greased the heads of all the women and children. Then he pulled the planks forming the walls of the houses out of the ground. He sharpened them [at one end, and] those which were very wide he split in two. He sharpened all of them. The last house of the village was that of the Raven. He did not pull out its wall-planks. He put the planks on to the backs of the women and children and said: 'Go down to the beach. When you go seaward swim five times round that rock. Then go seaward. When you see sea-lions you shall kill them. But you shall not give anything to stingy people. I shall take these children down. They shall live on the sea and be my relatives.'

Then he split sinews. The women went into the water and began to jump [out of the water]. They swam five times back and forth in front of the village. Then they went seaward to the place where Blue Jay and the men were boiling. Blue Jay said to the men: 'What is that?' The men looked and saw the girls jumping. Five times they swam round Blue Jay's rock. Then they went seaward. After a while birds came flying to the island. Their bills were [as red] as blood. They followed [the fish]. 'Ah!' said Blue Jay, 'do you notice them? Whence come these numerous birds?' The Raven said: 'Ha, squint-eye, they are your children; do you not recognize them?' Five times they went round the rock. Now [the boy] threw the sinews down upon the stones and said: 'When Blue Jay comes to gather mussels they shall be fast [to the rocks].' And he said to the women, turning toward the sea: 'Whale-Killer will be your name. When you catch a whale you will eat it, but when you catch a sea-lion you will throw it away; but you shall not give anything to stingy people.'

Blue Jay and the people were eating. Then that hunter said:

'Let us go home. I am afraid we have seen evil spirits; we have never seen anything like that on this rock.' Now they gathered mussels and carried along the meat which they had left over. In the evening they came near their home. [Blue Jay shouted:] 'Stikŭa, fetch your mussels!' There was no sound of people. Five times he called. Now the people went ashore and [they saw that] the walls of the houses had disappeared. The people cried. Blue Jay cried also, but somebody said to him: 'Be quiet, Blue Jay; if you had not been bad our chief's son would not have done so.' Now they all made one house. Only Raven had one house [by himself]. He went and searched for food on the beach. He found a sturgeon. He went again to the beach and found a porpoise. Then Blue Jay went to the beach and tried to search for food. [As soon as he went out] it began to hail; the hailstones were so large [*indicating*]. He tried to gather mussels and wanted to break them off; but they did not come off. He could not break them off. He gave it up. Raven went to search on the beach and found a seal. The others ate roots only. Thus their chief took revenge on them.

Beliefs of the Californian tribes

The tribes of California afford a strange example of racial conglomeration, speaking as they do a variety of languages totally distinct from one another, and exhibiting many differences in physical appearance and custom. Concerning their mythological beliefs Bancroft says:

'The Californian tribes, taken as a whole, are pretty uniform in the main features of their theogonic beliefs. They seem, without exception, to have had a hazy conception of a lofty, almost supreme being; for the most part referred to as a Great Man, the Old Man Above, the One Above; attributing to him, however, as is usual in such cases, nothing but the vaguest and most negative functions and qualities. The real practical power that most interested them, who had most to do with them and they with him, was a demon, or body of demons, of a tolerably pronounced character. In the face of diverse assertions to the effect that no such thing as a devil proper has ever been found in savage mythology, we would draw attention to the following extract from the *Pomo* manuscript of Mr Powers – a gentleman who, both by his study and by personal investigation, has made himself one of the best qualified authorities on the belief of the native Californian, and whose dealings have been for the most part with tribes that have never had any friendly intercourse with white men. Of course the thin and meagre imagination of the American savages was not equal to the creation of Milton's magnificent imperial Satan, or of Goethe's Mephistopheles, with his subtle intellect, his vast powers, his malignant mirth; but in so far as the Indian fiends or devils have the ability, they are wholly as wicked as these. They are totally bad, they have no good thing in them, they think only evil; but they are weak and undignified and absurd; they are as much beneath Satan as the "Big Indians" who invent them are inferior in imagination to John Milton.

'A definite location is generally assigned to the evil one as his favourite residence or resort; thus the Californians in the county of Siskiyou give over Devil's Castle, its mount and lake, to the malignant spirits, and avoid the vicinity of these places with all possible care.

'The coast tribes of Del Norte County, California, live in constant terror of a malignant spirit that takes the form of certain animals, the form of a bat, of a hawk, of a tarantula, and so on, but especially delights in and affects that of a screech-owl. The belief of the Russian river tribes and others is practically identical with this.

'The Cahrocs have some conception of a great deity called Chareya, the Old Man Above; he is wont to appear upon earth at times to some of the most favoured sorcerers; he is described as wearing a close tunic, with a medicine-bag, and as having long white hair that falls venerably about his shoulders. Practically, however, the Cahrocs, like the majority of Californian tribes, venerate chiefly the Coyote. Great dread is also had of certain forest-demons of nocturnal habits; these, say the Cahrocs, take the form of bears, and shoot arrows at benighted wayfarers.

'Between the foregoing outlines of Californian belief and those connected with the remaining tribes, passing south, we can detect no salient difference till we reach the Olchones, a coast tribe between San Francisco and Monterey; the sun here begins to be connected, or identified by name, with that great spirit, or rather, that Big Man, who made the earth and who rules in the sky. So we find it again both around Monterey and around San Luis Obispo; the first fruits of the earth were offered in these neighbourhoods to the great light, and his rising was greeted with cries of joy.'

Father Gerónimo Boscana gives us the following account of the faith and worship of the Acagchemem tribes, who inhabit the valley and neighbourhood of San Juan Capistrano, California. We give first the version held by the *serranos*, or highlanders, of the interior country, three or four leagues inland from San Juan Capistrano:

'Before the material world at all existed there lived two beings, brother and sister, of a nature that cannot be explained; the brother living above, and his name meaning the Heavens, the sister living below, and her name signifying Earth. From the union of these two there sprang a numerous offspring. Earth and sand were the first-fruits of this marriage; then were born rocks and stones; then trees, both great and small; then grass and herbs; then animals; lastly was born a great personage called Ouiot, who was a "grand captain". By some unknown mother many children of a medicine race were born to this Ouiot. All these things happened in the north; and afterwards when men were created they were created in the north; but as the people multiplied they moved toward the south, the earth growing larger also and extending itself in the same direction.

'In process of time, Ouiot becoming old, his children plotted to kill him, alleging that the infirmities of age made him unfit any longer to govern them or attend to their welfare. So they put a strong poison in his drink, and when he drank of it a sore sickness came upon him; he rose up and left his home in the mountains, and went down to what is now the sea-shore, though at that time there was no sea there. His mother, whose name is the Earth, mixed him an antidote in a large shell, and set the potion out in the sun to brew; but the fragrance of it attracted the attention of the Coyote, who came and overset the shell. So Ouiot sickened to death, and though he told his children that he would shortly return and be with them again, he has never been seen since. All the people made a great pile of wood and burnt his body there, and just as the ceremony began the Coyote leaped upon the body, saying that he would burn with it; but he only tore a piece of flesh from the stomach and ate it and escaped. After that the title of the Coyote was changed from Eyacque, which means Sub-captain, to Eno, that is to say, Thief and Cannibal.

'When now the funeral rites were over, a general council was held and arrangements made for collecting animal and vegetable food; for up to this time the children and descendants of Ouiot had nothing to eat but a kind of white clay. And while they consulted together, behold a marvellous thing appeared before them, and they spoke to it, saying: "Art thou our captain, Ouiot?" But the spectre said: "Nay, for I am greater than Ouiot; my habitation is above, and my name is Chinigchinich." Then he spoke further, having been told for what they were come together: "I create all things, and I go now to make man, another people like unto you; as for you, I give you power, each after his kind, to produce all good and pleasant things. One of you shall bring rain, and another dew, and another make the acorn grow, and others other seeds, and yet others shall cause all kinds of game to abound in the land; and your children shall have this power forever, and they shall be sorcerers to the men I go to create, and shall receive gifts of them, that the game fail not and the harvests be sure." Then Chinigchinich made man; out of the clay of the lake he formed him, male and female; and the present Californians are the descendants of the one or more pairs there and thus created.

'So ends the known tradition of the mountaineers; we must now go back and take up the story anew at its beginning, as told by the *playanos*, or people of the valley of San Juan Capistrano. These say that an invisible, all-powerful being, called Nocuma, made the world and all that it contains of things that grow and move. He made it round like a ball and held it in his hands, where it rolled about a good deal at first, till he steadied it by sticking a heavy black rock called Tosaut into it, as a kind of ballast. The sea was at this time only a little stream running round the world, and so crowded with fish that their twinkling fins had no longer room to move; so great was the press that some of the more foolish fry were for effecting a landing and founding a colony upon the dry land, and it was only with the utmost difficulty that they were persuaded by their elders that the killing air and baneful sun and the want of feet must infallibly prove the destruction before many days of all who took part in such a desperate enterprise. The proper plan was evidently to improve and enlarge their present home; and to this end, principally by the aid of one very large fish, they broke the great rock Tosaut in two, finding a bladder in the centre filled with a very bitter substance. The taste of it pleased the fish, so they emptied it into the water, and instantly the water became salt and swelled up and overflowed a great part of the old earth, and made itself the new boundaries that remain to this day.

'Then Nocuma created a man, shaping him out of the soil of the earth, calling him Ejoni. A woman also the great god made, presumably out of the same material as the man, calling her Aé. Many children were born to this first pair, and their descendants multiplied over the land. The name of one of these last was Sirout, that is to say, Handful of Tobacco, and the name of his wife was Ycaiut, which means Above; and to Sirout and Ycaiut was born a son, while they lived in a place north-east about eight leagues from San Juan Capistrano. The name of this son was Ouiot, that is to say, Dominator; he grew a fierce and redoubtable warrior; haughty, ambitious, tyrannous, he extended his lordship on every side, ruling everywhere as with a rod of iron; and the people conspired against him. It was determined that he should die by poison; a piece of the rock Tosaut was ground up in so deadly a way that its mere external application was sufficient to cause death. Ouiot, notwithstanding that he held himself constantly on the alert, having been warned of his danger by a small burrowing animal called the *cucumel*, was unable to avoid his fate; a few grains of the cankerous mixture were dropped upon his breast while he slept, and the strong mineral ate its way to the very springs of his life. All the wise men of the land were called to his assistance; but there was nothing for him save to die. His body was burned on a great pile with songs of joy and dances, and the nation rejoiced.

'While the people were gathered to this end, it was thought advisable to consult on the feasibility of procuring seed and flesh to eat instead of the clay which had up to this time been the sole food of the human family. And while they yet talked together, there appeared to them, coming they knew not whence, one called Attajen, "which name implies man, or rational being". And Attajen, understanding their desires, chose out certain of the elders among them, and to these gave he power; one that he might cause rain to fall, to another that he might cause game to abound, and so with the rest, to each his power and gift, and to the successors of each forever. These were the first medicine-men.'

Many years having elapsed since the death of Ouiot, there appeared in the same place one called Ouiamot, reputed son of Tacu and Auzar – people unknown, but natives, it is thought by Boscana, of 'some distant land'. This Ouiamot is better known by his great name Chinigchinich, which means Almighty. He first manifested his powers to the people on a day when they had met in congregation for some purpose or other; he appeared dancing before them crowned with a kind of high crown made of tall feathers stuck into a circlet of some kind, girt with a kind of petticoat of feathers, and having his flesh painted black and red. Thus decorated he was called the *tobet*. Having danced some time, Chinigchinich called out the medicine-men, or *puplems*, as they were called, among whom it would appear the chiefs are always numbered, and confirmed their power; telling them that he had come from the stars to instruct them in dancing and all other things, and commanding that in all their necessities they should array themselves in the *tobet*, and so dance as he had danced, supplicating him by his great name, that thus they might be granted their petitions. He taught them how to worship him, how to build *vanquechs*, or places of worship, and how to direct their conduct in various affairs of life. Then he prepared to die, and the people asked him if they should bury him; but he warned them against attempting such a thing. 'If ye buried me,' he said, 'ye would tread upon my grave, and for that my hand would be heavy upon you; look to it, and to all your ways, for lo, I go up where the high stars are, where mine eyes shall see all the ways of men; and whosoever will not keep my commandments nor observe the things I have taught, behold, disease shall plague all his body, and no food shall come near his lips, the bear shall rend his flesh, and the crooked tooth of the serpent shall sting him.'

In Lower California the Pericues were divided into two *gentes*, each of which worshipped a divinity which was hostile to the other. The tradition explains that there was a great lord in heaven, called Niparaya, who made earth and sea, and was almighty and invisible. His wife was Anayicoyondi, a goddess who, though possessing no body, bore him in a divinely mysterious manner three children, one of whom, Quaayayp, was a real man and born on earth, on the Acaragui mountains. Very powerful this young god was, and for a long time he lived with the ancestors of the Pericues, whom it is almost to be inferred that he created; at any rate we are told that he was able to make men, drawing them up out of the earth. The men at last killed their great hero and teacher, and put a crown of thorns upon his head. Somewhere or other he remains lying dead to this day; and he remains constantly beautiful, neither does his body know corruption. Blood drips constantly from his wounds; and though he can speak no more, being dead, yet there is an owl that speaks to him.

The other god was called Wac, or Tuparan. According to the Niparaya sect, this Wac had made war on their favourite god, and had been by him defeated and cast forth from heaven into a cave under the earth, of which cave the whales of the sea were the guardians. With a perverse, though not unnatural, obstinacy, the sect that took Wac or Tuparan for their great god persisted in holding ideas peculiar to themselves with regard to the truth of the foregoing story, and their account of the great war in heaven and its results differed from the other as differ the creeds of heterodox and orthodox everywhere; they ascribe, for example, part of the creation to other gods besides Niparaya.

Myths of the Athapascans

The great Athapascan family, who inhabit a vast extent of territory stretching north from the fifty-fifth parallel nearly to the Arctic Ocean, and westward to the Pacific, with cognate ramifications to the far south, are weak in mythological conceptions. Regarding them Bancroft says:[4]

'They do not seem in any of their various tribes to have a single expressed idea with regard to a supreme power. The Loucheux branch recognize a certain personage, resident in the moon, whom they supplicate for success in starting on a hunting expedition. This being once lived among them as a poor ragged boy that an old woman had found and was bringing up; and who made himself ridiculous to his fellows by making a pair of very large snow-shoes; for the people could not see what a starveling like him should want with shoes of such unusual size. Times of great scarcity troubled the hunters, and they would often have fared badly had they not

---

[4] *The Native Races of the Pacific States*, vol. iii.

invariably on such occasions come across a new broad trail that led to a head or two of freshly killed game. They were glad enough to get the game and without scruples as to its appropriation; still they felt curious as to whence it came and how. Suspicion at last pointing to the boy and his great shoes as being in some way implicated in the affair, he was watched. It soon became evident that he was indeed the benefactor of the Loucheux, and the secret hunter whose quarry had so often replenished their empty pots; yet the people were far from being adequately grateful, and continued to treat him with little kindness or respect. On one occasion they refused him a certain piece of fat – him who had so often saved their lives by his timely bounty! That night the lad disappeared, leaving only his clothes behind, hanging on a tree. He returned to them in a month, however, appearing as a man, and dressed as a man. He told them that he had taken up his home in the moon; that he would always look down with a kindly eye to their success in hunting; but he added that as a punishment for their shameless greed and ingratitude in refusing him the piece of fat, all animals should be lean the long winter through, and fat only in summer; as has since been the case.

'According to Hearne, the Tinneh believe in a kind of spirits, or fairies, called *nantena*, which people the earth, the sea, and the air, and are instrumental for both good and evil. Some of them believe in a good spirit called Tihugun, "my old friend", supposed to reside in the sun and in the moon; they have also a bad spirit, Chutsain, apparently only a personification of death, and for this reason called bad.

'They have no regular order of *shamans*; anyone when the spirit moves him may take upon himself their duties and pretensions, though some by happy chances, or peculiar cunning, are much more highly esteemed in this regard than others, and are supported by voluntary contributions. The conjurer often shuts himself in his tent and abstains from food for days till his earthly grossness thins away, and the spirits and things unseen are constrained to appear at his behest. The young Tinneh care for none of these things; the strong limb and the keen eye, holding their own well in the jostle of life, mock at the terrors of the invisible; but as the pulses dwindle with disease or age, and the knees strike together in the shadow of impending death, the *shaman* is hired to expel the evil things of which a patient is possessed. Among the Tacullies a confession is often resorted to at this stage, on the truth and accuracy of which depend the chances of a recovery.'

Conclusion

In concluding this survey of representative myths of the Red Race of North America, the reader will probably be chiefly impressed with the circumstance that although many of these tales exhibit a striking resemblance to the myths of European and Asiatic peoples they have yet an atmosphere of their own which strongly differentiates them from the folk-tales of all other races. It is a truism in mythology that although the tales and mythological systems of peoples dwelling widely apart may show much likeness to one another, such a resemblance cannot be advanced as a proof that the divergent races at some distant period possessed a common mythology. Certain tribes in Borneo live in huts built on piles driven into lake-beds and use blow-pipes; so do some Indians of Guiana and contiguous countries; yet no scientist of experience would be so rash as to advance the theory that these races possessed a common origin. It is the same with mythological processes, which may have been evolved separately at great distances, but yet exhibit a marked likeness. These resemblances arise from the circumstance that the mind of man, whether he be situated in China or Peru, works on surprisingly similar lines. But, as has been indicated, the best proof that the myths of North America have not been sophisticated by those of Europe and Asia is the circumstance that the aboriginal atmosphere they contain is so marked that even the most superficial observer could not fail to observe its presence. In the tales contained in this volume the facts of Indian life, peculiar and unique, enter into every description and are inalienably interwoven with the matter of the story.

In closing, the author desires to make a strong appeal for a reasoned and charitable consideration of the Indian character on the part of his readers. This noble, manly, and dignified race has in the past been grossly maligned, chiefly by persons themselves ignorant and inspired by hereditary dislike. The Red Man is neither a monster of inhumanity nor a marvel of cunning, but a being with like feelings and aspirations to our own. Because his customs and habits of thought differ from ours he has been charged with all manner of crimes and offences with which he has, in general, nothing to do. We do not deny that he was, till very recent times, a savage, with the habits and outlook of a savage. But that he ever was a demon in human shape must be strenuously denied. In the march of progress Indian men and women are today taking places of honour and emolument side by side with their white fellow-citizens, and many gifted and cultured persons of Indian blood have done good work for the race. Let us hope that the ancient virtues of courage and endurance which have stood the Indian people in such good stead of old will assist their descendants in the even more strenuous tasks of civilization to which they are now called.

* * *

The most obvious omission in Spence's survey of the Indians of the North are the Eskimo (or, as they call themselves, 'Inuit', 'the people'). The name Eskimo, meaning 'eaters of raw flesh', was donated them by the Algonquian-speaking tribes to the south. The Eskimo did indeed masticate uncooked flesh, principally of caribou, moose, and the mammals of the sea, whales and seals. Of the linguistic group Eskimo–Aleut, the Eskimo themselves were the last of the tribes to wander over the Bering land bridge, in about 3,000 BC, and retain the distinctive eye fold of the Mongols.

During the dark days of the Arctic winter, Eskimo life was inward and village-based, with entire families living in one-room houses (made of earth, or earth and stone and whalebone, or ice), rarely venturing outside for days on end. Not surprisingly, shamanic religion, story-telling, and the crafting of religious objects was well developed among the tribe with home-bound days to fill.

Their religious ideas were not formalized, their festivals and ceremonies few in number. The main religious gathering was an impromptu ecstatic séance held by the shaman (angakok), who while beating a drum would fall into a trance in which he could communicate with the spirit world. Usually the angakok's prophecies were trivial and domestic, but on occasion assumed tribal importance, relating messages from the spirits which told of the movement of shoals of fish or the advance of bad weather. Aspirants for the role of shaman were required, on reaching puberty, to wander a deserted region alone, where in his anxiety and hunger the *tornaq*, or spirit, would appear. The frightened candidate would be promised visions, and on returning to his family would serve an apprenticeship to an experienced magician.

The Eskimo had no gods as such, with the partial exception of the Old Woman Who Lived Under the Sea, known as Sedna, and also called Arnakuagsak, Nerrivik, and Nuliajoq. Unlike most peoples, where the Great Goddess was an Earth deity, to the Inuit, whose life and survival depend on the sea, Sedna was a water spirit. She was born to two giants, and she grew rapidly, having an insatiable appetite for flesh. One night she started to eat the limbs of her sleeping parents. On awaking, the horrified parents put Sedna in their *umiak* (skin-covered canoe) and paddled far out to sea, where they threw her overboard. She clung desperately to the side of the canoe, whereupon Sedna's parents cut off her fingers, which turned into fish, seals and other creatures as they fell into the water. Sedna herself slipped beneath the surface, to become the demonic ruler of the ocean depths. It was Sedna who caused the storms of the sea, it was Sedna who controlled the migration of the sea's animals.

When Inuit hunters were unable to find food, the angakok would send his spirit down into the sea to plead with the goddess. To reach Sedna's underwater realm of Adlivon the spirit of the angakok first had to survive an icy whirlpool, then get past a cauldron of boiling seals, evade a snarling guard dog, and cross over an abyss on the thinnest of arches, before arriving at Sedna's tented palace on the seabed. There, the spirit would sing a hymn of pleading and contort itself to amuse the sulky dark lady. Eventually, she would be induced into helping, telling the spirit that either the Inuit must move to another location or where she would send them prey to catch.

With so few gods, the Eskimo relied on spirits to guide them. There was no concept of a supreme spirit (as, for instance, the Sioux had with Watanka Tanka and the Iroquois with Manitou); befitting a clan-centred culture, the Eskimo considered that each family had an ancestral spirit to guard them. Some Eskimo cultures believed that the ancestral spirits had an overlord, rather like the Europeans of the medieval era believed in a king of the fairies. The ancestral spirits would provide information in dreams about good hunting, and sometimes allow humans to understand the speech of animals and birds. This was sensible practice by the ancestral spirits, for the dead lived in an unhappy harsh underworld, rather like this world, only darker. The spirits of the dead needed a share of the catch of their descendants, given as offerings, to stave off hunger. But animals and birds were not mere sources of food; they too had spirits and souls, they too were worthy of respect, and were to be charmed into the traps of man.

Unlike the Inuit, the fishermen and hunter-gatherers of the Northwest – principally the Haida, Kwakiutl, Tlingit and Tsimshian – had a high degree of social organization, living in large permanent villages in which families were divided into groups dedicated to a totem, usually an animal, with which an ancestor had had a special relationship. Thus there were Salmon people, Beaver people, Killer Whale people and so forth. The totem – a sort of family crest – was carved on a pole placed to the front of the lodge.

Totem creatures figured large in the region's mythology, but were neither fully human nor fully animal nor fully spirit. In the mythology of the Northwest Coast a bear, for instance, could act like a human but change into Bear at will, meaning it had spirit character. The fisher tribes had a vague conception of a pre-eminent spirit power, the Chief of the Sky People (called by Spence, 'Sky-god'), who, along with Sun, Moon, the Old Woman Under The Sea, and the trickster Raven, were full deities. But none were formally worshipped. There were no temples, no regular ceremonies in the region. Heroes tended to have supernatural powers, for example Stoneribs, the boy who kills the sea monster Qagwaii (a killer whale) by jumping inside him and killing him from within with a bow and arrow.

The Raven is a reminder that many primitive societies of North America have conceived of creation as an act of trickery. According to the Haida, the Raven (also known as Yetl or Hoya) stole the sun from his grandfather Nasshahkeeyalhl and made the moon and stars from it. The Raven then divided night and day, made lakes and rivers, filled them with salmon, planted trees on land and placed animals in them. In a giant clamshell he found some timid creatures, which he released onto the beach, singing all the while. These were the first men. Quickly becoming bored with his discovery, Raven scoured the world for their female counterparts, finally finding some women caught in a chiton (a seashell). He put the women with the men and was much entertained by their interactions.

Raven might be creator and provider, but he is always unable to resist lechery and mischief. He never truly creates; he steals, discovers and fiddles things about. Raven, as Spence notes, is not the only trickster of the Northwest. Mink and Blue Jay also take the role. Tricksters were feared, respected and admired. Some animal spirits of the region, though, such as the bird-spirit known as Crooked Beak of Heaven were only to be dreaded, and kept at bay by the rituals of the Shamans' Society. Any animal-spirit, however, was capable of retribution if maltreated. If people, for example, tortured a salmon or threw away excess fish, retribution from the spirits would ensue. The British Museum ethnographer Cottie Burland (1905–1983) recorded a story from Nass River, British Columbia, which illustrates the dire consequences of a lack of regard for nature:

It tells how, in a canyon near the head of the river, there was a wonderful place that the tribes people could always visit to find salmon and wild berries. The villagers who lived nearby were wealthy enough to trade with others and much respected. As time went on, the younger people forgot the old traditions; sometimes they killed small animals and left the carcasses for the crows and eagles to eat. Their elders warned them that the Chief in the Sky would be angered by such foolish behaviour, but nobody heeded them. In one case, when the salmon season was at its height and the fish were swimming up river in their myriads, some of the young men of the Wolf Clan thought it amusing to catch salmon, make slits in the fish's backs, put in pieces of burning pitch pine, and put them back in the water so that they swam about like living torches in the river. It was spectacular and exciting, and they did not think about the cruelty to the salmon, or the waste of a good food. The elders as usual protested and as usual the young people took no notice. At the end of the salmon run season the tribe made ready for the winter ceremonies. But as they prepared they heard a strange noise in the distance, something like the beating of a medicine drum, and grew worried. As there was nothing very threatening about it, the young people said, 'Aha, the ghosts wake up, they are going to have a feast too.' The old people guessed that the young men's thoughtlessness in ill-treating the salmon had brought trouble on the tribe. After a while the noises died down, but within a week or two the beating of drums became louder and louder. Even the young warriors became very careful about what they did, because they were frightened. The old people noted the young men's fear, and said it would be their fault if the tribe perished. Eventually a noise like thunder was heard, the mountains broke open, and fire gushed forth until it seemed that all the rivers were afire. The people tried to escape, but as the fire came down the river, the forest caught fire and only a few of them got away. The cause of the conflagration was said by the shamans to be entirely due to the anger of the spirit world at the torture of the salmon.

Perhaps the most famous ceremony of the Pacific Coast tribes was the potlatch. At the ritual, the host gained increased status by giving away symbols of his wealth, or by showing contempt for it – notably, by clubbing female slaves to death. Although the potlatch was manifestly a means of demonstrating personal power (and by extension, the power of the host's tribe) the ceremony had a definite religious aspect, frequently to do with mourning the dead. For the Tlingit the potlatch, which might last over a week, could help the spirit of a dead chief move from his 'Earth Walk' into the spirit land.

In describing the Californian tribes to the south of the Pacific Northwest as speaking 'a variety of languages', Spence understated the actuality: the Native Americans within what is currently cartographic California spoke between 75 and 100 tongues. His source, Bancroft, was wrong in claiming the tribes to be 'pretty uniform' in the main features of their theogenic beliefs. While the tribes of the north and central area held a belief in a creator, the tribes of the south were noteworthy for being among those Native Americans with no cosmology. The world is not born, because it has always existed. Consequently, the bulk of the southern Californian origin myths consists of a history of mankind, at first as a single tribe, then many tribes.

The tribes of California provided the last tragic footnote in the story of the independent Native American. In 1911 a Yahi man stumbled out of the Sierra, following the deaths of his relatives. He had had no previous contact with whites. Billed as 'The last wild Indian', the Yahi man was taken to the University of California, Berkeley, where he was studied closely by the anthropologist Alfred Kroeber. Forbidden by tribal custom to give his name to strangers, the Yahi was named Ishi. He died five years later of tuberculosis. At least he was the ward of someone who knew about and respected Californian Indians; Kroeber was the author of the monumental *Religion of the Indians of California*, 1917.

'The great Athapascan family' of the subarctic referred to by Spence is linguistically related to the tribes of the Northwest. Today the Athapascan language family is usually known as 'Na-Dene', 'na' meaning 'people' in Tlingit and 'dene' meaning people in numerous Athapascan languages.

The caribou-eating, warlike Chipewyan of the tundra and boreal forest were the dominant regional tribe, who extended their influence in historical times by being both middleman and provider in the fur trade. The Chipewyan held that animals, spirits and other animate beings lived in a non-earthly realm of inkoze simultaneously with their physical existence. Pre-birth and post-life humans were part of inkoze; knowledge of this other world could be obtained during physical life, however, by dreams and visions. Powerful animals, meanwhile, sacrificed their physical being for the use of the people. This model of sacrifice proved sufficiently similar to the Christian concept of God's sacrifice through His Son to allow a smooth integration of Christianity into the religion of the Chipewyan. Today, most Chipewyan are simultaneously animists and Christians.

AN A–Z OF THE CHIEF GODS, SPIRITS AND MYTHICAL BEINGS OF NORTH AMERICA

ADEE/IDO: Thunderbird (Pacific Northwest)

AIRSEKUI/ARESKOUI: The Great Spirit (Huron)

AKYCHA: Spirit of the Sun (Eskimo)

AMOTKEN: The creator, an old man dwelling in heaven, and father of the people (Selish)

ANGPETU WI: The spirit of the Sun (Sioux)

ANINGAN: The Moon (Eskimo)

ATAENTSIC: The Sky Woman, granddaughter of the Chief-Sky-Rulers (Iroquois)

ATIUS TIRAWA: The creator and supreme deity (Pawnee)

AWAHOKSHU: The Abode of the Spirit Power (Pawnee)

AWONAWILONA: The Sun-Father, and also, like *Wakonda*, the all-pervader (Zuñi)

BEAR: Master of animals, chief of the underworld, and a culture hero. Particularly revered by the Algonquins, and the Ute, who believe they are closely related to the animal, which features prominently in Ute myths

BRIGHT STAR: 'Mother-of-all-Things', a personification of Venus (Skidi Pawnee)

CORN MAIDENS: The most important deities of the people of the Southwest pueblos, who accompanied the first humans when they emerged from the underworld (Hopi/Zuñi)

COYOTE: The prototypical trickster, found throughout most Native American cultures. Exists in animal and human form, always male, and sometime a beneficent culture hero

DAGANOWEDA: Hiawatha (Iroquois)

DEOHAKO: The Sister Spirits of Corn, Beans and Squash (Iroquois)

DELGETH: Flesh-eating antelope (Navajo)

DZONOKWA: The Cannibal Woman (Northwest)

GEYAGUGA: The Moon god (Cherokee)

GITCHE MANITOU: The All-Father (Iroquois)

GLUSCAP/GLOOSCAP: Variously creator, trickster, transformer and culture hero (Algonquian, Wabanki)

GREAT HARE: A demi-urge, creator, transformer, trickster and culture hero. Sometimes personified as Rabbit (Algonquian)

HAHAI-WUGTI: The Spider Woman (Hopi)

HA-WEN-NHYU: The Great Spirit (Iroquois)

HASTSHEHOGAN: Along with Hastneyalti, the principal *yei* or benevolent deity (Navajo)

HASTSEYALTI: With *Hastshehogan*, one of the two main *yei*, and a creator of man (Navajo)

IATIKU: One of the Sisters who created man, the other being *Nautsiti* (Acoma)

IKOTIMI/ICTNICKE: Spider, a trickster (Sioux)

ISAKAWUATE: Old Man Coyote, the trickster (Crow)

ISHTINIKE: Trickster-culture hero (Ponca)

ISTEPAHPAH: A devouring monster (Creek)

KETCHIMANETOWA: The Great Spirit (Fox)

KEMUSH/KUMUSH: 'The-Old-Man-of-The-Ancients' who, at the bidding of *Morning Star*, created the Earth from the ashes of the Aurora Borealis (Klamath/Modoc)

KOMOKUMS: Trickster-transformer (Modoc)

LUDJKATAKO: The Giant Turtle (Creek)

MALSUM: Brother to *Gluscap*, a destroyer (Algonquian)

MANABOZHO: A variant of *Nanabozho* (Northeast)

MATCHI MANITOU: The personification of the 'medicine-spirit' (Chippewa)

MENAHKA: The Great Spirit (Mandan)

MICHABO: The Great Hare (Algonquian)

MORNING STAR: After the Sun the most important of the celestial divinities among the Plains tribes, being a personification of Venus (Skidi Pawnee, Blackfoot and others)

NAHURAK: Generic name given to the animal spirits who lived in five houses, namely Pahuk, Nakiskat, Tsurapako, Kitsawitsak and Pahua

NANANBOJO/NANABOOJOO: The *Great Hare* (Potawatomi)

NANABOZHO: The Great Rabbit (Northeast)

NANOOK/NANUQ/NANUE: The Bear, Ursa Major and the Pleiades star group (Eskimo)

NA'PI: The creator, the 'Old Man' (Blackfoot)

NEGAKFOK: The spirit of the cold (Eskimo)

NESARU: The Power Above (Arikara)

NAUTSITI: With Iatiku, one of the Sister co-creators of man (Acoma)

NOKOMIS/NOOGUMEE: Earth goddess and the mother of *Great Hare* (Menominee/Micmac)

ONATAH: The spirit of corn (Iroquois)

PAH: The spirit of the Moon, set in the west by *Tiráwa* to shine at night (Skidi Pawnee)

PALULUKON: The Great Serpent (Hopi)

PASIKOLA: The Rabbit, the trickster (Creek)

QAMAITS: The Supreme Being of the Bella Coola of the Pacific Northwest, who almost uniquely in the North America held the major deity to be feminine

RAVEN: The Trickster in various North American Indian cultures, especially in the North-west. Also known as *Yetl* and Hoya

SEDIT: Coyote, the trickster (Wintun)

SEDNA: The Great Sea Mother (Eskimo)

SEQINEK: The spirit of the Sun (Eskimo)

SHAKURU: The spirit of the Sun (Pawnee)

SISIUTL: A water spirit, characterized as a monstrous serpent (Kwakitl)

SPIDER-WOMAN: An underworld being who, in the mythology of the tribes of the Southwest, various creates human life or equips humans with the necessary skills for survival, such as weaving (Hopi, Navajo, Keresan)

TAWESKARE/TAWISKARO: The evil Creator-Twin (Huron)

THUNDERBIRD: A mythical bird who is the creator of storms and messenger of the gods

TIRAWA: The Great Spirit (Pawnee and Delaware)

TORNAQ: A guardian spirit (Eskimo)

TORNGASOAU: The immortal, supreme being (Eskimo)

TRICKSTER: Creator, joker and culture hero, commonly characterized as Coyote, Raven, Crow, Hare or Rabbit. Frequently buffoonish, devious and sexually predatory

TSENTSA: The good creator-twin (Huron)

UKTENI: A magical water snake (Natchez)

WAKONDA/WATANA TANKA: The Power Above, the Great Spirit, the Great Mystery (Osage/Sioux/Omaha)

WAXCPINI: The trickster (Cree)

WINDINGO: Giant cannibals (Ojibwa)

YETL: The Raven, a trickster (Pacific Northwest)

TRIBES BY REGION

The Arctic

Tribes Polar Eskimo, Greenland Eskimo, Igulik Eskimo, Southampton Eskimo, Labrador Eskimo, Netsilik Eskimo, Mackenzie Eskimo, Alaskan Eskimo, Caribou Eskimo, Baffin Island Eskimo, Aleut, Ingalik, Inupiaq

Major Languages Eskimo –Aleut

Major myth types Tricksters, sea goddess, shamans

Subarctic

Tribes Chipewyan, Koyukon, Dogrib, Beaver, Kutchin, Abitbi, Carrier, Cree, Han, Slave, Tutchone, Yellowknife, Naskapi, Kalapuya, Notka

Major Languages Athapascan

Major myth types Trickster, Earth Diver, transformer

The Northwest Coast

Tribes Tlingit, Haida, Kwakiutl, Chinook Haida, Hupa, Karok, Nootka, Alsea, Bella Coola, Chilcotin, Cowlitz, Gitksan, Haisla, Heiltsuk, Salish, Quileute, Tsimshian, and Yurok.

Major Languages Salishan, Na-Dene
Major myth types Transformer, trickster, stories based on lineage, heroic myths, Bear myths

California
Tribes Hupa, Pomo, Yurok, Chumash, Maidu, Miwok, Modoc, Ohlone, Patwin, Pomo, Salinan, Wintun, Costanoa, Dieguno, Serrano, Shasta, Yurok, Yokuts, and Yuki.
Major Languages Penutian
Major myth types Origin myths, animal myths, tricksters and transformers

Southwest
Tribes Apache, Pueblo, Navajo, Coahuiltec, Jemez, Mojave, Yuma, Tanoan Pueblos, Papago
Major Languages Uto-Aztecan-Tanoan
Major myth types Emergence myths, migration myth, trickster

The Great Basin
Tribes Shoshoni, Paiute, Nez Percé, Spokane, Bannock, Ute, Skitwash, Yakama, Chemehuevi, Goshute, Washo
Major Languages Uto-Aztecan
Major myth types Trickster, hero and heroine, transformer, dying gods

The Plains
Tribes Sioux, Blackfoot, Assiniboin, Crow, Omaha, Cheyenne, Arapaho, Kiowa, Comanche, Arikara, Caddo, Gros Ventre, Kansa, Lipan, Mandan, Missouri, Nez Percé, Plains Cree, Pawnee, Osage
Major Languages Siouan, Caddoan, Na-Dene
Major myth types Culture hero, trickster, stories and legends featuring buffalo

South-east
Tribes Cherokee, Choctaw, Chickasaw, Creek, Seminole, Biloxi, Natchez, Alabama, Calusa, Quapaw, Timucua, Yuchi
Major Languages Muskogean

Major myth types Culture hero, emergence myths, trickster and tales featuring councils of animals.

North-east

Tribes Micmac, Abenaki, Mohawk, Oneida, Onondaga, Cayuga, Seneca, Conestoga, Conoy, Delaware, Powhatan, Montauk, Pequod, Narraganset, Wampanoag, Massachuset, Mohican, Huron, Ottawa, Menominee, Sauk & Fox, Winnebago, Potawatomi, Miami, Illinois, Shawnee, Erie, Tuscarora, Minga, Maliseet, Ojibwa, Tobacco

Major Languages Algonquian-Titawan-Kutenai, Iroquois-Caddoan

Major myth types Trickster stories, culture hero

BIBLIOGRAPHY

Stephen E Ambrose, *Crazy Horse and Custer, The Parallel Lives of Two American Warriors*, 1975

Virginia I Armstrong (ed.), *I Have Spoken: American History through the Voices of the Indians*, 1971

Dawn E Bastian and Judy K Mitchell, *Handbook of Native American Mythology*, 2004

John Bierhorst, *The Mythology of North America*, 2001

Black Elk, *Black Elk Speaks: Being the Life Story of a Holy Man of the Oglala Sioux*, 2000

Franz Boas (ed.), *Indian Myths and Legends from the North Pacific Coast of America*, 2002

Dee Brown, *Bury My Heart at Wounded Knee: An Indian History of the American West*, 1970

Cottie Burland, *North American Indian Mythology*, 1965

George Catlin, *Life Among the Indians*, 1875

Duane Champagne (ed.), *The Native North American Almanac: A Reference Work on Native North Americans in the United States and Canada*, 2001

Ella C Clark, *Indian legends of the Pacific Northwest*, 1953

Jeremiah Curtin, *Creative Myths of Primitive America*, 1899

——, *Seneca Indian Myths*, 1922

Natalie Curtis, *The Indians Book*, 1907

Angie Debo, *A History of the Indians of the United States*, 1971

Ella C. Deloria (comp.), *Dakota Texts*, 1932

Vine Deloria, Jr, *Red Earth, White Lies: Native Americans and the Myth of Scientific Fact*, 1988

Mike Dixon-Kennedy, *Native American Myth and Legend*, 1996

D M Dooling (ed.), *The Sons of the Wind: The Sacred Stories of the Lakota*, 1984

George A Dorsey, *The Pawnee Mythology*, 1906

George A Dorsey and Alfred L Kroeber, *Traditions of the Arapaho*, 1903

Mourning Dove, *Coyote Stories*, 1933

Richard Erdoes and Alfonzo Ortiz (eds), *American Indian Myths and Legends*, 1984

—— (eds.), *American Indian Trickster Tales*, 1998

Sam D Gill and Irene F Sullivan, *Dictionary of Native American Mythology*, 1992

Bill Grantham, *Creation Myths and Legends of the Creek Indians*, 2002

George Bird Grinnell, *Pawnee Hero Stories and Folk-Tales: With Notes on the Origin, Customs and Character of the Pawnee People*, 1889

——, *Blackfoot Lodge Tales: The Story of a Prairie People*, 1892

Ulrich W Hiesinger, *Indian Lives: A Photographic Record from the Civil War to Wounded Knee*, 1994

Arlene Hirschfelder and Paulette Molin, *Encyclopedia of Native American Religions*, 2000

Frederick W Hodge (ed.), *Handbook of American Indians of North Mexico*, 2 Volumes, 1907, 1910

Alvin M Josephy, Jr, *The Indian Heritage of America*, 1968

Alvin M Josephy, Jr, *500 Nations*, 1994

Jon E Lewis, *The Mammoth Book of Native Americans*, 2004

Luther Standing Bear, *Land of the Spotted Eagle*, 1933

Margaret Mead, *The Changing Culture of an Indian Tribe*, 1932

James Mooney, *Myths of the Cherokee*, 1995

Howard Norman (ed.) *Northern Tales: Stories from the Native Peoples of the Arctic and Subarctic Regions*, 1998

Michael Leroy Oberg, *Native America: A History*, 2010

Morris Edward Opler, *Myths and Tales of the Jicarilla Apache Indians*, 1938

Arthur Caswell Parker, *Seneca Myths and Folk Tales*, 1923

Paul Radin, *The Trickster: A Study in Indian Mythology*, 1956

Bill Reid, *The Raven Steals the Light: Native American Tale*, 1984

David B. Rockwell, *Giving Voice to Bear: North American Indian Myths, Rituals, and Images of the Bear*, 1991

Dean Snow, *The American Indians*, 1976

Matilda Coxe Stevenson, *The Zuñi Indians: Their Mythology, Esoteric Fraternities, and Ceremonies*, 1905

William C. Sturtevant (ed.), *Handbook of North American Indians*, 1978–2001

Stith Thompson, *Tales of the North American Indians*, 1929

Frederick W. Turner III, *The Portable North American Indian Reader*, 1974

Ruth Underhill, *Red Men's Religion: Belief and Practices of the Indians North of Mexico*, 1965

Frank Waters, *The Book of the Hopi*, 1963

James Wilson, *The Earth Shall Weep*, 1998

Bill Yenne, *The Encyclopedia of North American Indian Tribes*, 1986

INDEX